D1003819

TEACHING AND LEARNING
THE LOVE OF GOD

JOSEPH RATZINGER

Teaching and Learning the Love of God

Being a Priest Today

Selected Writings

With a Foreword by Pope Francis
and an Introduction by Gerhard Cardinal Müller

Edited by Pierluca Azzaro and Carlos Granados

Translated by Michael J. Miller

IGNATIUS PRESS   SAN FRANCISCO

Original Italian edition:
Insegnare e imparare l'amore di Dio

Spanish edition:
Enseñar y aprender el amor de Dios
con ocasión del 65.° aniversario de la ordenación
sacerdotal del Papa emévito
© 2016 Libreria Editrice Vaticana;
© 2016 Biblioteca de Autores Cristianos
Madrid, Spain

German edition:
Die Liebe Gottes lehren und lernen: Priestersein heute
© 2016 Libreria Editrice Vaticana; © 2016 Verlag Herder GmbH,
Freiburg im Breisgau, Germany

Cover design by Roxanne Mei Lum

CONTENTS

FIRST MASS

Jubilee Homilies

APPENDIX

FOREWORD

By His Holiness Pope Francis

Every time I read the works of Joseph Ratzinger/Benedict XVI, it becomes clear to me that he pursued theology "on his knees" and still does: on his knees, because we see that he is not only a preeminent theologian and master of the faith, but a man who really believes, really prays. We see that he is a man who embodies holiness, a man of peace, a man of God. And so he embodies in an exemplary way the essence of all priestly work: that deep rootedness in God without which all organizational talent, all supposed intellectual superiority, all money and power are useless. He embodies that constant relation to the Lord Jesus without which nothing is true any longer, everything becomes routine, priests almost become salaried employees, bishops become bureaucrats, and the Church is not Christ's Church but something that we have created, a non-governmental organization that ultimately is superfluous.

The priest is the man who embodies "Christ's presence and ... bear[s] witness to his saving mercy", Benedict XVI observes in his *Letter Proclaiming a Year for Priests*. While reading this book, you will come to see clearly how much he himself, in the sixty-five years of his priestly ministry, has lived and continues to live this priestly activity in an exemplary way, has borne and continues to bear witness to it.

As Gerhard Ludwig Cardinal Müller has so authoritatively reaffirmed, the theological work of Joseph Ratzinger—and then later of Benedict XVI—assures him a place among such great theologians on the Chair of Peter as Leo the Great, the saintly Pope and Doctor of the Church.

With his renunciation of the active exercise of the Petrine ministry, Benedict XVI decided to place himself now entirely at the service of prayer: "The Lord is calling me 'to scale the mountain', to devote myself even more to prayer and meditation. But this does not mean abandoning the Church; indeed, if God asks me this it is precisely so that I may continue to serve her with the same dedication and the same love with which I have tried to do so until now", he said in his final, moving Angelus message. From this perspective I would like to add also to the correct observation by the Prefect of the Congregation for the Doctrine of the Faith that perhaps today in particular, as Pope Emeritus, he gives us in an especially clear way one of his greatest lessons of "theology on his knees".

Then maybe Benedict XVI, right from *Mater Ecclesiae* convent to which he has retreated, can testify further and in an even more illuminating way to the "decisive factor", the interior center of priestly ministry that deacons, priests, and bishops must never forget: namely, the fact that the first and most important ministry is not conducting "current business" but praying for others, unceasingly, with body and soul. Just as the Pope Emeritus does today: continually immersed in God, his heart always directed toward him, like a lover who thinks at every moment of the beloved, regardless of what he is doing. So His Holiness Benedict XVI shows us with his witness what true prayer is: not the activity of many persons who are considered especially pious but perhaps not well suited to solving practical problems—the "business" that the "more active" regard as the decisive element of our priestly ministry, thus restricting prayer to a "leisure time activity". Nor is prayer just a good practice with which to soothe one's conscience or a pious method of obtaining from God what appears necessary for us at a particular moment. No. Prayer is—as Benedict XVI says and testifies in this book—a more decisive factor: it is the intercession that the Church and the world—especially at this truly historical turning point—need today more than ever, need like bread, indeed, more than they need bread. For prayer means that one entrusts the Church to God, conscious that the Church does not belong to us but to *him* and that, precisely for this reason, he will never abandon us; because prayer means entrusting the world and mankind to God. Prayer is the key that opens God's heart; the only one that succeeds in bringing God over and over again into this world of ours; and also the only one that succeeds in leading mankind and the world over and over again to God, like the prodigal son to the father who loves him so much that he is just waiting to be able to hold him again in his arms. Benedict knows that prayer is the first duty of a bishop (Acts 6:4).

So true prayer is therefore accompanied by the awareness that without prayer the world loses not only its orientation, but also the true source of life: "Without a connection to God, we become like satellites that have left their orbit and then hurtle randomly into the void and not only destroy themselves but also threaten others", Joseph Ratzinger writes at one place in this book, thus offering us one of his many magnificent images.

Dear confreres! I take the liberty of saying that if one of you should ever have doubts as to what the center of gravity of his office is, its meaning, its usefulness; if he should ever have doubts about what people really expect of us, then he might reflect on the pages set before us here. What people expect of us is in fact, above all, what is described and witnessed to in this book: that we should bring Jesus Christ to them and lead them to him, to the fresh, living water for which they thirst more than for anything else, which he alone can give and nothing else can replace; that we lead them to true, perfect happiness when nothing else can satisfy them; that we lead them to realize their most secret dreams, which no worldly power can promise to fulfill!

It is no accident that the initiative for this book originally came from a layman, Professor Pierluca Azzaro, and from a priest, Father Carlos Granados. They have my cordial thanks, my best wishes, and my support for this important project—as does Father Giuseppe Costa, director of the Libreria Editrice Vaticana, which is publishing the *Complete Works of Joseph Ratzinger*. No accident, as I already said, because the book that I am presenting today is aimed at priests and lay faithful alike, as is demonstrated by the following page from the book, among others, which I would like to offer to clerics and laity as a final, moving invitation to read it: "By chance I recently read the account in which the great French author Julien Green describes how he converted. He relates that he was living in the period between the world wars just as a man lives today, with all the concessions that he makes for himself, no better and no worse, shackled to pleasures that are against God's will, so that, on the one hand, he needs them in order to make life bearable and yet, at the same time, finds this same life unbearable after all. He looks for some way of escaping, strikes up relationships here and there. He goes to the great theologian Henri Brémond, but it remains just an academic discussion, theoretical hair-splitting that does not help him make headway.

He becomes acquainted with two great philosophers, the married couple Jacques and Raïssa Maritain. Raïssa Maritain refers him to a Polish Dominican. He goes to him and again describes to him this fragmented life. The priest says to him: And do you approve of living this way? No, of course not! You would like to live differently, then; you regret it? Yes! And then something unexpected happens: the priest says to him: Kneel down. *Ego te absolvo a peccatis tuis*—I absolve you. Julien Green writes: Then I noticed that deep down I had always waited for this moment, had always been waiting for there to be someone, sometime, who would say to me: Kneel down, I absolve you. I went back home, I was not a different man; no, I had finally become myself again."

Franciscus

INTRODUCTION

The Catholic Priesthood

Beyond the Crisis—Toward Renewal

By Gerhard Cardinal Müller
Prefect of the Congregation for the Doctrine of the Faith

When we speak about the priesthood, our thoughts turn spontaneously to the many examples whom we have encountered on our vocation journey, priests who have made their mark on our faith story. We heard our call without any merits of our own and seek to do justice to it every day despite our weaknesses; their testimony is a shining example that makes this special calling take shape before our eyes.

The light that shines forth in these examples comes from the life and the person of Jesus Christ. The priests who are his witnesses point to him. Of course we cannot think of the priesthood of the New Covenant without referring to the Lord Jesus—to the one who gave this gift to us in his capacity as "merciful and faithful high priest" (Heb 2:17)—and to the days in which this gift sprang from his heart.

After the dark days of the Passion, on the evening of Easter Sunday, when the disciples have barricaded themselves in the house where they are, the risen Lord appears and stays in their midst. They recognize him when he shows them his hands and his side with their glorified wounds. Hope springs again in the disciples; their despair turns to joy. Before, they were stunned, close to death. Now they reawaken and live. The sight of Jesus and his words about his ascension into heaven and return to the Father set them back on their feet and send them out into the whole world, to proclaim to all nations what he has taught them and to baptize them in the name of the Father and of the Son and of the Holy Spirit (cf. Mt 28:19).

That is also the moment when the crucified and risen Lord reveals to the Eleven the actual foundation of the Catholic priesthood and expresses its most profound meaning: "'Peace be with you. As the Father has sent me, even so I send you.' And when he had said this, he breathed on them, and said to them, 'Receive the Holy Spirit. If you forgive the sins of any, they are forgiven; if you retain the sins of any, they are retained'" (Jn 20:21–23).

With these words, which are brightened by his faithful, merciful look, the risen Lord cheers the hearts of the disciples again. In them he brings to completion what happened in the Easter event: the transition from darkness to light, from death to life, from fear to hope, from the end to a new beginning.

This encounter with the look and the words of the risen Jesus causes the disciples to experience the transition to the New Covenant that began at their first encounter with him. Everything now makes a qualitative leap, and this lays the cornerstone for overcoming every crisis. Thus even their crisis of faith in relation to his mission as Messiah is overcome—the crisis in which they all abandoned him in the tragic hours when he was handed over to sinners. Also overcome is the crisis of their apostolate, in which they ran away and were scattered like a flock without a shepherd.

Abandonment and scattering are overcome. Gathered around the presence of the risen Lord, the disciples are once again united. So their faith is united again, and their mission gains renewed impetus from the new root of the Passover.

By giving them a share in the mission and authority entrusted to him by the Father to build up the kingdom of God, new life from the Paschal Mystery is granted to those whom Jesus in the course of his public life chose and called as his apostles: Jesus "went up on the mountain, and called to him those whom he desired; and they came to him. And he appointed twelve, to be with him, and to be sent out to preach and have authority to cast out demons" (Mk 3:13–15).

This mission, which Jesus' enemies had reduced to "failure" at the stake of the ignominious Cross, is transformed from tragedy into salvation, contrary to all human expectation or prediction. It is the Easter miracle, the miracle of a new life that unforeseeably bursts into history, through and beyond the apparent defeat. The scandal of the Cross causes resurrection to blossom on its wood.

All the words of the commission that Jesus gave to his disciples are summarized in his Easter proclamation and show their full effectiveness in the post-Paschal activity of those who have definitively become apostles. Among their duties is also to make sure to hand on their mission and authority.

In this way it is plainly evident that even in apostolic times and in the transition to the post-apostolic Church, the office of shepherd and leader emerged, which in the three degrees of bishop, priest, and deacon was regarded by the whole Church as binding in carrying out the divine institution of the *sacramentum ordinis*.

All the disciples have a share in the universal salvific mission of the Father's Eternal Word-made-flesh, the Son of God. The apostles and their successors (in the episcopal, priestly, and diaconal ministry) receive the commission to build up the Church until the coming of Christ, until the end of time, by leading and serving her.

Thanks to the power of the Holy Spirit, the words and actions of the ordained ministers replicate sacramentally—as an efficacious sign—the words and actions of God. They speak and act with Christ's authority, and Christ speaks and acts through them. Thus Jesus can really say: "He who hears you hears me, and he who rejects you rejects me, and he who rejects me rejects him who sent me" (Lk 10:16; cf. 1 Thess 2:13).

In the same way, Paul, too, when he speaks about the apostles as "God's coworkers" (cf. 2 Cor 6:1) and "servants of Christ and stewards of the mysteries of God" (1 Cor 4:1), can interpret the apostolate as *ministerium reconciliationis*: "So we are ambassadors for Christ, God making his appeal through us. We beg you on behalf of Christ, be reconciled to God" (2 Cor 5:20).

Thus is accomplished before our eyes the founding of the sacramental priesthood, which is clear from the perspective of the theology of revelation, or, as *Lumen gentium* 10 puts it, the hierarchical priesthood, which by its very nature is essentially distinguished from the common priesthood of all the faithful.

This essential difference is described as follows: The bishop and the priest have a share in the power by which Christ himself builds, sanctifies, and leads his Body. The decree *Presbyterorum ordinis* says, "Wherefore the priesthood, while indeed it presupposes the sacraments of Christian initiation, is conferred by that special sacrament; through it priests, by the anointing of the Holy Spirit, are signed with a special character and are conformed to Christ the Priest in such a way that they can act in the person of Christ the Head" (PO 2).

In his first letter to the priests of the Church—with whom he performs the pastoral ministry—the apostle Peter opposes an incorrect interpretation of the statements about the priestly character of the whole Church and of all believers (1 Pet 2:5, 9) that contradicts the apostolic-sacramental ministry and warns: "Tend the flock of God that is your charge, not by constraint but willingly, not for shameful gain but eagerly, ... being examples to the flock", after the example of Christ, the "chief Shepherd" (1 Pet 5:2–4) and the "Shepherd and Guardian of your souls" (1 Pet 2:25). Here the Christological foundation and the apostolic classification of the episcopal and priestly ministry are clearly evident.

Following this teaching, which is rooted in tradition, the Second Vatican Council taught us anew to regard the Church as resting on a divine foundation. Through the mediation of Christ and of the Holy Spirit, the Church is living communion with God and with our neighbors in the truth, in life, and in love. As the People of God, the Body of Christ, the Lord's vineyard, and the flock of the Good Shepherd, the Church, the Temple of the Holy Spirit, is not an organization created by men that pursues religious or social goals; she is not a beneficent NGO, as Pope Francis said in his first homily on March 14, 2013. And at his General Audience on October 23, 2013, he reaffirmed: "The Church is sent to bring Christ and his Gospel to all."

Now in the risen Jesus Christ, she is truly Church, "the universal sacrament of salvation" (*Lumen gentium* 48, *Gaudium et spes* 45). In keeping with the mystery of the union of divine and human nature in the Person of the Son of God, she is made up of divine and human elements and thus has as her goal the unity of men with God and with one another.

In this sense the Second Vatican Council can rightly say: "For the nurturing and constant growth of the People of God, Christ the Lord instituted in His Church a variety of ministries, which work for the good of the whole body. For these ministers, who are endowed with sacred power, serve their brethren, so that all who are of the People of God, and therefore enjoy a true Christian dignity, working toward a common goal freely and in an orderly way, may arrive at salvation" (*Lumen gentium* 18).

These statements of Vatican Council II point out to us the nature of the priesthood, a priesthood whose identity goes back to the desire of Jesus himself, to his word and his Paschal activity. With his words and his faithful, merciful look, Jesus leads the apostles into *this* priesthood: he identifies them with *this* priesthood, and to *this* priesthood he entrusts them. *This* priesthood is handed down to us by the tradition of the Church: from the New Testament via the Council of Trent and down to the Second Vatican Council.

Through his Resurrection, Christ overcame the greatest crisis of faith that ever existed: the pre-Paschal crisis of the disciples and, in particular, the crisis of mission and apostolic authority and, consequently, also the crisis of the priesthood. So it is possible for us to overcome all historical crises of the priesthood, too, precisely and solely by looking to the Lord; toward the Lord to whom all power in heaven and on earth is given and who is with us always until the end of the world.

By responding to his look, which rests upon us and our priesthood, and directing our look toward him, immersing our eyes in those of the High Priest—the crucified, risen Lord—we can overcome every obstacle, every difficulty.

I am thinking especially of the crisis of the doctrine about the priesthood during the Reformation—a crisis on the dogmatic level, which demoted the priest to a mere representative of the congregation by eliminating the essential difference between the sacramental priesthood and the common priesthood of all believers. And I am thinking also of the existential and spiritual crisis that broke out in the second half of the twentieth century, in the time after the Second Vatican Council—but certainly not *because* of the council; we are still suffering from the consequences of that crisis.

Indeed, the council marked out the hierarchical structure of the Church—which is displayed in the various tasks of bishops, priests, and deacons—within the framework of a far-reaching ecclesiology that was thoroughly renewed on the basis of the biblical and patristic sources (cf. *Lumen gentium* 18–29). Its statements about the two sacred orders of the episcopate and the presbyterate (out of a ministry that is divided into three orders in all) were discussed in greater depth in the decrees *Christus Dominus* and *Presbyterorum ordinis*.

In this way, the council tried to open up a new path to an authentic understanding of the identity of the priesthood. How did it come about, then, that immediately after the council the priesthood went through an identity crisis that is comparable in history only with the consequences of the Reformation in the sixteenth century?

Joseph Ratzinger explains with great acuity that whenever the dogmatic foundation of the Catholic priesthood is lacking, the source that nourishes a life of Christian discipleship runs dry; not only that, but this also suppresses the motivation that leads to a rationally founded understanding of the renunciation of marriage for the sake of the kingdom of heaven (cf. Mt 19:12) and of celibacy as an eschatological sign of the world to come, which is to be lived out in joy and confidence by the power of the Holy Spirit.

When the symbolic relation that is part of the nature of the sacrament is obscured, priestly celibacy becomes the relic of a past that rejected the body and is denounced and opposed as the sole cause of the priest shortage. And with that, the fact that the sacrament of Holy Orders can be administered only to men, which is well known to the Magisterium and in the practice of the Church, disappears as well. A ministry that is understood in utilitarian terms is thus exposed in the Church to the suspicion that it legitimizes a claim to dominion that should be justified and restricted along democratic lines instead.

The crisis that the priesthood has experienced in the last few decades in the Western world is also the result of a radical unsettling of Christian identity vis-à-vis a philosophy that situates the ultimate purpose of history and of every human life within the world and thus robs it of its transcendental horizon and eschatological perspective.

Expecting everything from God and founding our whole life on God, who has granted us everything in Christ: this alone can be the logic of a path in life that follows Christ with complete self-dedication and shares in his mission as Savior of the world—a mission that the Lord accomplished in his suffering and on the Cross and that he has unmistakably revealed through his Resurrection from the dead.

Interdenominational factors must also be mentioned, though, as reasons for this crisis of the priesthood. As is evident already from his first essays, Joseph Ratzinger from the very beginning showed great sensitivity to the tremors that announced a genuine earthquake, namely, the naïve openness in many Catholic circles to Protestant exegesis, which came into fashion in the 1950s and 1960s.

Those on the Catholic side were often not aware of the preconceived views at the basis of the exegesis that resulted from the Reformation. So it happened that the Catholic (and Orthodox) Church was deluged with criticism of the priestly ministry, which—as some scholars thought—lacked all biblical foundation.

The sacramental priesthood that was completely geared to the Eucharistic Sacrifice—as reaffirmed at the Council of Trent—seemed at first glance not to be biblically justified, both terminologically and also with regard to the special powers of priests in comparison to laymen, especially the power to consecrate. The radical critique of worship—which strove to overcome a priesthood that had been reduced to the function of cultic mediator—seemed to pull the rug out from under priestly mediation in the Church.

The Reformation rejected the sacramental priesthood, because—purportedly—it would have called into question the uniqueness of Christ's High Priesthood (according to the Letter to the Hebrews) and marginalized the common priesthood of all believers (as described in 1 Pet 2:5). This critique was accompanied by the modern idea of personal autonomy and also by the individualistic practice that results from it, which regards any exercise of authority with distrust.

What theological view resulted from this? It was determined that Jesus, from a sociological-religious perspective, was not a priest with cultic functions and consequently—to use an anachronistic formulation—should be regarded as a layman. Moreover, since the New Testament uses no sacral terminology for ministries and offices but terms that were considered profane, this looked like effective proof of the unsuitability of a transformation that took place in the early Church—from the third century on—which changed those who performed only certain "functions" within the Christian community into illegitimate members of a new cultic priesthood.

Joseph Ratzinger subjects the historical criticism carried out by the Protestant theologians to a detailed critical examination of its own. He does this by distinguishing between philosophical and theological prejudices, on the one hand, and the use of the historical method, on the other. In this way he is able to show that with the achievements of modern biblical exegesis and a precise analysis of historical dogmatic development, one arrives quite reliably at the dogmatic statements that were minted especially by the Councils of Florence and Trent as well as by the Second Vatican Council.

What Jesus means for the relation of all men and of the entire creation to God—in other words, the acknowledgment of Jesus as Savior and universal Mediator of salvation, which is developed in the Letter to the Hebrews by means of the term "high priest" (*archiereus*)—was never something that depended on his membership in the Levitical priesthood and, therefore, had such membership as a prerequisite.

The foundation of Jesus' being and mission lies, rather, in the fact that he comes from the Father, from the house and the temple in which he dwells and in which he must be (cf. Lk 2:49). The divinity of the Word is what makes Jesus, in the human nature that he assumed, the one true Master, Shepherd, Priest, Mediator, and Savior.

He grants a share in this consecration and mission to the Twelve by calling them. They develop into the circle of the apostles, who lay the foundation stone for the Church's mission in history, which is an essential component of her nature. They pass on their authority to the shepherds of the universal Church and of the particular Churches that function at the local and regional level.

From the perspective of comparative religious history, the initial designations of the offices of "bishop", "priest", and "deacon" in the Christian communities of Gentile origin seem to have been terms from the profane realm. And nevertheless, in the context of the early Church, their Christological reference and their relation to the apostolic ministry cannot be disregarded.

The apostles and their disciples and successors appoint bishops, priests, and deacons by the laying on of hands and prayer (cf. Acts 6:6; 14:23; 15:4; 1 Tim 4:14). In the name of the supreme Shepherd, they are the shepherds and servants who visibly represent him; through them he himself is present in his capacity as *analogatum princeps* [criterion of comparison] of the shepherd and minister.

This results also in the spirituality of the priest, or of the bishop, as the case may be, who is consecrated by the Holy Spirit through the imposition of hands (cf. Acts 20:28). This spirituality is not the external addition of some private pious practices but, rather, the intrinsic form of the willingness to place oneself completely at the service of Christ and to refer to him with one's whole being and life.

The authentic nature of the sacramental priesthood lies in the fact that the bishop and the priest are servants of the Word who provide the ministry of reconciliation and as shepherds pasture God's flock. Inasmuch as they fulfill Christ's commission, Christ makes himself present through their works and their words as the sole High Priest in the Church of God that has gathered for the liturgical celebration.

The objections raised against the Catholic priesthood would make sense if the Church's priesthood was understood as an autonomous or even a merely supplementary mediation alongside or apart from Christ's mediation. Hence even Martin Luther's objections miss the central core of the binding dogmatic teaching about the sacramental priesthood.

One fundamental prerequisite for the recovery of priestly identity seems, therefore, to be availability: understanding oneself as a servant of the Word and a witness to God while following Christ and living in communion with him. The decisive attitude that Joseph Ratzinger warmly recommends to us on our journey is the following: "to keep contact with him [Jesus] alive. For when we look away from him, we inevitably fare as Peter did as he was walking toward Jesus on the water: Only the Lord's look can overcome gravity, but it really can. We always remain sinners. But if he holds us, the waters of the depth have lost their power."

This is precisely why it is so necessary, too, for a priest to have a well-grounded theological education and an ongoing relation to scholarly theology.

With the contributions in the present volume, Joseph Ratzinger shows a path that leads out of the crisis into which the Catholic priesthood had fallen for lack of suitable theological and sociological rudiments and motivations. A crisis that left many priests, who had begun their journey quite full of love and zeal, uncertain about their role in the Church. The present volume can be a rewarding reference work, not only for the scholarly theological definition of the sacrament of Holy Orders, but also for more in-depth, spiritual reflection on the vocation to the priesthood, for spiritual exercises for priests, and for preaching about the "ministry of a new covenant", the "ministry of the Spirit and of life" (cf. 2 Cor 3:6–8).

Pope Benedict XVI saw the proclamation of the word of God, which takes priority over all human activity, as the particular task of the episcopal and priestly ministry. Moreover, this is precisely what Pope Francis recalled on April 21, 2013, in a way that was poignant and equally emphatic, when he admonished those who are called to the sacrament of Holy Orders in the context of a priestly ordination ceremony: "Remember then that you are taken from among men and appointed on their behalf for those things that pertain to God. Therefore, carry out the ministry of Christ the Priest with constant joy and genuine love, attending not to your own concerns but to those of Jesus Christ. You are pastors, not functionaries. Be mediators, not intermediaries."

We can recognize, in the way in which these two great popes look at the priesthood, the way in which Jesus looks at his apostles. The way he looks at those whom he sends out, as in every era, to pasture his flock. This look is what distinguishes us and shields our priestly vocation from the world's distorted views of it, which are always incomplete and reductive. This look is what urges us on, with trust and confident hope, leaving the fogbank of every crisis behind us.

The look of the chief Shepherd is what renews his shepherds at all times and makes them free for the ardent mission to which he has called them despite their wretchedness and misery. Precisely the look and the words of Jesus are the constant source of priestly identity that enables us to overcome the desert of every crisis, so as to go toward the promised land that must be conquered anew every day: the promised land of his kingdom. We should draw on this look, on these words at every moment. Despite every apparent defeat, this is the point of departure from which we can start afresh again and again.

HOMILIES

Holy Oils: Signs of God's Healing Power and Diocesan Unity

At the Chrism Mass, 1978

The sign of oil, which gives this Mass on the eve of Holy Thursday its special orientation and character, is intimately connected with the mystery of Jesus Christ; for this name Christ—Χριστός—means in English: the Anointed One. This means that, in terms of the faith of the Old Testament, the early Church could not express any better what this Jesus was and is than to let this symbol of oil become his name. But what is actually expressed by it?

First, it incorporates primordial human experiences. Throughout the Mediterranean region, in Palestine as well as in Greece, Italy, and North Africa, oil was the symbol of vital strength in general. The fruit of the olive tree was the real fundamental food, even more than daily bread. It was at the foundation of the entire human diet. It was at the same time also the medicine with which strength and rest and peace were restored to the body. In the psalms we hear again and again this joy about the delightful qualities of oil, how it pours over the sunburned, weary, exhausted body and suddenly makes it experience again all the

"Die heiligen Öle—Zeichen der Heilkraft Gottes und der Einheit des Bistums", for the Chrism Mass on March 22, 1978, in the Liebfraudendom, Munich. Previously unpublished. [B 426]

gladness and strength of life. And thus, above and beyond this necessary service to life, oil then becomes also a cosmetic, the expression of joy in life. The necessary and the superfluous, which after all man needs, too, interpenetrate here inseparably. And so then it is understandable also that oil, as a carrier of vital strength, lies close to the divine; for God, after all, is God by being the power of life. Men of God, prophets, priests, and kings are anointed, they are "the anointed", and this now means more than that they have an abundance of olive oil; it is supposed to express the fact that the power of life itself stands over them. Jesus Christ, however, is the true Prophet, the true Priest, and the true King, and that is why only he now is the Anointed One in the full sense. *The fact* that he is the Christ became definitively clear to the Christians in the Resurrection. Here the oil, as a power opposed to death, had definitively proved its strength. He was obviously anointed with that stronger oil, for which olive oil can be only a sign, only a final offshoot. He stood in that vital power which was able to banish corruption, defy death, and bring him out of the grave as the Anointed One and set him up in the middle of mankind as the victor. Thereby it becomes apparent at the same time what sort of oil this new, different oil is, at which the fruit of the olive tree could only hint in its own way in everyday experience: the power of life itself, the Holy Spirit of God, who binds him as the Son with the Father and thus also rescues man from the claws of death. He is the One Anointed, no longer with the fruit of the olive tree, but rather with the thing that it symbolizes, with the power of life itself, with God's creative Spirit.

Consequently, oil acquired a new meaning in the Christian sacraments. Of course, the extent of its use in them—it plays a role in almost all the sacraments—still reflects its everyday status in the Mediterranean world, and so the sacraments still remind us also of the earthly life of Jesus, of the world out of which he steps to meet us. And in the extent to which the sign of oil is effective in the sacraments, we can still see something of the spectrum of hopes bound up with it: in the Anointing of the Sick, it is, so to speak, God's medicine; when it is used before Baptism, it is a reminder of one understanding of Christianity, in which Christian life is regarded as a competition, as an Olympic contest in the arena of history. The Christian is someone who prepares himself for the great wrestling match of life in the drama of history. The athletes who entered the arena anointed their body with oil, so that it would be soft, supple, strong, and lively, not dried out. The anointing at Baptism is supposed to suggest that the Christian is anointed by the Lord in order to enter into the drama of history as a wrestler and a winner. The anointing that is then administered after Baptism in Confirmation and Holy Orders recalls the anointing of priests, prophets, and kings.

But all this now acquired a new depth from Jesus Christ. When consecrated oil is put on the forehead and the hands of a patient on his sickbed, then it no longer expresses merely the earthly and so often vain hopes that were placed in olive oil in the ancient world; now it can be the sign for God's true medicine, for the entrance of Jesus Christ into the space of our suffering, our fears, and our needs. Then it expresses the fact that there really is an herbal remedy for death, that Jesus Christ has stepped into the night of death and stands in the night of our suffering as the true medicine of God; he carries us and gives us peace and assurance: that we are safe in God's hands forever.

And when we are anointed before Baptism for the contest of life, this means that he, who on the Cross fought the dramatic battle with the forces of hatred, envy, and despair, stands over our life as the power that carries us, that gives us life and does not allow us to dry out, that stands behind us and catches us when we get tired and leads us through this arena into his mercy. And over all this, of course, resounds then also the claim of these anointings, as it is formulated for instance in Saint Paul's remark: *"Christi bonus odor sumus in omni loco*—[In every place] we are the aroma of Christ" (2 Cor 2:15). This means: the stench of despair, of spiritual decay, of greed and hatred, all the powers that are ultimately corruption and destroy life, are now confronted by the new power of his life, and by accepting it, this dry rot of despair and hatred is supposed to be confronted by the fragrance of true life, trust in indestructible love, safety in the power of God's Spirit, which, so to speak, disinfect the world.

The ancient Church found all this depicted in advance in verses 1 and 2 of Psalm 133: "Behold, how good and pleasant it is when brothers dwell in unity! It is like the precious oil upon the head, running down upon the beard, upon the beard of Aaron, running down on the collar of his robes!" In this saying, which probably originated in one of the schools of wisdom in Israel, this delightful experience of oil permeating the weary body and making it fresh and lively again, becomes the image for the beauty of fraternal peace. Early Christianity, however, found in it a statement about the fraternal communion of the Church and her oneness resulting from the sacramental unity that comes from Jesus Christ. He is the true Aaron, and the oil that comes down from him is no longer merely an image for the delightfulness of life and for the beauty of fellowship; rather this new oil, the power of the real life of God's Spirit, establishes and creates the fraternal unity of the Church.

And so one final thing becomes visible: the Holy Spirit, symbolized by the oil, is love. And this is why he is the power counteracting death and corruption. This is why he is center of God himself, the unity of Father and Son. This is why he is the central link between Creator and creation. This is why he is the foundation of the Church and our peace. And so this Mass of the holy oils is, as a result of this, its inmost message, at the same time a feast of the Church and of her unity. Around the altar of the cathedral we celebrate the Holy Sacrifice of Jesus Christ. This one altar, which expresses our local Church of Munich and Freising, our diocese in its unity, is in turn a reference to Jesus Christ himself, who is simultaneously the living altar and the priest. We receive from and in this one cathedral the holy oils, which now go out so that the sacraments throughout the diocese come from this one center and thus appear visibly as the fruit of the one sacrament of the death and Resurrection of Jesus Christ. What happens today, in the consecration and distribution of the oils, fulfills what these psalm verses suggest: the outpouring of the holy oil over the whole body of the Church.

So I would like to thank once again all who represent here this unity of our diocese, who struggle day by day to live for and believe in this unity and to allow it to support them. The distribution of the holy oils is more than an external transport, which nowadays could be arranged in some other way. It is the interior process: that we become servants of life, that we carry on this outpouring of life-giving oil onto the whole body of the Church and thus place ourselves at the service of the fraternal unity of the Church, which was founded by her Head and lives by the strength that goes forth from him.

And this is why this day is in a special way also a feast of priests, who have made this carrying their life's work, whose whole life is actually this kind of repeated going out from the center, so that the oil will flow through the body and will grow into the strength that comes to us from the

Lord. As men we need what is definitive, but, conversely, the definitive can prove its worth only if again and again we return from our going forth and also seek the center and receive its strength anew. This is the reason why, according to the new order of the liturgy, priests renew their ordination promises at this time. It is as though we enter again into the center from which all our strength and mission come. We start again with the Lord, so that once more the life-giving oil might overcome the dryness of everyday routine and bring to life in us the joy of Christ's victory.

We do this in the presence of the whole believing Church; for just as the priests in their way support the Church, they are supported in their ministry by you, the faithful. Now when we renew our ordination promises, I ask you, dear brother priests, to do it in this spirit of prayerful entrance into the Lord, who alone can support us. And I ask you all, who as representatives stand for this whole diocese, to support us, too, with your prayers, so that in us the promising and at the same time challenging words of Saint Paul may be fulfilled more and more in us: "[In every place] we are the aroma of Christ" (2 Cor 2:15).

Becoming "Spiritual Clergymen" (Johann Michael Sailer) in the Breathing Space of the Spirit

At the Chrism Mass, 1979

In the letter that the Holy Father wrote to priests through-out the world for Holy Thursday, he tells of a custom that has developed in many localities behind the Iron Curtain where persecution left no priests. I had already learned of such an event some years ago from friends. It happens there that the people go to an abandoned church or, if one no longer exists, to a cemetery where a priest is buried. They place the stole on the altar or on the tombstone and pray together the prayers of the Holy Eucharist. At the place where the Consecration would occur, a deep silence ensues, which is sometimes interrupted by weeping. The pope then goes on and turns to us priests. He says: Dear brothers, when doubts about your vocation some-times assail you, when you doubt the meaning of it and ask yourselves whether it is socially unproductive or even use-less, then reflect on this fact. Think how much these peo-ple yearn to hear the words that only the lips of a priest can

"Im Atemraum seines Geistes 'geistlich Geistliche' (Johann Michael Sailer) werden", for the Chrism Mass on April 11, 1979, in the Liebfrauendom, Munich. Previously unpublished. [B 499]

pronounce. How much they yearn to receive the Body of the Lord. How anxiously they are waiting for someone to be able to tell them, "I forgive your sins." This "Eucharist by desire", in which the people in their abandonment reach out to the Lord in prayer, go out to meet him in their yearning, and thus in faith communicate with Holy Church and therein with the Lord himself, gives witness to the living Church, witness to the hidden closeness of the Lord, and witness to what priesthood means.

Contrasted with this humility of faith, how petty the recommendation of many theologians seems: in an emergency anyone can pronounce the words of consecration. In such a "Eucharist of desire", certainly more presence of the Lord occurs than in a presumed authority that tries to make even Christ and the Church into the product of our efforts. No man can dare on his own to use the "I" of Christ as his "I" without blaspheming. No one can say on his own authority: "This is my body." "This is my blood." "I absolve you from your sins." And yet we need these words as much as our daily bread. When they are no longer spoken, the daily bread goes stale and social achievements become empty. So this is the most profound and at the same time the most exciting gift of the priestly ministry, which only the Lord himself can give: not only to relate his words as words of the past, but to speak here and now with his "I", to act *in persona Christi*; to represent Christ's person, as the liturgy expresses it.

Basically we can derive from this the whole nature of priestly activity and the commission of priestly life. Certainly, even if a priest contradicts these words with his life, they are still effective, precisely because the "I" of Jesus Christ is what matters here, and not the man's ego. The man does not forgive sins, but HE does. The body of this or that man does not become present, but

His does. But at the same time it is clear that we cannot say such words without them making demands on our own life and requiring interior correspondence to what we are saying. Because if interiorly we were to chafe against what we represent, it would necessarily become a judgment upon us. Someone who is allowed to take the "I" of Jesus Christ on his lips must therefore above all believe it himself first. The priest must first and foremost be a *man who believes*. This is the center of all his activity, and if it is not present, then nothing real happens anymore. Certainly all sorts of business might continue, but he lacks what is essential, and the Church then becomes a leisure time association, and she becomes superfluous. And that is why the pope in this letter said very emphatically: People expect above all a priest with deep faith, a priest who prays, a priest who lives according to the program of the Beatitudes.

And now I turn to you particularly, dear brothers, for I become stuck at this point: "program of the Beatitudes"— do we really try to live according to them? Or have we not one and all grown thoroughly accustomed to the standards of the Western world, so that we take them entirely for granted as the life-style to which we, too, are entitled? Certainly, and thank God, there is the slogan, "live differently", find "alternative life-styles". But when you get down to the core, specifically when the Christian life is offered as this alternative, then with all these slogans we are just getting by with precisely what is considered normal today, and we fail to recognize that the Beatitudes, that the Church's faith and the way of life that it sets up, would be *the* alternative that of course would cut into our flesh, which we would have to accept in order for the faith to become believable. And the people are waiting for someone to believe before they do, because they, too, would find it nice if everyone could believe again and if they could dare again to believe: It is true, there is a God, there is a Christ who loves me even to my final hour. Albert Camus once said, "*Je n'aime pas les prêtres anticléricaux*—I do not like anticlerical priests." He, the anticlerical author, said this! But he wanted men with integrity. He did not want a person who, so to speak, plays down his own particularity and says, "Don't take it so seriously; I don't either. I already belong to this world of today." He looked for the man who has integrity, who is "himself", and who stands for what he is. This is the demand made of us not only by the Gospel but also by this era that is looking for alternatives. We ought to have again more often the courage to set this flirtation aside. Yes, all of us have played a little and flirted with this *prêtre anticlérical*, this anticlerical priest. A priest must have the courage to have integrity, to stand up for the alternative that he is, and to profess it. Connected with this also—we do not like to hear it, I know—is the pope's admonition that a priest should also be recognizable, even by his clothing.

In 1968, I experienced the student protests in Tübingen, and it was moving to see how these young people, who were publicly repudiating their parents and the world in which they had grown up, presented this dramatically even in the way in which they demonstrated, and they knew: What I am, I must also show; it must be expressed. And how very soon there were fellow travelers who found it very important to appear just the same way with a beard and similar accoutrements! I think that something important is going on there: an attitude that matters to people can never be merely interior; it must be displayed. Someone who hides makes no statement and kindles no fire, because you have to assume that he himself doubts whether what he once undertook is now the right thing and worth spending his life doing.

In this connection, the pope then wrote several very thought-provoking sentences about the topic of adaptation. He recalled the great priest figures of the modern era: Vincent de Paul, John of God, the Curé of Ars, Maximilian Kolbe. Each one of them was different; each one was a man of his time and proclaimed the Gospel to his time, proclaimed it with the caustic, healing rigor that is an essential part of it and must be applied to new wounds in every age. In this respect, they had adapted the Gospel and made it the Gospel of their time; not by hiding themselves or by devising strategies, but rather—as the pope said—because each one made an original response to the Gospel, because each one, as himself, as this man, had wrestled interiorly with the Gospel and with the Lord and had found his response, which was then the Gospel response for that time.

Someone who wants to use the "I" of Jesus Christ must believe in it. And he who believes prays. And he who prays professes. And he who professes also lives accordingly. The pope said in this context: Let us be shepherds and not hirelings. Not the kind of men who calculate how many hours then remain for me and my private concerns. The only ones who need to do that are the ones whose profession is something that exists alongside their life. But being a priest is not something that we have to build for ourselves alongside our life as our own acquisition; it is our very life. And it can find no greater task than to be a witness to the love of Jesus Christ.

Another thought from the pope's letter struck me especially. He spoke about the need for us to convert again and again. He said this in connection with celibacy, but of course it applies to the whole spectrum of priestly and human life. Now we have nothing against that as a general statement. After all, it does not cost much to say: We are all sinners and we need forgiveness. But we are very sensitive and allergic to it when it becomes a question of *me* admitting that *my* actions need forgiveness. And only then are we talking about a real conversion. We find it very difficult to acknowledge that something that we feel is normal and has become a habit in life is not right and should be otherwise. When something has become for us a habit or even just a frequent act, then we would rather think that the norm is wrong than that we have gone astray. And I have observed that when a priest falls—interiorly or exteriorly is not the question here—when he can no longer be one with his commission, really and ultimately a silent, often unrecognized arrogance is always to blame. Not the sexual problems against celibacy or whatever else it might be, but this fact that we do not like forgiveness. That we cannot admit that over and over again we need conversion, change, and the Lord's forgiveness. And another odd thing occurred to me: we are all sinners. And often even those who are per se more virtuous and more competent are the ones who dislike forgiveness. Nevertheless, when someone refuses forgiveness in his life, he becomes poisonous, no longer at one with himself, no longer at one with the world and with God; he becomes unhappy and aggressive because the unforgiven sin is at work in him.

Conversely, however often someone may have sinned, if he has the simplicity of heart that admits it and allows itself to be forgiven, then he finds joy and peace of mind and becomes one with himself. The Lord is reconciliation, and to refuse reconciliation means to reject the Lord himself. So again and again we are that Peter who does not like to let anyone wash him. And yet we can participate in the Lord only if we let ourselves be washed.

The particular symbol of today's Holy Mass, which sin-
gles out one part of the mystery of Holy Thursday, is the
sign of oil. Christ got his name from it—Χριστός means
"the Anointed One". And so the chrism is the sign of
the Holy Spirit, for the new anointing that is given to
him and pours out from him. A priest should be above
all a *spiritual man*. The [early nineteenth-century] Bishop
of Regensburg, Johann Michael Sailer, once said that
we needed "spiritual clergymen". At this point it now
becomes immediately apparent again that such a reflection is not a matter of private conversation, so to speak, in
priestly circles; rather, it concerns *all* of us, because only all
of us together can build the living Body of Jesus Christ,
because only all of us together can give each other the
breathing space of the Holy Spirit. And if people in secular
professions, if you, dear brothers and sisters, need priests
who believe-in-advance and believe-first, we need you to
believe-with. And we need you to support and correct us
by your patience, so that we recognize: we are needed,
and that itself will restore our faith again.

So let us join at this moment in praying that the Lord
may touch us all with the anointing of the Holy Spirit.
That he may grant to us to live in the breathing space of
his Spirit and thus become living Church.

Eucharist and Pentecost as the
Origin of the Church

At the Chrism Mass, 1981

The Cenacle on Mount Zion in Jerusalem, to which we turn our attention in a special way during these days, is the scene of two decisive events in the history of our salvation. In it the Eucharist was instituted; in it Christ distributed himself so as to become the Bread of Life for all ages. In it, however, the sending of the Holy Spirit, the first Pentecost, also took place. With the sign of the disciples speaking in all languages, which prefigured the Church, that extends beyond the boundaries of all languages, beyond the boundaries of all places and time, and builds a new, boundary-transcending unity, the communion of the People of God. These two things intrinsically belong in the same room, the two things are *one* coherent event, both are the founding of the Church. For the Church can exist only because Christ imparted himself to men, because he communicated himself to them and thus leads them in communion with one another into the unity of his Body, into the new organism of his love. On the

"Eucharistie und Pfingsten als Ursprung der Kirche", for the Chrism Mass on April 15, 1981, in the Liebfrauendom, Munich. Previously published under the title "Der Heilige Geist in der Eucharistie", in *Predigten und Fürbitten*, vol. C/1, ed. Winfried Blasig (Zurich, 1985), 110–15. [B 607]

other hand, Church can exist only because the Holy Spirit in turn breathed on the clay, so to speak, and because he brings together the people who stand beside each other and opposite one another, so that they might be the new organism that Christ wants to create in this world.

Eucharist and Pentecost together are the origin of the Church. The Church can exist only because she is Christ's organism, because she comes from him. But she can exist only because this organism is animated by God's Spirit, also. This Spirit is the Spirit of Christ's Body, and in it he is Spirit-made-flesh again and again. In terms of these connections, we should understand the fact that the Holy Father invited the bishops throughout the world to preach today at this Mass about the Holy Spirit, about his Pentecostal mystery. The external occasion for this is the commemoration of the Council of Constantinople, which 1,600 years ago formulated Christendom's common profession of faith in the Holy Spirit. This profession is like the vital sap in the Church's organism, the marrow of her identity, in which she finds herself again and again and is herself. And this is why the commemoration of the Council of Constantinople is not just one jubilee among others for Christianity, the recollection of something long past, but rather is a re-calling in the fullest sense of the word: calling to mind and entering into the inner truth, into the real source of life that supports us and makes us Christians. Holy Spirit and Eucharist, Pentecost and Holy Thursday belong together; one helps us to understand the other.

So let us try, in terms of the Pentecostal mystery, to understand the Holy Spirit better; and, in this mystery, the Eucharist and our mission as baptized Christians and as priests in the service of Jesus Christ. If we look at the Pentecost event, the Holy Spirit is manifested as power to gather, power to transform, and power to send.

He is power to *gather*. He brings together again the
scattered disciples, whom fear and selfishness have driven
apart. He comes to them when they have gathered and
fits them completely into a unity. This corresponds to
his inmost nature. God is love, the Bible tells us. But if
he is love, then that means that he is I and Thou, that he
is responsive self-offering and self-giving. And it means
that I and Thou do not remain a separated opposition
but that they are profoundly one in love. The revelation
of the faith tells us that the unity that love creates and
that we call God is a deeper, nobler, more radical unity
than the unity of something indivisible, than the smallest
unit of the material world. That is why "being Triune"
and "being One" is not a contradiction; it follows from
the nature of love. Where there is love, there is con-
frontation and there is unity. This is not a contradiction
but, rather, the consequence of the fact that God is love
and that love is the primordial reality, the divine. God is
Father and Son, but as Spirit he is unity, he is love that
does not destroy the opposition, and yet does not leave it
as opposition, either, but rather creates from it the most
profound unity. The Holy Spirit is Gathering, and this is
the sign of him, his nature throughout all of history. We
recognize him by the fact that there is gathering, unification. "He who does not gather with me scatters" (Mt
12:30). Faith that comes from the Holy Spirit is always
gathering; unification that binds together again what has
been scattered. And so priestly ministry is above all a
ministry of unification, a ministry of gathering.

Here we are led another step farther. Only someone
who is recollected can collect. Someone who is torn, who
lives superficially, is scattered amidst all the many distractions of everyday activity; someone who has no interior
unity but is torn apart by all the pressures and strains that

pull at us—how is he, the unrecollected man, supposed to be able to collect? Only someone who is recollected himself and has the habit of recollection can convey recollection to others, can radiate that peace and inner unity which in turn re-collects and unifies. Recollection means emerging from distractions, seeking the laborious path leading to the center. Gathering is the transition into what unites us all. Gathering means entering at that point where men are one with each other and can touch each other in the first place; at the point where God is in man's heart, the ground and unity of us all. Gathering means going down through the disturbances and distractions to this unifying center. This cannot happen without self-control, the patience that seeks this center again and again.

From this perspective, dear brothers in the priesthood, it becomes evident that gathering, being recollected ourselves, is a decisive part of our priestly ministry. We cannot carry it out correctly if we ourselves are unrecollected, distracted, torn, superficial men. I believe that there is a danger for all of us that, given the many tasks that rush in on us, that are important to us and engross us, we have a guilty conscience when we look for an hour of recollection. We think that we really work as priests only when we do things that can be checked off the list and presented as finished projects. Yet the West, our country, the world is afflicted with this activism which tears people apart in their jobs and causes them to become so poor and empty interiorly, so unrecollected, and, therefore, so hostile toward each other. Learning to become recollected men is not an escape from pastoral work but the indispensable center of it. Seeking again and again throughout the day's work the hour of recollection, the path to the center. For this above all is what people expect of us: that when they meet us they do not find another agitated person, but something of the recollection, peace, and quiet of the things that abide and make us interiorly calm and free.

The Holy Spirit gathers, and he calls us to seek recollection, not as a waste of time, but as entrance into the mystery of life, into the real support without which works become futile and empty. The Holy Spirit gathers: this also means, however, that he gathers us into our common profession of the faith, into the common Catholic form. One of the risks we run, which make the Church so uncomfortable, is that everyone wants to have his private faith and his private theology; the idea that there should be a different theology for men and for women, for workers and for scholars, and God knows for what else. And by these private theologies of ours, by the Jesus that we ourselves have devised, we evaluate the faith of the Church, we evaluate what the pope says and what the bishops say. But Christ exists only in the We; for he is in his Body, which means in the communion of those who have become his organism and his organs. He is not found in the privatized ego but only in the first-person-plural form, in the common form that is expressed in the common profession of the faith. We speak about the Holy Spirit as gathering. In the confusion of the fourth century, when the ecclesial communion in the East seemed to be almost totally destroyed and dissolved into the private theologies of a wide variety of circles, he created the gathering form of the creed and from it the common Catholic form and, thus, the unity of what had been torn apart. When we speak about him in this way, we too have to relearn the selflessness that does not measure the faith by what we ourselves have devised but, rather, recognizes that theology is the interpretation of the common faith and is measured by it. Our private faith is not the standard for the Church; rather, the common word spoken by the Church is the standard for our faith and measures whether it has truly become We-Faith in the gathering power of the Holy Spirit. This is what we must seek again: this gathering form that then receives and supports us in advance as a space of unity beyond so much that is private and diverse, a space in which there is something that supports from the very foundation and unites among the differences.

"In my Father's house are many rooms" (Jn 14:2), says the Lord. And if we really believe in terms of the common We of the Church, then it is evident that there are many rooms and many ways in which we can find a home in the faith. But then they are no longer opposing bunkers in which we defend our little discovery but, rather, rooms of the one house in the gathering power of the Holy Spirit.

The Holy Spirit is *transformation* [*Verwandlung*]. The Mass, which begins as gathering, has its climax in the consecration [*Wandlung*]. Bread of this earth becomes the Body of Christ, the bread of eternal life. What shines forth in the distance ahead of us, the new heaven and the new earth, is reality here. "Behold, I make all things new" (Rev 21:5). Bread, the fruit of the earth and of our work, becomes his Body. HE is in it, the One who gives himself to us as the beginning of the transformation of the world, as the beginning of *our* transformation, since we are supposed to enter into this transformation. In the Eucharist, Christ is not added, so to speak, to the bread as a second thing, so that he would now be there with it. After all, he is not one thing alongside something else; he is the source, the root, the creative power of the whole. When he touches a place, there is not something else besides what was there before but, rather, a new creation takes place; things then become new. That is also why being a Christian cannot be a little Sunday world in addition to our workaday world, something that we build as an addition in some devotional corner of our life; rather, it is a new foundation, it is transformation that changes us.

The decisive work of the Holy Spirit is transformation. For this reason, being a Christian is continual conversion. Conversion is correspondence to the transformation in the Eucharist. Tradition designates both with the one word *conversio* and thus expresses the intrinsic unity of the two events. We can be Christians only if we submit to this process of new creation, of transformation, by regarding Christianity, not as a pious supplement, but as the power that defines our whole life, a power that we allow to penetrate every routine action as a new, transforming form in us. We should become Christ's wheat—the bread of Jesus Christ—with him, as Saint Ignatius of Antioch said. Becoming wheat means letting oneself sink into the earth, letting oneself be taken, and not remaining shut up in one's own privacy. It means letting oneself be permeated by the forces of the earth and from on high. Letting oneself be changed in them, letting oneself be decisively transformed by what comes to us as a challenge: by God's trials, by his gifts, by yearning, by the good things and the difficult things that people give us to bear. And growing, becoming new in this maturation process. It means taking in God's sun and the earth's water—in the power of the Spirit—and allowing them to ferment in us, so that we become Christ's good bread. It means accepting the oven—of afflictions, too—and being ground down by everyday troubles. Or to use another image: in order for a cluster of grapes to become good wine, it has to drink a lot of sunlight. This, dear brothers and sisters, dear confreres, is our task: to drink a lot of sunlight, so that we become good wine. To expose ourselves again and again to the sunlight of the word of God, of God's appeals, but also to the storm and the wind and the water, the only way in which we can become a cluster that is ripe and produces good wine to drink.

And finally: the Holy Spirit is *mission*. At the end of the Mass come the words, *"Ite, missa est."* Go, it is mission! And it is not wrong that this key word in tradition gave the name "Mass" to the whole event, because this whole thing is mission, because all of God's deeds always exist for others, also. The Holy Spirit always works under the banner of For; he never merely comes to someone privately; rather, he always comes so that something can be handed on. He is always the mission, the appeal to hand on. And so we should take into ourselves anew this law of For. It is depicted in Sacred Scripture when the Holy Spirit appears in the image of the fiery tongue. Fire is the power that warms and brightens. "Did not our hearts burn within us ... while he opened to us the Scriptures?" (Lk 24:32). Only someone who himself is burning can kindle. We must become burning Christians. We must make that journey of the disciples of Emmaus with him, in which we let him make us burn with his word, in which we submit to and expose ourselves to the fire that makes separated elements molten and combines them and creates unity.

The Holy Spirit is also message [*Wort*]. The end of Sacred Scripture tells us something about his language. There it says, "The Spirit and the Bride say, 'Come!'" (Rev 22:17). And this is his message—Come, Lord Jesus! He calls to Christ. And that is how we recognize the Holy Spirit, the fact that he calls to Christ. And for this reason, he remains a power that points forward; he wants to complete the Incarnation; he wants to make all mankind into the Body of Jesus Christ. He wants to bring to its fullness what was begun in Nazareth. This is why the Holy Spirit is the true renewal and the true rejuvenation of the Church, because he leads us to the future, to the coming of Jesus Christ. Of course this rejuvenating power always has fidelity as its origin, too; for something that has no roots cannot grow or live and therefore cannot be rejuvenated, either.

The Holy Spirit says, "Come!" Wherever he is, there is Advent, setting out into the true future, into the new creation. He is the only one who, by calling Christ over, can renew the earth. Let us try to learn his language and call on Christ by calling on him. Let us go forth to meet the true future of the world: gathering, unification, transformation. Let us go toward that power which renews the face of the earth.

By Surrendering Ourselves, We Also Find Ourselves

Farewell Meeting with Priests and Deacons, 1982

Introductory Remarks

Statio

Dear confreres!
Dear brothers and sisters in the Lord!

With all my heart I welcome you all here at this hour in the Cathedral in Freising, and I would like to say a cordial "God reward you" for the fact that we are able to see ourselves gathered together here in this great fellowship of the presbyterium, the spiritual ministry in our diocese, to experience ourselves together as Church, and that by many sacrifices we have arrived at this hour, so as to thank the Lord together for his mercies and to call them down on us anew.

"Indem wir uns hingeben, finder wir auch uns selbst", a farewell homily to priests, published under the title "Halten wir zusammen, bleiben wir beieinander", in *Wir leben von Ja: Dokumentation der Verabschiedung vom Joseph Kardinal Ratzinger* (Munich: Pressereferat des Ordinariats, Munich and Freising, 1982), 16–22; and previously in *Ordinariatskorrespondenz*, Munich, no. 7 (February 18, 1982); and under the title "Ein Abschiedswort an die Priester: Indem wir uns hingeben, finden wir auch uns selbst", in *Zeitfragen und christlicher Glaube: Acht Predigten aus den Münchner Jahren*, 2nd ed. (1982; Würzburg, 1983), 82–91. [B 665]

We have gathered at the altar at which we once said "Adsum": "I am ready, Lord, as you have called me", and at which we gave our hands into his hands and our path into his. We did not know and could not know along what paths he would lead us, but we knew that his hands are kind and that we could entrust ourselves to him. In this hour we say again Yes to him: Lord, take me as I am. Make me what you want me to be.

Homily

Dear confreres in the episcopal and priestly ministry!
Dear deacons and colleagues in pastoral work!
Dear candidates for the priesthood!
Dear brothers and sisters in the Lord!

Within the context of my new ministry, I recently encountered the fate of a priest from a very distant land in which the beauty and difficulty of our calling in our time was reflected in a way that I found moving. In his student days and in his first years as a priest, he was an enthusiast who had joyfully discovered God's word and calling; he had journeyed ever farther into this word, and in his conversations, lectures, and meetings, and through the witness of his own life, he had become a leader and guide to many.

Because much was expected of him, they sent him again and again to barren ground, which made sowing the word difficult. And since he now realized that there was no demand for his sowing, that it trickled away with no results, the burden of this futility lay more and more heavily on his heart. The gloom of such futile efforts was compounded by all the questions that were besetting the whole Church at that time: Is this assignment really necessary now? Do we not need a completely different Church and an entirely different ministry? Should everything not be different? And likewise he sensed also the burden of loneliness that had grown heavier, the question of whether there is any meaning to celibacy, which he had not desired in the first place but had only accepted for the sake of the other calling.

It had grown dark around him—and so he left. He wanted at last to be a man like all the others: just himself, free from the all-too-heavy burden of God's word and God's Church. He found a meaningful and at the same time well-paying profession as an insurance agent and in that way was able to continue using his skill at conversation and meeting with people. As he now approached people with his new job and no longer communicated the word of God to them but, rather, tried to do business with them, he sensed how inferior this quite reasonable start was to what he had done before. And he said: I noticed that God had given me my persuasiveness, not in order to make business deals with people but, rather, in order to proclaim his word.

What he was now doing, although it was good in itself, was nevertheless paltry compared to talking to people about what really matters, about the question of how we can be men and can live correctly as men. How second-rate, how petty was the security that he now offered compared with the question about what really matters, the firm ground on which we can live and die. And so he looked for something else, became a social worker, and could now talk with people about their humanity again and advise them about it.

Incidentally, it seems to me very characteristic of our time, a time in which everything is geared to technological security and scientific certainty, that advice and counseling have acquired such importance in it. Evident in this search for advice and counseling, which has given rise to a whole network of widely varying counseling services—in contrast to all the security know-how—is the space of the human freedom for what really matters to us, that cannot be calculated or mastered by technology and therefore can only be served in freedom, by considering carefully the other's freedom, in advice that calls for freedom and encounters it.

But the question arises: What happens if the counselor himself is only guessing about what man is like? If he himself must guess, can he not also betray himself as he does so in darkness? Might it be that the blind man is leading the blind? Is our therapeutic and yet helpless society, precisely in its search for the right advice and the path of freedom that cannot be calculated, not in fact similar to the society of men that the Lord pitied because they were "like sheep without a shepherd"?

Back to the priest who was employed as a social worker: he counseled people. But he noticed how this, too, was much less than what he had done before, because now he could only try with his feelings, with his common sense and his private experience, with certain statistically average values of psychology and sociology, to point out paths in a profoundly impenetrable darkness. So finally he found that he, like the prodigal son, despite all his quiet leaving, had nevertheless been on the way to the Lord once more, had been approaching him, and had found him again in the exquisite greatness of his ministry. He could say to him anew: "Adsum", Here I am, Lord, take me back, as you took Peter back, since he, too, never stopped loving you after all in the midst of his weakness. He had recognized again how precious this ministry is, which offers people not this or that, but what they live by, "a ministry in which we offer not only ourselves and our own wretchedness, but what he, the Lord of all life, can give." We can really lead people, as we heard earlier in the reading, to the green pastures, to the inexhaustible living waters, the waters of life, which God alone knows and gives, and into the truth of Jesus Christ and of his Church.

I think that reflected in the life story I have just described is something of the grace and the tribulation of the way that we all travel as servants of Jesus Christ in this time, even though, thank God, our outward journeys generally are not so dramatic. After the enthusiasm of setting out, again and again there is the problem that Moses had to deal with on Israel's journey: the longing for Egypt, the temptation to wonder whether it would not have been better simply to remain in Egypt, to be like anyone else, to do one's own thing and not always to have to walk holding his hand, not to be exposed to the desert of his callings and the apparent monotony of the bread and of the water that he provides.

But still, by God's mercy, things like scales fall from our eyes over and over again in the recognition that precisely by giving ourselves to him we also find ourselves. By acknowledging his right to us, by acknowledging people's right to our fidelity and, consequently, allowing ourselves to be given, we give what really matters, we have the privilege of leading to the waters of life and fulfilling the most beautiful human potential: giving to another person what we live by, the meaning that supports us, the hope that sustains us, the certainty with which we can truly live and die.

Dear brothers, this hour of leave-taking is and must be above all else an hour of thanksgiving. The episcopal ministry is burdened today with all sorts of conferences, meetings, and paperwork. It was nice, and still is, when you can then go out to the parishes, when you can experience and see the living Church, how present the Church is even today, how happy she makes people, too, how much she gives them space in which to live, even today.

Of course I know that in doing so the bishop experiences, so to speak, only the Sunday side of the congregation and that behind this feast-day side there is a meager, much more laborious workday. It takes a lot of seemingly unproductive hours, many laborious workdays, and also a lot of being burdened by what really does not seem to be part of the ministry. It takes a lot of care and toil to make the community grow, to build up ministries in it, to teach it to love God's word and to help it to come together in harmony. It takes patience, many disappointments, and again and again new willingness to serve.

But, on the other hand, the Sunday side is not just an appearance; it is the fruit of these many hours of toil. After the hours of routine with their futile efforts and their darkness, the Church is kept alive in this way; she can celebrate Sunday and be Sunday for the people, so that again and again they will make the effort to go on and build up the living Church and place themselves at the service of Jesus Christ and of his living Body. For this great togetherness which, despite all the drudgery, is blessed, I would like to say today a very cordial, "May God reward you!"

Because in our humanity the things that we begin are never accomplished, human thanks always assume the form of a request as well. While thanking you for this service of solidarity in the proclamation of Jesus Christ, who makes himself present so forcefully and consolingly today in our being together, I would like to ask you for this above all else: Let us keep going, let us stay together! The priesthood is a ministry that can be performed only in the first person plural. Therefore I chose as my motto *Cooperatores Veritatis* [Co-workers in the truth], in which this We of our service is expressed: only by being brothers and sisters of Jesus Christ, only by entering into the great fellowship of those who are called and by being the We of the presbyterate of a diocese can we as individuals carry out our ministry to the whole and for the whole.

Let us keep going! I ask this of you with all my heart. Let us keep going in the deaneries. Let us look out for each other when an individual becomes tired. Let us call on each other. Let us speak with one another. Let us support one another. Let us help each other. Let us exchange our charisms and so make the ministry easier for each other by giving one another what we can give. Let us stand by each other, and let us not talk ourselves into partisan divisions.

It is good and right that there are different charisms and, thus, different ways also of understanding the ministry. The Church needs this, because there are different sorts of people. But let us not become divided as a result. Even so let us stand by one another, let us not shatter that basic trust in one another that we live by a common faith, by a common mission, that despite all the external differences we nevertheless think and work on the basis of this common foundation and for its sake; only by doing this can we belong to one another and make each other productive. Let us stand by each other. Let us keep going—we can do so through all our differences by standing by what truly supports us together, by standing by our Lord, by standing by Jesus Christ. Let us love him, let us approach him again and again.

Praying the Breviary, personal prayer, meditation on his word—all these things are not just external, incidental habits that have grown up over the course of history; these are the signposts that show us the way to what is decisive. Only when we have in the deepest possible way this foundation of our common togetherness can we then tolerate various sorts of differences, because the essential thing behind them is never called into question, because we are all with him, because we are all in Jesus Christ's boat.

Let us abide with the Lord. Let us not break off our deep interior relation to him. Let us live it out, so that it can support us. And let us abide with each other, too, in the sense that we do not try to divide Christ and his Church. Let us not invent for ourselves a Jesus of our own who is supposedly better than the real one who encounters us in his Body, the Church. Let us not invent a better Gospel that we pit against the difficulties and failings of the Church. Let us believe that Christ willed to live in a body and that this body is human. Let us believe that he is present only in the We of the community that he has led through all the troubles throughout history and that we can truly have his word only in this We, in the togetherness of the Church's faith; only in this way can we personally discover this word again and again, ever more deeply, in its inexhaustible greatness. Let us stand by each other in the concrete Church, in the Church with the bishop, with the communion of bishops, with the pope, and there let us live out the one Gospel of the Lord, which is the strength of us all. Any other attempt could only cause new division. Let us thank the Lord that he leads us again and again into this unity, and let us seek it over and over and again with all humility and patience.

The harvest is great, the Lord says in today's Gospel. I can still hear how the Holy Father shouted this saying to the crowd that had gathered on the Theresienwiese [during his pastoral visit to Germany], especially to the large number of young people who were present, and how he interpreted this saying about the harvest so profoundly that God implanted it in the people, and now it is to grow and mature in the sunlight of God's truth and love. The harvest is great—so it is even today. It can be dismaying when we see in conversation with young people this question about a better life, about an alternative, about truly fundamental meaning, when we recognize what a harvest stands ready and is waiting for laborers even today in this questioning and seeking, when we see what sorts of birds also swoop down on this harvest and try to harvest it for themselves. The harvest is great. And we can thank the Lord that he called us to serve in this harvest, within the limitations of our ability, which we can and must humbly accept again and again.

"The harvest is great, but the laborers are few. Therefore pray the Lord of the harvest to send laborers into the harvest." This is also my final great request to all of us, that in keeping with our Lord's command we ourselves might fervently send up this prayer to him again and again as our common concern, that we might pray to him fearlessly, as he taught us to pray. Such a petition will not be left unanswered. If the statistical trend of the last fifteen years had continued as was projected, in 1981 only 130 students would have started to study theology in the major seminary, but in fact there were 542. We should not make too much of numbers, but this does show that there are no irreversible trends, that there is something new, a new start that statistics could not predict because they cannot calculate freedom. And there are many dioceses today in Germany that are already gratefully saying: We are no longer suffering from a shortage of beginners.

A new awakening has begun. This means that we can pray, we are allowed to pray and to trust. Let us do so with all our heart! Let us do so while turning to the Lord. But let us do so while turning to one another, also. Let us do so not only with words but with our whole being. Let us invite people, young people, to undertake this bold venture of the Word and this great service which is difficult and therefore beautiful. We know that even the generation gap cannot be an obstacle, and many have found this path through an older priest in whom they encountered fulfilled humanity and reliability and mature goodness. Let us venture to speak to them, to invite them without any violence to their freedom, with our words, with our message, with our being. Let us do this full of trust that the Lord is waiting for our petition so that he can act for us.

And let us thank the Lord once again that he called us to stand in his presence and serve him. Lord, we have placed our hands in yours. Lead us as you will. Call men into your service so that your harvest might grow in our times.

Toward a Supportive Christianity

On the Patronal Feast of the Priestly Society of Saint Salvator

Straubing, 1998

Gospel: Luke 14:1, 7–14

Dear sisters and brothers in the Lord!

Saint Paul once said in the Letter to the Romans: We do not know what we should pray for; the Holy Spirit himself must tell us (cf. Rom 8:26). I think that this is the experience of all of us. We want to pray. But the great words of the Church's faith are too far removed from our lives and cannot simply become our words. And we ourselves live in such a way among everyday things, so far removed from God, that the attempt to speak with him very soon dries up. The Spirit has to teach us the right words. We have just prayed to him to inspire us with his breath, so that we might understand him and learn to speak to him. To learn to pray is to go to the school of the Holy Spirit. He teaches

"Für ein Christentum, das trägt", homily for the patronal feast of the priestly society of St. Salvator on August 30, 1998, in the Basilica of St. Jacob, Straubing, *Communio: Mitteilungen an die Freunde und Förderer der Priesterbruderschaft St. Salvator in Straubing* 2 (1999): 2–3. [B 1084]

us to pray in many different ways: for example, continually through the events in our life. Sometimes there is a need, a sorrow, so that we cry out to him, because we need more help than anything that men can do. Or there may be a joy that brings us to the point where we must say to the Eternal Lord a word of thanks that extends far beyond all human thanksgiving. He teaches us to pray through our life, when we are watchful enough to sense these quiet promptings that sometimes can be very loud, also. But he also teaches us to pray when we become familiar with Sacred Scripture; he teaches us to pray, above all, through the liturgy, which is the great school in which the Holy Spirit would like to lead us into prayer. So let us try, with two sentences from today's liturgy, to go to this school. The first major petition that we just heard today in the Church's prayer (for the Twenty-Second Sunday in Ordinary Time) and presented to God reads: "Insere pectoribus nostris amorem tui nominis." Place deep into our hearts the love of your Name. Lovers like to say in silence the name of the beloved person, which for them is much more than a word. In this name he is partly present, in this name they touch the beloved himself. By naming him in his absence, they direct their lives toward him and feel that they are brought into communion with him. Clearly the liturgy would like something like that to happen between us and God. That he himself might become dear to us and that in addressing him by name we might touch him and draw near to him. But is something that is easy for us to do with people who are spiritually close to us really going to work with God?

When we talk about his name, we probably think first of the great story of the burning bush, where God speaks to Moses and sends him to the pharaoh and to his own people. Moses resists because of the magnitude of this task,

and he says in a world full of gods: How then am I supposed to speak of You; who are You really? Do You have
a name that I can say: so and so is the one who is sending
me? And God grants this request and says, "I am who am.
That is my name."

This name is a mystery. And yet it is a name; for it
means that God allows himself to be addressed, that we
can call upon him with this word, that he has come within
earshot of us, that he no longer stands aloof and inaccessible behind the clouds, so that we ask, "Does he really
exist or not?" He has entered, so to speak, the world's
address book and now has a name, too, that is like a sort of
telephone number. It is possible to speak to him, and we
know that he listens to us. He has a "name".

Of course that was only a beginning on Mount Sinai,
which appears obscure to us and is remote from us. The
real, definitive burning bush stood in Bethlehem and on
Golgotha. Now it is no longer just a mysterious word
that God gives us so that we can address him; now he
has become one of us, he has taken on flesh, he belongs
to us in the history of this world, and from now on he
is one of us. He himself, the God who became man, is
God's callability, his nameability, his living name and his
human name. For this reason Jesus is much more than
just a word. In this name we touch this reality that God is
now really here, we can speak with him, that he is one of
us. The name Jesus completed the name "I am who am,
Yahweh." Jesus is an extension of this name and is now
no longer called merely "I am" but, rather, "I am the one
who saves you."

Latin speakers translated this with the word *Salvator*,
which means the same as Jesus, and the Germans rendered
it with the word *Heiland*: the one who heals me, to whom
I can come. If we let these connections resonate in our

soul, then we could very well begin to start a conversation with God and say, for instance:

So you let us address you, then. You are not merely the distant geometry of the universe. You are here; you know me. It is not true that we must assume that God is so great that we miserable creatures on this tiny planet are of no interest at all to him, because he has other things to do. No. Precisely because he is great, he has a heart for everyone and room for everyone. You let us talk to you, God; you care about me, about me, too, even when things go badly for me and also when I am happy. You always care about me. In today's Gospel, you tell us that you descended to the last place.

Thus the name Jesus leads into conversation with God, leads to the prayer of the Priestly Society of St. Salvator, which for eight hundred years now has been a prayer association of priests and laymen. Its concern has been, in terms of this name, precisely to lead people into dialogue with the Redeemer, the Savior. And this word, Savior, as a translation of Jesus, has become a word of love, a word spoken by the heart. Of course words of love demand discretion. One cannot display them in the great market-place; if we do, they are devalued and become mawkish. And unfortunately it has happened in the last century that too much sentiment has been invoked where there was none in the first place, so that we can scarcely pronounce the word *Heiland*, Savior, because it appears mawkish to us. But today we run the opposite risk.

Nowadays we would like to make Christianity exclusively a matter of head knowledge. But a Christianity that is merely discussion, organization, and a bit of morality does not support us; we cannot grow fond of it; it does not provide joy and strength for our life. In order for the faith to support us and not to be a burden, it has to touch the heart, we must be able to grow fond of God. And so on this feast day of the Salvator Brotherhood, we want to call the Lord Jesus by his name, ask him to make us grow fond of this name again, so that by our fondness for this name we might again sense his own closeness and so that this might bring joy to our heart, the joy of being loved, of not being alone, which remains and guides us even in hours of darkness.

In the prayer for today two petitions then follow; I would like to explain briefly only the first of them: "Bind us more and more to you", it reads in German; the Latin text speaks about "religionis augumentum", an increase in religion, a request that religion might increase and grow. And we know that there is every reason today to make such a request. For although there is a great demand for superstitious and religious sorts of practices, religion itself is diminishing. We see this in the churches that are becoming emptier (not today, thank God), in the dying convents, in the parishes to which pastors can no longer be assigned because there are no priests left, in the absence of God in the public square. The attempt to banish the cross [from classrooms] was only one symptom of the conviction that God is supposed to disappear from public life. But there are other symptoms too: for instance, the tone in which people frequently speak publicly and in the media about God or about religion, at best with a bit of condescension and often with malicious glee and arrogance; they have to show that they are above all that, that they are more enlightened and no longer pursue such things. But this decline in religion is by no means leading people to higher ground: humanity is disappearing more and more. In Albania, in Russia, in the countries where religion has been trampled on for decades, we see that man was also trampled on in the process. Humane sentiments were destroyed and replaced by cold-hearted coarseness. The Church Fathers once said that insensitivity was the real sin and the distinctive mark of the pagans. Are we not also in danger of falling into this insensitivity, this heartlessness? Religion is declining, and if we reflect on this and are realistic, we must simply admit that there is reason to pray for its growth, that its importance might be recognized again, that respect for what is holy, for what is sacred to people, might become the norm again instead of malicious glee; that the importance of God might be recognized again and that we might perceive again that wherever he is excluded, man suffers.

In the German Missal, as I have already said, this petition for the increase of religion is worded: "Bind us more and more to you." That is a free translation, but essentially it is quite correct, for religion, *re-ligio*, means the bond with, dependence on the origin, on the living God. Nowadays we do not like to hear the word "bond", because we like freedom. But it is true, nevertheless, that the man who is bound to no one deteriorates and his life becomes empty. Man lives by his relationships, which give him worth and dignity. The saying "Tell me who your friends are, and I will tell you who you are" is in fact the truth. Someone who has false relationships or none at all deteriorates. Someone who never had the privilege of saying "Mother" lovingly to a mother and never experienced a mother's love, someone who never had the privilege of trusting in a father, has an internal wound that will trouble him for the rest of his life. And someone who has never experienced God's goodness is again deeply wounded, for he is missing the place, the relationship that puts all the other relationships in order. Without a connection to God, we become like satellites that have left their orbit and then hurtle randomly into the void and not only destroy themselves but also threaten others.

"Bind us more and more to you": this is a prayer to the Holy Spirit and for the Holy Spirit. For he is the one who fastens man to God; through him God enters into man and touches man. He leads us to one another; he is the living atmosphere of God that carries us to him. He alone can show us the true trajectory of our life. And so this petition, which is a prayer to the Holy Spirit, should be the petition for this year dedicated to the Holy Spirit: "Bind us to you", touch us from within, so that we perceive again that you exist. Give us a sense of and a taste for what is good and true, for you, for the living God. Let us experience the power of your presence in our hearts; let us be glad about the faith. Show me the trajectory of my life, so that I might walk aright.

In conclusion, let us look once again at the Gospel: at this Gospel about the last place. At first it appears to be like a rather petty prudential rule: "Be careful, do not take the first place", or even as the expression of inhibited humility. But that is not the meaning of the passage at all, because it is a parable. And like almost all of Jesus' parables, it is a bit of a disguised autobiography of Jesus himself, in which he shows his way, his inner being. He is the First, the Creator, the Origin of all things, the Lord. But he descended, came down to us, descended to the last place. He descended into the night of suffering, abandonment, mockery, and death. He went to the last place in the world. What was the real reason why? Because he is needed there the most, because there are people there who lack all love, who are calling for the healing Savior. He descended also for the sake of us who are not in the last place, descended in order to heal our pride; for pride is the real sickness of man. It was the sin of Adam, who wished he did not need God anymore but wanted to be like a God himself and wanted to vie with God. And that is, after all, the temptation of our

time, too, that we would like to vie with God, that we
wish we did not need God any more. We can manage by
ourselves. But by thinking and living this way, by leaving
him out and thinking that we do not need him, we put
ourselves in the wrong place, namely, in the place of the
lie. In reality we do need him; we cannot exist without
him. And precisely this is the greatness of man, that God
alone suffices for him. He came as Savior to heal us.

When we begin to grasp this, then we begin to grow
fond of him, then we will begin to love his name, then we
will become praying people, then the Holy Spirit works in
us—and then we love the right way.

PRIESTLY ORDINATION

Acting *in Persona Christi*

The Threefold Ministry of the Priest

Freising, 1977

Dear candidates for Holy Orders,
dear brothers in the episcopal and priestly ministry,
dear brothers and sisters in the Lord!

The day of priestly ordinations is the harvest day of a diocese, one of the high points in its life. For this day demonstrates how much faith is alive in a local Church, how much
hope-filled courage that can give young men the strength
and the joy to entrust themselves to the Lord's service in the
knowledge that the common faith of the Church will support them in it. At the same time, it is a day that decides the
life, growth, or withering of a diocese. For if the Eucharist
were no longer the living center of a local Church, then
everything else in her would slowly and inevitably dry up,
too. And it is not true, either, as we may sometimes be
inclined to think, that there is a sort of competition between
priestly ministry and the new lay ministries, for which we
are grateful. Rather, the saying of Saint Paul is still true:
When one member suffers, the whole body suffers, and

"Handeln 'in persona Christi'—vom dreifachen Amt des Priesters", for the
priestly ordination in St. Mary's Cathedral, Freising, on June 25, 1977. Previously unpublished. [B 380]

75

when one rejoices, it benefits the whole (cf. 1 Cor 12:26). Only the two together can be alive and grow. If the Church no longer receives her vital force from the altar, then the word of God and the proclamation of the word also lose the soil in which they are rooted and drift off into theoretical, academic talk that cannot give strength. If the attitude of repentance can no longer approach the authoritative word of absolution that can be spoken in the name of the Lord in the power of the sacrament, then the repentant attitude, too, trickles away into insignificance and meaninglessness. If young men no longer enter the Lord's service, fewer and fewer young people will be reached by the power of his word and his signs. Then the burden that weighs on our priests will become still heavier, so that in the wear and tear of everyday routine they are less and less able to radiate the power of the Gospel, to hold up its gladdening luminosity to the present time, and this would necessarily begin a downward spiral of dying off, the end of which would not be difficult to figure out. So this is an hour of deliberation, of an interior demand on the faith, hope, and charity of us all. But at the same time, it remains and should remain an hour of thanksgiving; for the fact that the Lord willed to call four young men, that they found their way to the altar, that like Peter they dared to climb out of the boat of this world's routine and to walk toward the Lord on the sea, trusting that the power of his hands will keep them.

And now I turn to you, dear candidates for Holy Orders. As the *Roman Pontifical* stipulates, I would just like to remind you once again briefly of what you meditated on during these years and took to heart again in these days of your retreat. You know that the Second Vatican Council, in order to make visible the one full meaning of the priestly ministry, presents it in the threefold form of teaching, sanctifying, and shepherding (cf. PO 4–11).

First, there is the *ministry of teaching*, or, as we prefer to call it, the *ministry of proclamation*. During these years of study, you have thought and lived and, now and then probably, also suffered your way into the word of God, so as to be able to hand it on. And I ask you: Keep thinking and living your way into this word. For only inasmuch as it is alive in you and you live in this word can you hand it on and make it bear fruit. And here I would like to read to you what the *Pontifical* says about this: "Let them meditate on your law day and night, so that they may believe what they have read, teach what they have believed, and practice what they have taught."

Then there is the *ministry of sanctification, priestly ministry in the narrower sense*, the ministry of the sacred signs, the seven sacraments, centered on the celebration of the Eucharist. On his own, no man could speak the words that are true only on the lips of Jesus Christ: "This is my body." "This is my blood." Only by his authority, only supported by the empowerment that he himself alone can give, can a man pronounce these words of salvation and consecration that the world needs so much. The language of tradition says that the priest speaks them *in persona Christi*, "in the role of Jesus Christ". But you know that this role, which could burn us up if we do not correspond to it inside, can be adopted correctly only if we enter into it interiorly. If we represent the Lord not only externally in word and gesture, but also from within and give ourselves over to him.

And finally there is the *ministry of shepherding*, which was entirely renewed and transformed at the moment when Jesus, the only true Shepherd, appeared as Lamb. He made good the irrevocable power and the irrevocable claim of his truth and his word and became close to us through the equally irrevocable power of his love. May he grant you the ability to be shepherds in this way: to make known the irrevocable claim of his word and to make it livable in a new way in this world by making good this claim by the power of our humble love, which is united to the Lord's love and subject to it. This alone gives rise to true authority that is neither tyranny nor arbitrariness but the entrance of truth into the world, which is at the same time love. May the Lord of us all, the "Shepherd of our souls" (cf. 1 Pet 2:25), grant that you yourselves, day by day, may find the way that you will show to those entrusted to you and that thus shepherd and flock together may arrive at the destination: eternal life, Christ, our Lord.

Gestures of Priestly Ordination

Imposition of Hands and Anointing of the Hands

During the Ordination of Five Priests from
the Jesuit Order in Munich, 1977

Reading: 2 Kings 5:14–17

Dear brothers and sisters,
dear candidates for Holy Orders!

Priestly ordination is not only a celebration for a few select
men, but a celebration of the whole Church, of the whole
People of God. For we all live dependent on one another,
not only physically but also intellectually and spiritually.
The Church, the fact that each one of us is Christian,
could not continue to exist unless the Eucharist was celebrated, the sacraments administered, the word of God
proclaimed, unless, in a word, there were men who make
themselves completely available for the service of Jesus
Christ and of his Gospel. But the converse is also true:
the priest could not continue his ministry, could not each
day find fresh courage to be the messenger of the Lord

"Gebärden der Priesterweihe—Handauflegung und Salbung der Hände",
for the ordination of five priests for the Jesuit Order in the Church of St.
Michael in Munich on October 8, 1977. Previously unpublished. [B 392]

79

and of a task in which he always falls immeasurably short, were it not for the space of faith in which he can hear his call; were it not for the space of prayer that supports and strengthens him; were it not for the space of hope and love that responds to him and again and again leads him anew through times of discouragement and failure.

The Second Vatican Council quite rightly spoke about the universal priesthood of all Christians. But that does not then mean, as it is sometimes misunderstood, that everyone can do everything or that all are assigned to the same task, but, rather, this very fact means that each of us must follow his calling, that we are all appointed for each other, and that, since no one can do everything, only all of us together as the one body of Christ can fulfill anew his entire mission in his grace again and again in every age.

In the liturgy of priestly ordination, this participation of the universal priesthood is expressed by the Litany of the Saints. We all pray, we all cry to God for mercy, we all wrap these young men, so to speak, in the mantle of prayer. We call on the saints, that they may be like a living rampart around their vocation and at the same time a living door that opens to them the way to people's hearts and to God's Heart. We call on these saints, but it is also up to us to place ourselves beside and among them, so that with them we might become this rampart and this door. And so the Litany of the Saints can become for us all an examination of conscience, too, whether we are still doing this sufficiently. There is an old proverb that says, "Omne malum a clero", all evil comes from the clergy, and the French theologian Louis Bouyer wrote a while ago in a rather bitter book that there is really no crisis of the *Church* today at all, but only a crisis of the *priests* and nuns who have grown weary of their calling and now in their weariness of heart have the desire to go back and be like everyone else, a longing for ordinariness. There is a lot of truth in that, yet it is oversimplified. For, after all, the priest does not continue on his own, but, rather, he remains standing because around him the Church's faith supports him, calls and challenges him, gives him a door, and is a protective wall for him. If we complain so much today about a crisis, then all of us, every one of us, must ask in this hour whether we have always been sufficiently aware of this; whether we knew that we all have to support one another, that we must continually try to be mindful that we should give back the courage of the faith, too, and not just receive it; that we should open the doors of the heart and prepare the ways, so that someone who is in danger of becoming discouraged can see how much yearning, how much demand there is for Christ's message, even today in this world.

And now I turn to you, dear young friends. You know that in recent years an immense amount has been written about the priesthood: good and poor, useful and useless things. The Church's liturgy tells what priesthood actually is, above all with gestures, and it thereby makes us aware that there is something incomprehensible about it that our words can never exhaust. It makes us aware that the essence of priestly ministry can be grasped, not with the understanding alone, but only with understanding and heart, with mind and senses. With the senses, too! In the Church's liturgy, the body prays along. We have forgotten a little too much that prayer, too, is not merely a matter of the heart but, rather, makes demands on the whole indivisible man, that the body, too, by its gesture must hold itself out to the Lord and express the fact that we are turned toward him. The body expresses what comes from the heart. But it is also true, conversely, that the way in which we dare to express ourselves leaves its mark interiorly. So it is no wonder that finally, at the central point of the liturgy of priestly ordination, words fall silent and the gesture speaks.

I would just like to call to mind very briefly the two central gestures of priestly ordination, which make visible much more than we can ever say: the imposition of hands and the anointing of the hands. Both are related to two principal human organs, the head and the hands. First, there is the imposition of hands, with which the bishop and then the whole presbyterate covers the head of the *ordinandus*. The human head is, on the one hand, the place where the control room of his thoughts is found, so to speak, where mind and body mesh the most and the most mysteriously. And precisely in this place where a person is, as it were, the most recollected in himself and where the inner, hidden store of his mind plays out, he is at the same time the most open: eye, ear, and mouth; he takes the world into himself and carries himself out into the world through his word and his watching. This head with its senses, its interpenetration of sense and mind, is grasped in the imposition of hands. First of all, this is a gesture of occupancy. It is supposed to belong to the Lord. Its thinking, hearing, seeing, speaking should be at his disposal. It is a gesture of protection, like a roof of prayer that is set up over you. And a gesture of opening, like the antenna that opens up into God's Spirit and makes its way through the roof of prayer. Augustine said that through the Church's prayer the sacraments are administered, that this prayer of the Church is the space through which the Lord enters us.

Then there is the anointing of the hands. Anthropologists have made us aware of how much the hands express what is human about a human being. In man's nearest animal relatives, they are tools for grasping and striking. In man, in comparison to that, they have become incredibly weak, and he could confront only the smallest animals

with the strength of his hands. And at the same time, they
have become immeasurably stronger. With the work
of his hands, man has transformed this world; with his
hands he has stamped the features of the mind on stone in
his artistic activity. With his hands he can pray and he can
bless. Your hands will be anointed and dedicated to the
Anointed, Jesus Christ. They are now supposed to be, as it
were, the hands that Jesus Christ has in this world. Instead
of tools for striking and grasping, in which we take the
world as our own possession and try to wield our power
over it, they are to become hands of prayer, blessing hands.
And thus this sign of anointed hands actually expresses
everything that priesthood means and is: You are to carry
the Body of the Lord, announce absolution, lead people to
worship, and be prayerful yourselves, and you are to bless.

Earlier we listened to the reading about Naaman the
Syrian, who was healed of his leprosy in the Jordan. There
is a deep, subterranean connection between what we heard
in it and what is taking place here, and almost every single
feature of this story appears to be a foreshadowing of the
mystery of Jesus Christ. One feature above all in this story
has become dear to me, although for a long time I read past
it and it seemed at first like a superficial detail. It is reported
that Naaman, the healed man, wants to give thanks. And
at first he wants to do so with money, in keeping with his
position. But he is forced to acknowledge that that is not
enough in this case, that another order of magnitude is in
play here, compared to which money is always too little,
regardless of how much of it there is. He has to acknowledge that compensation is not enough here; only he himself suffices. So from that hour on he wants to be a servant
of the living God, to be truthful by becoming a worship-
per, someone who knows that he is indebted and thereby
transforms himself and the world. As a sign of the fact that

from now on he belongs to God, he has two mules loaded with earth from Israel. That strikes us at first as somewhat pagan; it recalls the notion that God is bound to his earth and that therefore you have to take some of it along. In truth, something very deep emerges from this: God is available to us not simply as we suppose him to be and as we ourselves want him to be. For us he is discoverable as he gave himself to us. And he gave himself to us through the history of his holy people, in which the earth of Israel is a prelude to the sacred earth of his Body, of his holy Church. We cannot be God's servants any way we please, but only in this sacred earth of his Body, his Church. And so, may God grant you to belong to this sacred earth forever more and thus to prepare the new earth, in which everything will be worship and, consequently, truth, freedom, and peace.

Becoming an Offering with Christ
for the Salvation of Mankind

Freising, 1978

Dear candidates for Holy Orders,
dear brothers in the episcopal and priestly ministry,
dear brothers and sisters in the Lord!

What is priestly ordination, really, and what is the priesthood into which it initiates? These are questions that have been posed to us anew in the debate in recent years, and we must learn anew the answer to them. The Church's liturgy gives the answer in prayer and significant gesture; it outlines it in advance in the four questions that inquire into the readiness of the candidates and thus pace off the interior space of the demands and the gift of the priesthood.

It would lead too far afield if we tried to reflect now on all of them. The last question actually summarizes in itself the essence of all the others, and we should look at it a little so as to understand in greater depth the meaning of this moment. It reads: "Are you resolved to consecrate your life to God for the salvation of his people, and to

"Mit Christus Opfergabe werden zum Heil der Menschen", for the priestly ordination in St. Mary's Cathedral, Freising, on July 1, 1978. The full text as yet unpublished; excerpt in *Mitarbeiter der Wahrheit: Gedanken für jeden Tag*, ed. Irene Grassl, 3d ed. (Würzburg, 1993), 187–89; a summary in *Ordinariatskorrespondenz*, Munich, no. 24 (July 6, 1978). [B 443]

unite yourself more closely every day to Christ the High Priest, who offered himself for us to the Father as a perfect sacrifice?" Although it is not said explicitly, the Eucharistic commission is behind this as the center of priestly existence. The priest exists in order to confect the Eucharist, to celebrate God's banquet among men, to be, as it were, the official who invites people to God's wedding to give him joy in this world. But the way in which the question is formulated in German is important. It does not say, "Are you ready to *do* or *make* this and that?" Rather, it says: "Are you ready to *become* an offering with Christ?" What is demanded here is not doing but being. And only in these depths in which a man allows himself to be touched and is personally ready to come into play can he correspond with the Lord's gift. Eucharist is more than a party, the priest's coffee-klatsch, a convivial gathering. It is the festive gift of God, in which he himself comes to us and, beyond all that we can do or make, touches the true depths of our life.

When we reflect further on this, the nature and extent of the demand that we are talking about becomes evident. The first thing to become clear is what I would like to call the "non-arbitrary character of the Eucharist". This means: It is not something that we ourselves—for instance, the pastor or the bishop—think up and do, but, rather, in it the Lord gives us more than any of us could give. In it happens something that none of us can invent or make. In it a gift is entrusted to the priest that is and remains a gift for him, too, in his faithful care. This, I think, should always be the first thing. The greatness of the Eucharist, which surpasses all other events in the world, consists not in all of our planning, however interesting it may be, but in what precedes our planning. In the fact that the Lord himself acts in the prayer and activity of the Church throughout history. What matters first of all is that we become servants of this greater plan, that we learn to go beyond ourselves and to bear the gift that none of us could ever invent and for which we are all waiting, nevertheless, for we all have a longing, whether or not we consciously acknowledge it, to step out of the mere contrivances devised by our minds and made by our hands and to become the festive gift that we cannot invent, that can only be gift.

The fact that this is so, that there is something here that we cannot make but can only hand on, by no means implies, however, that now we are merely passive, that we neither can nor should contribute to it ourselves. Quite the contrary: precisely because there is something greater here, our entrance into this preceding, greater event is all the more a demand made on all the dimensions of our self. Part of this, first of all, is simply the external preparation, making sure again and again that the external space for the celebration of the holy mysteries is there and is worthy, that the necessary services take place, that the people are gathered, that festivity and solemnity are promoted, that the people become able and willing to spend their time on something that is not an earthly business. When we say this, that such various external services are necessary, too, in order for this greatness to be, it already suggests also that there can be no Eucharistic service without the constant proclamation of the word of God, without the preparation of the interior space in which this word speaks to us. In recent years the Church has worked hard to make the Eucharist understandable and transparent for everyone. And that is a good thing. But at the same time we have necessarily noticed that there is a limit to it. Even when ever so much along these lines is done: you can never listen to the Eucharist and let it wash over you like a tabloid newspaper or the news on the radio. It always requires

more, a deeper and greater understanding, and if we tried
to create this in the Eucharist itself, it would be too late.
Then we end up having to talk more and more, until
finally we cover up the great impact of the sacred action
with words, talk it to pieces, and ultimately have still said
too little. Listening to the word of God must precede the
Eucharist; the senses and the heart must be prepared for it.
For here there has to be a listening and an understanding
that includes the heart also and the whole person, who
grasps more than his intellect alone could perceive.

Another part of it is leading people on the path of conversion, so that they learn to acknowledge their sins and
to receive forgiveness. Part of the predicament of our time
is that we have to dispute guilt more and more. Indeed,
man cannot bear guilt unless there is forgiveness in sight
somewhere. Then he denies it. But then he is living contrary to the truth. And someone who lives contrary to the
truth crumbles interiorly. He can bear his truth, the truth
of guilt, only if a new, greater truth comes to him. The
truth of God that is called forgiveness. This is the other
major aspect of priestly ministry, that we have the privilege of speaking this word of forgiveness and can thus
make truth possible for man and create life. This should
penetrate your heart today, this gift: the privilege of speaking the word of forgiveness, the word of blessing, and the
word of consecration.

Let us return again to the question in the rite of ordination. It says [in German]: "Are you ready to become an
offering with Christ ...?"

At first we resist such a formulation as a description of
the innermost meaning of priesthood. It might seem to
us extravagant, ultimately exaggerated, and untrue. But
that is because we associate "offering" or "victim" with a
false concept, for instance, the notion of endless torments

that people then for some reason consider to be a way of worshipping God. Or the notion that sacrifice was an achievement that Christ offered sufficiently and that we need not and cannot add anything more to it. On the contrary, the remark of Saint Augustine should alert us: "This is the sacrifice of Christians: Many are one Body in Christ." God does not want something of us, he needs nothing, he is the Creator of all things. He wants from us something that only his creature can give him anew: our love. Thus offering or sacrifice does not mean this or that torment, this or that achievement, but, rather, it means that we emerge from the fundamental law of egotism, self-assertion, self-sufficiency, and that we commend ourselves to the new law of Jesus Christ, who is the man for others and the Son of the Father in the eternal exchange of triune love. Because we cannot do this by ourselves, the offering of Christians means precisely this: allowing Christ to take us mercifully by the hand and to lead us into the inner unity of his organism, his holy Church, and thus, in union with him, to become like God. For God himself is not a self-enclosed Ego but, rather, is real only in the mutual self-giving of Father, Son, and Spirit. To become an offering means to allow oneself to be drawn into this mystery and so to drink the festive wine of Jesus Christ, the wine of divinity. From this perspective, we can then understand also the hard work that it takes to let oneself be taken again every day out of the self-enclosed ego and be fitted into the whole of his Body. The real, primary thing is not the toilsome aspect but, rather, this great transformation into the mystery of triune love. The more we keep this great new thing before our eyes, the more we will understand tiresome, everyday routine as a gift that makes us rich and free, and not as a torment that restricts and demeans us.

From this perspective we can now understand also the next-to-last of these ordination questions [in the German edition of the *Roman Pontifical*]: "Are you ready to assist the poor and the sick, to help the homeless and the needy?" This is not outdated social romanticism that was imported into the priesthood after the fact; rather, if it is true that celebrating the Eucharist means drinking the wine of Jesus Christ, the wine of his triune love, allowing oneself to be fitted into his Body, emerging from mere self-sufficiency, then this always means precisely to be open to others, too, to those who are marginalized. To think and to live by him means, not to appreciate a man, in terms of his functionality, but rather to see him with the eyes of God who created us, with the eyes of Jesus Christ, who loves each one of us and suffered for him.

In past discussions about the priesthood, various views were expressed: some said that a priest is no longer a real professional today because he does not fit into a world of specializations, in which we cannot have someone who is there for everything in life; others said that if a priest is still to be a professional, he must also become a specialist, for instance, a specialist for theological questions, who is available to the congregation for this purpose and advises it. I say: No. The greatness and ever-necessary character of the priest consists precisely in the fact that, in a world that has unraveled into specializations and consequently is ailing, suffering, and crumbling, he remains a man for the whole, who holds human existence together from within. After all, this is our great misery: that a man is no longer a man anywhere, but instead there is a special division for the elderly, for the sick, or for the children, and no one anywhere lives the fullness of human existence now. If the priest did not yet exist, then it would be necessary to invent the man who in the midst of the specializations is a man sent by God for men; who is there for the sick and the well, for the children and the elderly, for the weekday and the holy day, and who holds all this together thanks to God's merciful love. This is the truly beautiful, deeply human, and at the same time holy and sacramental thing about the priesthood, that for all the education that he needs, the priest is ultimately not one of many specialists but, rather, the servant of creatureliness, of humanness, who leads us together beyond the compartmentalization of life into the merciful love of God, into the unity of Christ's Body.

And so, dear young brothers, we wish to offer for you in this hour a heartfelt prayer that in all the toil involved in this word about offering and sacrifice, he will make you recognize again and again the wine of joy, the purpose for which all this happens. And that in all the fragmentation that this life brings every day to everyone and to you, too, he will grant you again and again the delightful experience of continuing in it the mystery of Jesus Christ, of leading people together, leading them to him, and thus holding human existence together, so that you become necessary with the necessity of someone who does not do some particular thing but, rather, cares about the very foundation of our life.

In this hour we all wish to pray that God might bless the Yes that these brothers of ours have just spoken in the presence of us all; that their ministry might be blessed as they now set out on their journey. Maybe after all another reason for the crisis in the priesthood is that congregations have supported their priests too little and did not make them feel how necessary they are. Let us then do it again! There will always be mistakes and weaknesses, but just when we discover them, let us seek one another all the more in the Lord! Let us support one another all the more, for the Lord's sake and by his help, so that the light of faith, the hope of life that he gives us, will not be extinguished in our homeland but will carry on. So that the festive joy of his love may brighten our life, so that we can be thankful people, Eucharistic people.

Giving the Answer of Life

The Example of Blessed Maximilian Kolbe

Freising, 1979

Dear brothers in the episcopal and priestly ministry,
dear candidates for Holy Orders,
dear brothers and sisters in the Lord!

The French theologian Marc Oraison relates in his memoirs in a way worth pondering how he found his path from medicine to the priesthood. As a surgeon he had had many successes in the battle against sickness and death, but also and inevitably he had an ever deeper sense of the limits of the medical arts and of their power. And then he writes: Given death, and seeing all that I was unable to do, I had an increasingly strong desire to make the Resurrection present in the sight of death, that is, to say Mass. For him, becoming a priest did not mean bidding farewell to what he had intended as a physician, but, rather, he saw in it the definitive, full answer to death, which is called

"Die Antwort des Lebens geben: Das Beispiel des seligen Maximilian Kolbe", for the priestly ordination in St. Mary's Cathedral, Freising, on June 30, 1979, in *Christlicher Glaube und Europa: 12 Predigten* (Munich, 1981; 2nd ed., 1982; 3rd ed., 1985), 45–52; previously in *Ordinariatskorrespondenz*, Munich, no. 22 (July 5, 1979); as a pamphlet with the title: *Die Antwort des Lebens geben* (Munich: Pressereferat der Erzdiözese München und Freising, 1979). [B 518]

resurrection: making Christ's Resurrection present, and ours in it, can be accomplished only in the power of the priestly mission.

Making the Resurrection present—I had to think of this phrase again when I had the privilege during the week after Pentecost of celebrating the Eucharist with Pope John Paul II in the concentration camp in Auschwitz–Birkenau. It was an exciting thought and an exciting experience, over this vast harvest field of death, on this killing field on which over a million people met their death, to live to see the presence of the Resurrection as the only true and only sufficient answer to it. It was exciting to experience how this memorial to hatred and inhumanity became a place of the triumph of the love of Jesus Christ and of love. And Father Maximilian Kolbe's sacrifice of his life, too, became comprehensible for the first time.

For it became evident that this death of his, the saying of the Mass of his life to its conclusion, was a sign of hope and a victory because it occurred out of faith in the Resurrection of Jesus Christ, because in terms of this faith it was an act of making the Resurrection present. Thus the pope could interpret the former scene of the most profound debasement of man as the place of the victory of love, where the power of Jesus Christ's love proved stronger than all destruction of things human.

The answer to an oft-asked question became clear to me as well. How often has it been said: Can anyone still believe in a good God after Auschwitz? I understood: Precisely because Auschwitz exists, we need faith, we need the presence of the Resurrection and of the victory of love; only the Resurrection can make the star of hope rise that allows us to live.

Making the Resurrection present—my dear young friends—this in fact describes completely the essence of what being a priest means. It means, most profoundly, being able to bring about this reality on the killing field of this world, in which death and its powers reap a continual harvest; it means bringing about the presence of the Resurrection and, thus, giving the answer of life that is stronger than death.

That is why celebrating the Eucharist of the Lord is and remains the innermost center of the priestly ministry, of the mission that you are receiving today: accomplishing in the Body and Blood of Jesus Christ his death and the victory of love. Thus your life must continually be measured with a view to this point and find its way starting from it. For celebrating the Eucharist, after all, does not just mean performing a ritual.

The prayers of the ordination liturgy say about this: "Imitamini quod tractatis"—"Imitate the mystery you celebrate." Let this event provide you with the measure and manner of your being, so that it might truly become the innermost center of your whole life.

Making the Resurrection present means that we ourselves live in it and on it. It can happen properly only if we are acquainted with the risen Lord. When the first election of an apostle was to be made in the Church after Easter, the fundamental criterion was: the one so appointed must know Jesus Christ, must have sat at table with him, must have been one of his followers, and must have met the risen Lord.

Only when we know Christ, when we accompany him on his paths, when we have learned to recognize his voice, when he speaks to our life, when we have encountered the risen Lord, do we live out the mission to make the Resurrection present in this world.

Therefore I can ask you once again at this hour to seek the fellowship of Jesus Christ continually, to live with him as your destination, to learn his ways, to hear his voice, to place your hands in his pierced side. Another part of this is the communion of Holy Church. For only in the communion of the Twelve and of the Seventy was it possible to walk with Jesus.

A Jesus whom we tried to seek apart from this communion would be a self-made Jesus. But in fact he lives only in the midst of the Church, which is his Body. By living as Church, believing in her and thus building her up, we encounter him. Making the Resurrection present, therefore, does not mean preserving the liturgy as though in a glass display case but, rather, that we continually carry life and love from it into the world and go out to the people so as to give them life and love.

Someone who believes in the Resurrection does not have to look out for himself and his self-fulfillment, for fear of missing something that life has to offer; rather he knows that infinity is his space, that he has no need to flee but can turn to others in service. The haste that attempts to exhaust the moment, the anxiety that fears missing out on life, is a sign of a world that does not know the Resurrection. Many people waste their time precisely by forcibly clinging to the moment. For their sake, we ought to be people who, based on their faith in the Resurrection, have time and are not afraid that life might treat them badly but, rather, are able to devote themselves fearlessly to serving their brethren in the great freedom of eternal love.

Celibacy, too, can be understood only from this perspective. It must never be based on a No or on skepticism, much less on misanthropy, for then it would not bear fruit and would be opposed to the intention of Jesus Christ. Quite the contrary: it must be a wholehearted encouragement to fidelity, encouragement to confidence. Its source has to be the courage that dares to live with a view to the eternity in which God's outspoken love embraces us unendingly.

During the visit to Poland, the Bishop of Katowice told me that his major seminarians, after the third year of their theology studies, have to work for a year in a mine or in a factory. And he reported that they all return from it fortified with a new joy; they not only lose all the petty haggling for advantages and comfort by facing and experiencing the difficulty of everyday life nowadays, but also and most importantly they hear people tell them again and again: We need a priest! We are waiting for him! Indeed, they themselves experience in the leaden monotony of our times the fact that the alternative, the light of the Resurrection, which alone can bring festive joy to this world, is truly a vital necessity.

I do not know whether seminarians doing a practicum here in Germany could hear our working people say anything like that. Maybe on account of our unbelief, all of us are too obstinate in our chase after the moment, after the things that life still might be able to give us, that time still might grant us. In truth, however, we need all the more urgently the freedom, the calmness that comes from faith in the Resurrection; we need unending space and the light of hope that can make our life free for the first time. And so the mission of this hour is for you to be witnesses of the Resurrection. "You shall be my witnesses" (Acts 1:8). With these words you go forth today.

But the Lord's words are never just a challenge; in the first place, they are always a promise. Grace and gift. And so there is another part of this commission: "I am with you always, to the close of the age" (Mt 28:20). The more we become witnesses, the more we can experience the grace of this presence even in the dark hours. So may the Lord who sends you be your light, your hope, and your fulfillment!

Peter: The Original Model
of Priestly Mission

Freising, 1981

First Reading: Acts 3:1–10
Gospel: John 21:15–19

Year after year the figures of the two apostles Peter and
Paul loom over priestly ordination as the original models
of priestly mission and as signs for the unity of the Church
in which this sending occurs. Through the liturgy of this
day they speak to us; they escort you, dear brothers, as
you set out on your path of ministry. Let us listen to what
today's readings may have to say along these lines.

A lame man is sitting there at the so-called Beautiful
Gate of the Temple, begging. He is asking for money to
pay for his living expenses, which he himself is not able
to earn. He is asking for money as a substitute for his freedom, which he does not have, as a substitute for his own
life, which is denied him. And now John and Peter come
along. How poor they are, with regard to what the man
is asking for. "I have no silver and gold." But how rich
they are with regard to something that he is not thinking
about and does not dare to ask for and yet is the essential

"Petrus—Urbild priesterlicher Sendung", for the priestly ordination in St.
Mary's Cathedral, Freising, on June 27, 1981, in *Heiligenpredigten* (Munich,
1997; new ed.: Donauwörth, 2005), 50–56. [B 624]

thing: "I give you what I have; in the name of Jesus Christ of Nazareth, rise and walk" (Acts 3:6). The unasked-for, unexpected, unrequested thing is given instead of the substitute. The essential thing is given to him—his own life. He is given to himself. From now on he can stand on his own two feet, can walk his own path, can leap (as the reading says), which is a sign of freedom; can enter the Temple, which means: saying Yes to God the Creator, joining in the Yes of creation, becoming Yes to himself and to his Creator.

"I have no silver and gold, but I give you what I have, in the name of Jesus Christ of Nazareth." This validly describes the substance of priestly ministry for all ages. "I have no silver and gold." Our task is not to change the world materially. In a time when we sense so deeply the material need, the hunger of many millions of people, in a time in which only what is quantifiable matters—that is, something you can reckon and calculate and take in hand as a fact—we feel immensely poor. And it is understandable that the temptation frequently arises to offer not just words, as it seems—words that are so empty and seem to be so little in comparison to the real needs of the world. We have to resist the temptation to transform the priesthood, too, into social service and political action, so as finally to give something tangible, something "real", so to speak.

But gradually we notice, too, that man hungers not only for bread and money, but also in fact hungers for a word, for the word in which we give a piece of ourselves, in which we give love—the real gift by which man lives. We begin to recognize that we sin if we hold back this real gift and bashfully hide it. And we perceive that even the millions of people in the world who are actually hungering are not content and are not treated fairly if we just hand them some money for bread. They, too—especially they—hunger for more, hunger for the word, hunger for the gift of our love. Moreover: our own word, our own gift, how weak it is! It can never be enough. We have—and this is the greatness of the priestly mission—more to give. We have something to give for which man does not ask and about which he often does not know and that, yet, is his real need. And this is why we are not allowed to direct our supply according to the demand, because by doing that we narrow man down, try to soothe him with the substitute, and keep him far away from the real thing that gives him back to himself. We have the name of Jesus Christ to give. And this name of Jesus Christ is the thing for which mankind hungers and asks in all its protests against the inadequacies of this world, even if it does not know it. It is the gift that can give man his freedom: to walk on his own feet, to walk and leap, to enter the Temple of the Lord, and to become a song of praise, to say Yes to his Creator, who in all the distress of this world is also our Redeemer and wishes to include us in his Yes.

To give the name of Jesus Christ is the everlasting substance of priestly ministry. Again and again it moves me deeply while distributing Holy Communion when I can say and must say: "The Body of Christ." When we give people and place on their hand something that is infinitely more than all that I myself am and have. When I can give them much more than I could ever give as a man, when I have the privilege of placing the living God himself onto their hands and into their heart. And it is an unheard-of thing to be able to say in the sacrament of Reconciliation, "I absolve you." You in the singular, not wrapped up in some collectivity in which we all say, "We are all sinners, you know", and: "Sure, God will be merciful to us all", while in reality, as a modern poet says, "we cannot stop chewing away on our undigested past." No, not in some collectivity in which I with my past and guilt and need am ultimately not affected. "I absolve you." A friend told me about a priest who was a Russian prisoner of war to whom a non-Catholic clergyman came with the request to make his confession. And he said to him, "Why are you coming to me?" The answer: "I do not want consolation but rather absolution." This is precisely what it means to give the name of Jesus, to give Jesus himself, and to say: You are free, your guilt does not matter any more, the burden of your past has been taken from you, you can stand and go your way and can go to God and can leap and sing praise. And what an unheard-of thing it is also to have the privilege at the hour of death of giving the anointing that leads to resurrection, to make the Resurrection present as the one real answer to death, so that in this hour, too, in which the final earthly lameness occurs, we can say: Stand up. You will rise, and you will go your way, and you will look into the eyes of your God, and you will praise him, and no one will ever take your freedom from you again.

To give the name of Jesus. This presupposes, of course, that we ourselves are standing in the name of Jesus, that he is invoked over us. And here the most profound mystery of priestly ordination becomes visible now, dear candidates for ordination! No one can speak in the name of Jesus on his own. He alone can empower us to do so. "I have put my words in your mouth", God said to Jeremiah at the beginning of his vocation (Jer 1:9). This is exactly what he is saying to you in this hour. "I put my words in your mouth." You will and may speak my words. You will say: "This is my Body! This is my Blood!" And you will say: "I absolve you!" With my ego? No man can empower himself to do that. Nor can any congregation, because, after all, these are the personal words of him alone. This can happen only in the sacrament, in the sacramental power

that he himself gives, and only in this way can the gift of
his name remain present in this world. I put *my* words in
your mouth. This is also what ultimately makes us free.
We do not need to invent the Church. And ultimately it
does not depend on my proficiency, my piety, my limited
ability to love. "I put my words in your mouth." And that
is why God could put up with it when Jeremiah contra-
dicted him and said, "Ah, Lord GOD! Behold, I do not
know how to speak, for I am only a youth" (Jer 1:6).
How often we quarrel with the Lord in this way, and his
answer remains: It is not about you. "I put my words in
your mouth." And therefore you are free, and it is all right
for you to speak, to proclaim the name of Jesus. The fact
that we can speak in his name also gives us that great interior calm, the peace, and the freedom without which this
ministry would be intolerable. But that does not mean, of
course, that we can just stand and look on, as it were, like
an indifferent loudspeaker. The meaning is fulfilled only if
we ourselves, too, really begin to think his thoughts and
thus to speak along in his words.

With that we have arrived at today's Gospel. The two
things that Jesus says to Peter: "Do you love me?" and
"Feed my sheep" (Jn 21:15–17), correspond to each other.
Loving and feeding are the same thing, according to this
wonderful saying of the Lord. Feeding or pasturing—
which means caring for souls—is done by loving, by loving together with the love of Jesus Christ. The sacraments
are still valid even without us. The word remains true,
even when it is turned against us. And often enough we
will need this as a consolation. But we can take care of
souls only by feeding, which means, by coming to love,
by loving together with him. And so we turn to the Lord:
Lord, you want me to speak in your name. Give me this
name. Give me to your name. Give me your name. And

I would like to ask you, dear brothers, to read again and
again these wonderful words about friendship with Jesus
that the Holy Father spoke to us priests in Fulda and to
let them come true in your life. And I would like to commend to you a remark by Pope Leo the Great, who once
said: "You must learn to find God's heart in Sacred Scripture, to hear God's heartbeat." Feeding means loving. Caring for souls means loving with the love of Jesus Christ,
and it means loving him, being loved by him! For that is
how he feeds us. This love of Jesus Christ is not something
saccharine, cheap, or convenient. Indeed, as the Gospel
tells us, it leads onward, for then we read: "Another will
fasten your belt for you and carry you where you do not
wish to go" (Jn 21:18). We must find and recognize Jesus'
friendship, God's heartbeat in Scripture. So that then,
when he fastens our belt and leads us where we do not
want to go, we still recognize him as our friend, still recognize God's heart, and know that even when he grabs hold
of us roughly, he is leading us into love, into salvation,
into freedom.

In conclusion I would like to put a little story that Hein-
rich Mann told in his autobiography. He reports that he
was in Italy one day, walking for a stretch on dusty roads
with a Capuchin friar. The latter asked him his denomina-
tion, and he replied that he neither believed nor denied,
because both were too lofty for him. At the end, when
they parted ways, the friar abruptly said to him, "Now
I will have to pray for you." This, too, seems to me to
be an image of priestly ministry. We are called again and
again, as God wills, to accompany people for a stretch on
the dusty roads of this world. And we are called then to
remember them and to include them in the intentions we
place before God, so that their way and ours become a way
of God. And it seems to me also to be an image for the

mystery of Jesus Christ himself: he walks with us on the roads of this world. He accompanies us. And at the end he says to each one of us—and in this hour he says it especially to you, dear candidates for ordination: "Now I will always think of you." He is always thinking of us. We are kept in his memory. That is our great confidence. Thereby we are given to his name, and his name is given to us. We go our way in this freedom and joy even in tribulation. May the Lord who today is taking you by the hand in this way always make this grace of his presence perceptible to you! May he help you to give the world the name of Jesus in your priestly ministry all the days of your life!

The Priest-Monk

One Who Prays for the People

Mariawald, 1991

The priesthood that Christ gave to his Church is one, but it is connected with many various charisms and many gifts, corresponding to the variety of people who are called to communion with Christ and are supposed to make up his Church. Today it happens that the sacrament of the priesthood encounters the charism of monasticism in its strictest form: the contemplative surrender to the Lord in a life of prayer and reflection on the things of God. Our notion of pastoral care has meanwhile become so pragmatic and so functional, too, that it is very difficult for us to imagine how these two things are actually supposed to go together: being a shepherd for people on behalf of the Lord and at the same time being a man of devotion and silence by leaving behind the activities of this world and turning in prayer to the living God. Nevertheless, the two things belong together, and if we just look at this coexistence we are preserved from a one-sided view of what it means to be a priest and we understand it more deeply. We can

"Der Mönchspriester—Beter für das Volk", for the priestly ordination of Brother M. Robert Hirtz on September 15, 1991, in Mariawald, *MIPB* 2 (2009): 49–52.

grasp this coexistence correctly if we go to the heart of it, which then opens up in various ways of actualization.

One thing that has frequently helped me to understand this is a responsory that the Church devised for Evening Prayer II for Pastors based on Old Testament texts. The responsory reads: "Hic est fratrum amator qui multum orat pro populo suo: This is a man who loved his brethren and ever prayed for them."

Being a priest means, on the basis of friendship and fellowship with Christ, becoming a friend for all one's brothers and sisters, also. The innermost act of this friendship with people is to bring all these people, all their cares, pains, sufferings, hopes, and joys, into the presence of the living God in prayer. The priest should, so to speak, gather up all the unresolved matters hidden in everyday activities, the things that oppress and threaten people in the events of this world, and carry them upward, so that they address the living God and make their way into his eye, his ear, and his heart.

The history of Israel's liberation, the history of mankind's salvation, begins with the fact that God hears the cry of Israel in need. Finally, he can no longer merely listen to it from a distance, because it wounds his heart, so that he comes down to redeem his people.

This, therefore, is the first and innermost task of priestly ministry: understanding, taking up, and transforming human matters in prayer, so that they become a cry that stands in the presence of God and draws him down again and again, because his heart is moved and he therefore wants to come to us and redeem us.

At the center of all Jesus Christ's pastoral ministry were the nights that he spent in prayer on the mountain, alone with his Father. From such a night of prayer face to face with the Father resulted the calling of the Twelve. Being on the mountain that way, he saw the ship of the Church, how it labors on the sea, on the waters of this world, and makes no progress against the head wind and seems to be sinking. And from that height, which is at the same time proximity, he got the ship on course again and continually speeds it on its way.

Finally there is the high-priestly prayer of Jesus Christ, in which he stands as the true High Priest in the presence of the living God, anticipates death, transforms it into love, and thus tears the veil between God and the world; all the pain of the world is taken up by him in love, resulting in peace and reconciliation. This high-priestly prayer continues during the night of the Garden of Olives and during the day of Calvary. There, in his loneliness on the mount of the Cross, the Lord brings the cry of the world into the presence of God and into his heart, so that he once again and definitively comes down and grants to the world resurrection and transformation. Repeating and imitating this high-priestly prayer of Jesus Christ over and over again in our needs, so that they become transformed therein, is central to the priestly mission. "One who loves his brethren and ever prays for the people" is a profound definition of priestly ministry. Dear Father Robert, that is why the Church prays on this day that you will love his people by the Lord, out of friendship with him, and that as a result of this friendship and fellowship you will always pray for the people.

The tradition of the Church viewed the story about Jacob's ladder, on which the angels ascended and descended, as an image of the interior prerequisites for Christian life and, thus, as an image of priestly life. The angels ascend and descend. This means that part of true friendship and fellowship with Christ is going up to him and bringing the things of this world into his presence. But that automatically includes bringing down again what we have received from him.

And so being a friend of the brethren always means also being a shepherd, leading them to good pastures, or as Saint Paul interprets it more clearly and comprehensibly for us: becoming stewards of the mysteries of God.

Prayer for the people leads to stewardship of the mysteries of God. The priest exists in order to bring the mysteries of God and, consequently, the Lord himself to the people. Bringing God to the people, installing him in this world as the one who descended with us, is the first and foremost task of a priest. He can and perhaps will have to do many other things as well. But if a priest were to begin thinking: first, there are so many problems to solve, God is not all that important, someday if we have time we will bring him back into play—then, of course, he would lose his way. For even though we do not see it and precisely when we do not see it, God is the truly necessary thing and the most necessary thing for people and for the world. When God disappears, man disappears.

The Shepherd Psalm of the Old Covenant, Psalm 23, described in unforgettable images this stewardship of the mysteries of God, that is, the bringing of God himself to the people and into this world: "You lead me to green pastures, to living waters. You anoint my head and prepare a table for me, and even in the dark shadows of the day of death you do not abandon me." Leading to green pastures, to living waters, means leading to the place where God's word is; conducting beyond all the talk of this world, beyond all the troubled waters of our information and ideologies, to the living water, to the words that really give us life and make the world green and fruitful again. We must allow the word of God itself to speak and not overlay it with our interpretations. We must offer the fresh water as God gave it to us, certain that his word is truth and that we need the drink of truth in order to live.

Anointing the head, preparing a table—these are images for the mysteries, the sacraments, in which Christ touches us and, so to speak, draws us into an embrace with him. In the sacraments he enters again and again into the world of the senses in order to touch us where we live and to lead us farther into eternity.

In the psalm there is a verse about the shadow of death. This leads us to a third perspective, which is closely related to today's feast. Indeed, we celebrate today the feast of the Seven Sorrows of the Mother of God. At first glance, it might seem like a strange date for such a joyful occasion. But this date is a particularly good date. In the Johannine scene of the Mother beneath the Cross, com-passionating, crucified with her Son, as it were, the Church recognized the fulfillment of Simeon's prophecy: "Your soul will be pierced by sorrow."

Mary stands beneath the Cross as someone who suffers with, and thus she has become the perennially valid anticipation of what the Church is, her living image. The Church's place is at the Cross of Jesus Christ: in communion with him, in the communion of the Cross; fruitfulness can come only from this place. The world needs compassion, but an active compassion that goes beyond our sorry strength, a compassion that draws the sufferings of the world into God's compassion with us—and thus into love, the only thing that transforms and redeems suffering and, yes, makes it valuable.

All too long now we have listened to ideologies that tell us: Christianity has it all wrong with its talk about the Cross; this pacifies and soothes people so that they do not rebel. We must not accept suffering, these ideologies tell us; we must do away with it. That sounds very nice. But when we look back at the extensive ruins of suffering "done away with", we see what insane arrogance there is in these claims. He who wants to do away with suffering must first do away with love. For love includes the fruitful transformations of suffering, without which there can be no alchemy of our heart, so to speak, by which we are drawn into God's love, by which we are drawn out of ourselves and thus become free for each other by God's power. No, we cannot do away with suffering. We see that this mad attempt almost succeeded in destroying love and holding it up as something stupid because it makes people dependent. Through such arrogance man is not elevated but dragged down beneath his own dignity into a soulless realm. We need the way that the Crucified One announces to us: communion with him, with his suffering. Only by drawing the suffering of the world into his divine compassion, into the Body that is the space of his love, does a healing transformation of the world occur: the redemption of man.

That is why part of the priest's mission is to suffer with the Lord, to understand the world's suffering, to help bear it, and to commend it to Christ, to place it into his redeeming love.

From ancient times the Church has given a blessing with the sign of the cross. For by Christ's Passion, the cross has become the hallmark of love. With her sign of blessing, the Church tells us where the source of all blessing, all transformation, and all fruitfulness is. Thus we can say, finally: The priest's task can be best described in the statement: The priest should be someone who blesses; he has received this ability and privilege from his Lord. But this task includes placing himself into the mystery of the Cross.

Dear Father Robert, in this hour, on the feast of the Sorrowful Mother of God, we entrust you to the Mother of our Lord, and the Church entrusts you to her, as Christ entrusted all future disciples to her in the disciple whom he loved. If you stand by her, you will stand well.

But do not forget, and let us not forget: conversely he also entrusted his Mother to John. He entrusts the Church to us priests. Only in great humility and in unconditional trust in God's grace can we dare to perform this ministry, but then live it also as a ministry of joy.

Therefore, as this feast day proclaims with its Gospel, remain standing by your Mother all the days of your life. Under her protective mantle, you will stand secure, because then you are in the shadow of Christ, in the light of the Resurrection.

Entering into the Mystery
of the Grain of Wheat

Rome, Saint Paul outside the Walls, 1993

Gospel: John 12:20–26

Dear candidates for ordination,
dear friends of the *Katholische Integrierte Gemeinde* (KIG,
   an apostolic association),
dear brothers and sisters in the Lord!

The words of the Gospel to which we have just listened
are Jesus' answer to reports of a request by pilgrims from
Greece who wanted to see Jesus. These men were driven
by their thirst for the living God. The gods of Greece,
who had long since lost their credibility, could mean nothing to them anymore, but even the god of the philosophers, however great and exalted in concept, was, after
all, merely a human thought, an attempt to advance to
the outer limit of what is conceivable and to cross over
into the mystery of the infinite. But they did not need an
invented god, a product of our own thinking; they sought

"Eingehen in das Geheimnis des Weizenkorns", for the ordination of five
candidates of the Integrierte Gemeinde in Saint Paul outside the Walls on
October 16, 1993, in *30 Jahre Wegbegleitung: Joseph Ratzinger, Papst Benedict
XVI. und die Katholische Integrierte Gemeinde*, ed. Arnold Stötzel, Traudl Wall-
brecher, and Ludwig Weimer (Bad Tölz, 2006), 82–85; previously in *Gemeinde
heute: Interne Nachrichten der Integrierten Gemeinde*, no. 1, *Das Heft vom Fest*, Bad
Tölz (1994): 35–41. [B 966]

the living God who is the truth, who shows that he is alive and illumines our minds and our hearts.

They had come to Jerusalem to worship him. They were pagans, but they had heard that the people Israel had been addressed and guided throughout its history by the one God, the Creator of heaven and earth, the God of all mankind. So they sought him there. But at the same time, they knew that he had bound himself to this people, to laws and rituals that could not be theirs, so that they seemed to be banished forever to the courtyard of the Gentiles, so to speak, and could look at him and had to believe in him only from afar.

Hanging over this hour of encounter, therefore, was the question that Maximus the Confessor formulated: Will the light, the great light of the living God, remain hidden under the bushel of the Law, encased in it? Or can it be put on a lampstand so that it illumines everyone in the house of creation?

This is the question that arises over and over again, particularly in our hour of a new paganism and also of a new longing for God: Is the light of God, the light of Jesus Christ, hidden under the bushel of our habits, our indifference, under the flood of our words, so that beneath them the word can no longer shine forth? Or can it emerge and once again become light for all who live in God's house, in his creation?

Jesus' answer goes far beyond the moment of the question. It looks into the great expanse of history. He says: Yes, you Greeks will see me, I will speak with you, and you will speak with me. Your language will become mine, and it will become a lampstand from which the light of the Gospel, God's light, shines into the world. When I am lifted up, I will draw you all to myself, not just you few pilgrims; I will be there for everyone. And all of you are to be with me, are to stand in the light and in the life of God. But precisely because it is about everyone, because it is not just about this hour but about history as a whole, it is not enough for me to speak now with a few people and to have a conversation that passes by, like so many of the conversations that you Greeks like so much. You seek the living God. Life, however, can be given only by living. More has to happen, therefore, than mere talk.

This is why Christ enters into the fate of the dying grain of wheat, so that the husk might break open and the mature fruit might emerge from the husk. This is why he enters into the mystery of the Cross, so that, when lifted up above and beyond the whole world, he might become visible to all and speak to all and give to everyone more than words: himself and, in himself, the life of the living God.

He enters into the Cross and Resurrection because only in that way does he become completely word and life. Through the Cross and Resurrection, he is no longer bound to this or that place, but is with everyone and gives them more than talk, gives them the life of the living God. And this is the only way it can happen, in this surrender of his life; only in this way does the grain of wheat break open and the fruit develop down through all the ages of history.

The Gospel of John continues with a series of sayings about "keeping and losing life" in which the Lord then extends this teaching to his disciples. They will go out and bring him, the Crucified and Risen One, to the people, as we can experience it so awesomely and dramatically here in this place where Paul, the Apostle to the Gentiles, gave his life with Christ and for Christ and, thus, with him for the world. They, too, cannot come with mere talk. They can bring him only by laying their life down in his, by surrendering themselves with him to the law of the dying grain of wheat, and, thus, through their own life bringing the living Word himself.

Because this is so, the messenger of Jesus Christ can therefore never be merely a public speaker or a specialist proposing a particular theory. Therefore the ministry of the messenger is a sacramental ministry, which means a ministry in which word and being belong to each other. And here again this cannot take the form of him giving himself in a heroic deed—what difference would he make?—but, rather, he must allow himself to be taken by the Lord, to die into him; in this way the Lord comes through him to the people. We call this sacrament, the fact that beyond all his own activity, beyond all his own ability and knowledge, this mystery of death occurs, this transfer of ownership to him, being accepted by him, so that he speaks, lives, and is present through us.

In the rite of priestly ordination, which we are experiencing right now, this is depicted in a very vivid way especially in the ceremony of robing the candidate in liturgical vestments. The candidate is robed, a passive verb; I myself cannot take them as my own, as we heard in the Second Reading: No one takes the priesthood upon himself. Indeed, that would just be his own act, and in the end he would remain merely what he has to give with his sorry ego. I must be robed. I must be taken by Him, so that He may be there through me.

Thus this ceremony of being robed signifies precisely the immersion of my ego in him. "Take me away from myself and give me to you as your own"—I leave myself to you, so that you might act and work through me and be among the people. This, of course, this self-abandonment, this allowing the ego to be immersed and to disappear in him, and so too this placing of my own will in his, very profoundly contradicts our attitude toward life—and I suppose this has been the case in every age. For, indeed, this ego is precisely what we want to assert; we want to fulfill it, put ourselves forward, have ownership of our life, and thereby draw the world into ourselves and enjoy it and leave a trace of ourselves in such a way that this ego persists and keeps its importance in the world.

It is characteristic of the present era that the so-called single life is on the increase and an ever greater, ever more dominant sector of the population is made up of persons who enter no lasting relationship but are just "I" and lead only this life of their own. And, indeed, there is something like an almost traumatic fear of fruitfulness, because the other might take our place away, because we feel that our share of existence is threatened. And ultimately this retreat into wanting to be only myself is fear of death, fear of losing life, all that we have and are.

But as the Lord tells us in the Gospel: Precisely this desperate attempt to possess the ego entirely after all, to possess at least this and as much of the world as can possibly fit into this ego—leads to it becoming withered and empty. For man, who is created in the image of the triune God, cannot find himself by closing himself up in himself. He can find himself only in relation, in going out, in self-giving, in the gesture of the dying grain of wheat.

Becoming a priest means that we accept in a very specific way this call of the Lord from today's Gospel, that we say Yes: Lord, take me as I am, make me as you want me to be; I give myself into your hands, I make myself over to you. The Gospel concludes with the saying: "If anyone wants to be my servant, he will be where I am, and the Father will honor him." Being a priest means becoming *diakonos Christou*, the servant of Christ; and this means not being at my own place, at the place sought out by my ego for itself, but rather: being where he is.

I think that this is actually the quintessential description of priestly ministry: Being where he is; seeking him, being at his disposal, belonging to him, walking with him, living with him, and this means again and again: being in the mystery of the Cross and Resurrection. For this is his permanent place, the place of his suffering in the world and at the same time the place of his glory, because right from this allowing-oneself-to-break-open proceeds the divine mystery of fruitfulness and the shining forth of God's life into this world.

Then comes this wonderful promise: "The Father will honor him." We do not look for honor from men, we are not status seekers. For then we have to bow also to people's opinions, submit to public opinion, which is considered an instrument of freedom but in truth is genuine slavery that lifts people up and drops them again. Again and again people are enslaved by making themselves comfortable with this opinion and seeking their ephemeral, fragile honor. That is not what we seek. The truth will make you free and enable you to get out of the endless search for opinions. We look to the truth of God, to the mystery of Jesus Christ, and by being with him we are certainly at the place of insignificance, at the place of the Cross in this world, but precisely thereby in God's glory, in the light of his face upon this world. If we seek God's honor, seek the truth, we stand in his honor. And this is authentic salvation, freedom, and life, not only for us but for others.

Dear friends, you said Yes: "I am ready." In this hour we pray for you, that the Lord may bless this Yes, that again and again you might find anew the place where he is and may be in him and through him and with him as his servants for the people, so that you might thus constantly be honored by God.

"A Body You Have Prepared for Me"

Porto Santa Rufina, La Storta (Rome), 2000

Dear brothers in the priesthood,
dear candidates for ordination,
dear brothers and sisters!

On this festive occasion, two feast days of the Church coincide and help us to understand better the reality, the event of this day: the feast of the Forerunner of the Lord, John the Baptist, and the great Eucharistic feast of the Church, Corpus Christi.

Saint John described himself as "voice", a voice that calls to repentance, that calls to conversion; a voice that invites listeners to prepare the ways on which Christ can then come as King and Savior. The Church Fathers connected this self-definition of the precursor as voice with the most significant title of Christ, which appears in the Fourth Gospel: Christ—Saint John the Evangelist tells us—is the Logos, the Word, the creative self-expression of the Father. Christ is the Word, and John is the voice that serves to make audible this eternal Word that became flesh, so that it

" 'Finen Leib hast du mir bereitet' ", for the ordination of the deacons and priests of the priestly brotherhood of the Missionaries of St. Charles Borromeo on June 24, 2000, in the Cathedral of Porto Santa Rufina, La Storta (Rome), a German translation by Karl Pichler of the original publication: "Un corpo mi hai preparato", *Tracce: Litterae Communionis*, no. 7 (July/August 2000): 83–86. [B 1154]

becomes accessible, so that it becomes present in our world. We can say that Saint John, who is the voice for this Word, lives a life of service, a life not for himself, but a life of self-surrender, a life of sacrificing himself for someone else.

Saint John is the Word's voice. If we reflect on this connection between voice and Word, we can understand, first of all, that being in service, diaconal existence, is not a transitory thing, not just a temporary matter in life, in the sacrament of Holy Orders: it is a permanent dimension, for priests, too, and for the bishops and for the pope, because Christ himself remained a servant, and Saint John, his precursor, is entirely voice for someone else, he lives, not for himself, but for another. To be in service, to be a servant, to be a deacon is a fundamental dimension of the sacrament of Holy Orders, and you who are receiving this ordination today are thus entering into a profound communion with the story of Christ, prefigured and exemplified in the precursor. John is voice, is servant, stands at the service of the Other. So we can understand also that the service of the Word includes not only the task of preaching, the task of catechesis, of religious dialogue, and so on; it is not only a task but an existential and essential reality in the life of the deacon, of the priest. We can be the voice of the Word only if our life is permeated by the Word, if we live it in the Word. The Greek Fathers said that our existence must be an existence for the Word and of the Word. To put it another way, the words that we can proclaim are convincing only if our own life is word, is nourished by the Word, lives on the Word.

On His Breast

We can think in this way about the moving story of the Last Supper, in which Saint John tells us that the beloved disciple leaned on the Lord's breast. This statement reminds us of the beginning of the Gospel, the fact that the Son comes from the bosom of the Father, that he is in the Father's bosom and therefore lets us see the Father. Being at the service of the Word presupposes standing in this profound relation with him who is the Word, leaning on the Son's breast, as he is on the Father's breast, drinking the Word from his heart, living in proximity to his heart, drinking from it the Word of life. Saint Paul tells us the same thing in other words when he says that we must enter into the mind of Christ. What is the mind of Christ? Paul answers: He humbled himself even to the Cross. And by the very fact that he humbled himself, he overcame Adam's pride, the pride that destroys mankind. In the humility of this descent even into death he transformed human misery; by surrendering himself he became in reality the Lord of heaven and earth. And then we hear the word of the Lord: Only the one who loses himself truly finds himself; he who wants to keep his life for himself loses it, and he who loses his life finds it. Losing one's life is the great movement of love, which is the movement of the deacon, the movement of Saint John the Baptist, and finally the dynamic of Christ himself. Let us enter into this mind of Christ and so let us learn the Word, so as to become in our life word of Christ and word of life.

With that we have already come to the other feast that we celebrate today: the Feast of Corpus Christi, the feast of the Body of the Lord. It is a feast that originated in the Middle Ages, and therefore the sixteenth-century Reformers, and to some extent the reformers of the liturgy in our century, too, looked down on it in a certain sense: a medieval concern—so they used to say and so they say— cannot be a great, profound thing. Let us ask ourselves, therefore: Does this feast really add something new to the great Eucharistic tradition that preceded it? The new feature that appears in the thirteenth century is the cult of Eucharistic adoration: with the establishment of this feast begins the use of the monstrance, of processions, of the tabernacle, and thus also of the silent conversation before the tabernacle, in which we really encounter the Lord: we see his presence, hear his word, sense that he is present. According to the Reformers of the century of the Reformation, all this is false, a major error, because the Eucharist, under the form of bread and wine, is created in order to be eaten, not to be contemplated; the Lord (they say) intended only the celebration of the meal and the fellowship in that celebration.

New Food

At this point we must ask ourselves, however, what fellowship is, what communion is, and how we can eat this Bread, the Lord himself. What we eat in Holy Communion is not a piece of matter; this food is an entirely different food: it is the Son of God who became man. Eating this new food therefore does not mean eating something; it is an encounter of my I with the I of the Son of God, it is a heart-to-heart communion. Eucharistic Communion is not something external: Communion with the Son of God, who gives himself in the Host, is an encounter with the Son of God and, therefore, a form of communication and adoration. We can receive it only by adoring, by opening up our whole existence to his presence, by opening ourselves so that he becomes the strength of our life. Saint Augustine describes this when he speaks about his visions, in which he heard the Eucharistic Lord say to him: This is a different food; you are not to assimilate me, but you are to be assimilated by me. To receive Communion is therefore to adore. Adoration is not something incompatible with Communion; it is the depth of Communion, and only by adoring do we truly enter into fellowship with Christ. Thus, through adoration, fellowship with Christ is immeasurably deepened. We know what blessings have come with silent adoration in our parish churches; we know that the greatest saints of love were nourished by adoration of Christ truly present, because by adoring him they learned his love, because they ate and drank his love unto the end, and because they themselves became living love. We can receive Communion correctly only when our Communion expands, deepens, and is made concrete in adoration that really receives the mystery of this presence.

Of course, the adoration that participates in the Eucharistic mystery that is the innermost dimension of Holy Communion has another, much deeper connection with the mystery of the Lord's will. Indeed, we must ask ourselves: How is it possible that Jesus becomes food, that we can eat Jesus? It is possible only because he, in his act of love unto the end, in the Cross and in the Resurrection, transformed himself into a being that lives in the Spirit who enlivens, as Saint Paul says: In his Cross, in his self-surrender, in his Resurrection he became the life-giving Spirit, and thus he is sacrament for us. This gift that makes him food, a life-giving Spirit, is adoration.

Transformation of the World

The Eucharist is therefore not a meal in which something is distributed, but, rather, it is the presence of this transition to the life-giving Spirit, it is the presence of this dynamism of going to the Father. The Lord is the one who opens the door, as the Letter to the Hebrews says: only by entering upon this way, the Lord's way of transformation, only by entering into this great act of adoration in which the world must be transformed in love, can we participate correctly in the Eucharistic mystery. The Eucharistic mystery is fulfilled as follows: not only the transformation of bread and wine, but our transformation and the transformation of the world into a living host. And when we priests, at the moment of Consecration, pronounce the Lord's words— "This is my Body, this is my Blood"—when the Lord lends us his mouth in order to pronounce these words that transform bread and wine, we say these words to ourselves and to the world and ask the Lord to transform us, so that we ourselves might become adoration, a living host. Saint Thomas says that the ultimate content of the Eucharist is *caritas*, love. The presence of the Lord serves to transform us and the world into adoration, that is, into an act of love that glorifies God.

In conclusion I would like to mention the beginning of Jesus' life, as it is described in the Letter to the Hebrews. This letter tells us that the Incarnation is accomplished in a dialogue between Father and Son. The Son says: "Sacrifices and offerings you have not desired, but a body have you prepared for me.... Then I said: Behold, I have come" (Heb 10:5, 7). This word sums up the whole life of Jesus: it proclaims the Incarnation and the crucifixion in one word. You prepared a body for me, behold, I come. It is the priestly word, it is the life of Christ. And when we receive ordination to the priesthood, we enter into this word, dear friends, and we too say at this moment: You prepared a body for me, behold, I come, I do not want to give something or other, one part or another; you prepared a body for me, I would like to give myself: Behold, I come.

At this moment we pray for you all, dear brothers, so that your whole life might be settled in this word and in this way you can be true deacons, true priests of Christ. You prepared a body for me, you gave my very self to me, behold, I come.

DIACONAL ORDINATION

Making the Deacon Jesus Christ Present in the Age of the Church

Munich, September 1977

First Reading: Amos 8:4–7
Second Reading: 1 Timothy 2:1–8
Gospel: Luke 16:1–13

Dear brothers and sisters,
dear candidates for ordination!

The readings for today, the Twenty-Fifth Sunday in Ordinary Time, and the Gospel that we have just heard harmonize in a quite astonishing way with the diaconal service for which you, dear friends, wish to make yourselves available at this hour and from now on.

First the thrilling, mighty voice of the prophet Amos cried out to us; the Church Fathers call him a trumpet, a sort of signal of judgment that tries to awaken us from the sleep of our selfishness, our desire for possessions, our craving for power. With a keenness that is unusual even in the Old Testament, Amos shook the consciences of the rich and the landowners and exhorted them to reflect that one day they would stand before God to give an accounting.

"Den Diakon Iesus Christus in der Zeit der Kirche vergegenwärtigen", for the ordination of permanent deacons in the Liebfrauendom, Munich, on September 17, 1977, *Diakon Anianus*, no. 39 (July 2005): 31–32. [B 386]

He was profoundly aware of the fact that this whole land had been handed over to the People of Israel, that no one could own it for himself alone, but, rather, that all ownership is given for mutual benefit. And so this reading goes together well with the parable of the unfaithful steward, with which the Lord intends to make us aware that we are all merely stewards; the owner is God. And what we have is given to us all only so that we might serve each other thereby. The Gospel confronts us with the question of whether we can be worthy of the great gifts—truth and the closeness of God—if we do not manage correctly the small gift, namely, the things of this world.

Both readings, however, lead to the words of the Church's prayer that reads: "Lord, you summed up the whole Law with all its commandments in the one precept to love God and neighbor." The true divine law, which is supposed to rule and purify the world, is love. Being Christian does not mean being subject to a multiplicity of commandments that ultimately no man can keep track of anymore; rather, being Christian means entering into this one thing, into the center of the love that has come from God and is now expected of us, and to live our way into it in its many demands and forms in everyday life.

And so, behind all this, the figure of the true steward, God's true, faithful steward, becomes visible, namely, Jesus Christ, who devoted himself to us all. He, the Son, became our deacon. This is a central aspect of the mystery of Jesus Christ, the fact that the Lord of us all is deacon: a servant who goes around and serves us and thus reveals to us the mystery of God's love. The greatness of the diaconal ministry that you now receive consists of the fact that it is commissioned to make the deacon Jesus Christ present in the age of the Church. Making the deacon Jesus Christ present means representing and accomplishing the mission of his love in the Church. That is why the first and foremost duty imposed on you is to carry on the signs of the love of Jesus Christ. Care for the sick and the suffering. Visiting them and giving them what no technology and no medicine is capable of giving them: the presence of compassion and common life; the power of understanding, which teaches them to believe in God's love even in suffering; the willingness to help of one who by his sympathy makes even suffering meaningful and worth living. And you are charged with caring for the poor; and also with accompanying people along their final way in this world as the expression of our reverence for the mystery of the human body and of human life, which is destined for immortality, and as part of our love for those who in this dying process have lost a little of themselves.

In terms of the sacrament, being a deacon means making present the mystery of the diaconate of Jesus Christ, his love in the Church.

It only seems that the New Testament reading from the First Letter to Timothy does not fit into this larger context that the First Reading and the Gospel have set up for us. In the middle of it is a shining sentence in which all the sublimity of the Christian view of God and of man is plainly evident: "God desires all men to be saved and to come to the knowledge of the truth." God loves everyone. He does not have first- and second-class children; rather, he cares about them all, because they are all his creatures. That is why his salvation and his love are meant for all who bear a human countenance.

But because this is so, the truth of the Gospel must go out and be proclaimed to the whole world. For this passage gives us to understand that the salvation [das Heil] of mankind is the truth. In merely human terms, too, this is already clear; for if I live in falsehood, then I live contrary to reality, then I live contrary to myself, contrary to what I authentically am. And if I live contrary to reality, contrary to my authenticity, then I trip myself up, then I am torn and destroyed, and that means: I am in trouble [*im Unheil*].

At the same time, though, we can say that salvation is love. For man's trouble is being unloved, being forgotten, the loneliness that destroys his life, that does not allow him to come to the wealth that opens up in being together, in the mystery of love.

The truth is salvation; love is salvation. These two things do not contradict each other but belong together, because the one God is truth *and* love. That is also why the prophet made his social criticism, not out of some ideology or other, not out of the envy of those who have come off badly, not out of resentment, but in terms of God's truth, which love discloses. And the central point of his critique is that he accuses people of forgetting the holy day of God's rest, the day of freedom that he granted to all mankind, that they are unwilling to recognize the rhythm of life that he gave us and, instead, set the contrasting tempo of self-seeking and greed and arbitrariness.

The love of Jesus Christ cannot be made present without the word of faith. The two belong together. All the services of love that we spoke about earlier—visiting the sick, caring for the poor, consoling the suffering, accompanying people on their final journey—all these services of love cannot happen without the word that gives them meaning and makes the love a certainty. Truth without love would be no truth at all, but then, too, love without truth becomes grim and finally a brutal ideology and cannot save.

Precisely because you embody the deacon Jesus Christ, the Lord's loving service, the service of the word is entrusted to you, also. Just as the services of love spread the Gospel, so too something of the love of Jesus Christ must shine through in the services of the word that you perform in the school, in the pulpit, in adult education, or wherever it may be.

All service of the word must ultimately be anchored in this sentence: "God loves all men and wants everyone to be saved." Being a deacon means having the privilege of making the deacon Jesus Christ present in the life of the Church. In this hour we are all praying for you, that he will bless the way for which you have prepared, that it may become a blessing for the entire holy Church of God. And we pray that what is said in the Church's concluding prayer today will come true in you and in us: "Grant us, Lord, that what we receive in the sacrament and profess in faith may become truth in us."

Telling Others the Gospel Vividly

Munich, February 1978

Reading: 2 Timothy 1:8b–10
Gospel: Matthew 17:1–9

Dear candidates for ordination!
Dear brothers and sisters in the Lord!

The Second Vatican Council moved the office and ministry of the deacon to the center of ecclesial life in a new way. This may seem contradictory in a time in which service professions are disappearing, and not just outwardly: behind this phenomenon stands a deeper and very comprehensible objection to service. Service seems to be a product of man's dominion over men and, therefore, an attack on equality, equal dignity, and the freedom of man. And it is certainly true that in every age there has been abuse of dominion, the abusive division of men, denial of the equal dignity given to them by the Creator. Yet we see more and more clearly that the abolition of service cannot be the answer to this; for we men are created in such a way that we need one another, that we can live only by being from one another and, consequently, only in being for one another, too; that therefore without service our life

"Das Evangelium lebendig weitersagen", for the ordination of deacons in the Liebfrauendom, Munich, on February 19, 1978. Previously unpublished. [B 419]

cannot continue. And if we no longer like to serve each other, then the only thing left for us is to make some other arrangements for this necessary interdependence, by placing ourselves at the service of machines, in the service of anonymous systems, and then through them letting ourselves be connected to each other somehow after all. Then we serve the machine, the system, at a considerable loss of freedom, and furthermore we pay for the whole thing with an impoverishment in our human interrelations, in the truth that brings people together.

In this situation the Church looks to Jesus Christ, who became a deacon for us. He, the Lord of the world, became a deacon, a servant. He set the table for his disciples, and he washed their feet. He transformed the world by exercising dominion as a service; by the fact that he, as Lord, served and became the servant of all. So he gives us the courage to serve freely, gives us the courage to assume the true dignity and freedom of a man by serving and, thus, to set up a new sign in this world. If the Church wants to be the Church of Jesus Christ, she needs the representation of the deacon Jesus Christ. She seeks him in two forms: first in the ministerial deacon, who remains a deacon, a servant, for his whole life and thus represents the deacon Jesus Christ visibly in our time and accepts his call. She needs him also, though, in the sense that every subsequent clerical ministry must be *diakonia*. It is not just an old custom that diaconal ordination is situated on the way to priestly ordination. A priest who stopped being a deacon would no longer perform his priestly ministry correctly, either. And a bishop who did not remain a deacon would no longer be a real bishop. And a pope who was not a deacon would no longer be a true pope. The diaconate is and remains a dimension of every clerical ministry, because the Lord who sustains all these ministries became himself our deacon and remains such in the Holy Eucharist until the end of all days.

If we now ask for more details about what is meant by this diaconal ministry, we receive an answer right in today's readings. First they tell us: "He called us with a holy calling" (2 Tim 1:9). The diaconate is founded first on his call, and it stands forever upon it. With that the reading makes a transition at the same time to today's Gospel about Christ's Transfiguration; for this whole Gospel is centered on the voice of the Father, which certifies the Son as the fulfillment of the Law and the Prophets, of Moses and Elijah, when it says: "This is my beloved Son, listen to him" (Mt 17:6). Out of God's ray of light that fell that day into the hearts of the disciples, these words remained with them as an abiding call: "Listen to him." And from that hour on they knew that they were standing then in this light of God, that they were in the realm of the Transfiguration, the transformation of the world, when they abided in this word and walked ever deeper into this word. Their whole life from that hour on was an entrance into this word, "Listen to him"; an ever deeper listening to the Son, to Jesus Christ, so as to make other people hearers, too. Because they themselves were hearers, they were able to give the voice of God to others: "Listen to him", and make the peoples of the globe hearers of Jesus Christ and thus lead them into the light and splendor of the Transfiguration. Being a deacon means living in terms of this point; it means being a hearer of the Word, a hearer of Jesus Christ.

One main task of the deacon, according to Church tradition, is the proclamation of the Gospel at all levels and in all forms. He is supposed to be an evangelist. He is supposed to offer people the bread of the Word, the bread that gives them meaning, on which man lives no less than on earthly bread. The deacon is supposed to be an evangelist; but he can only proclaim what he has heard—and if he has heard. He can tell others the Gospel vividly only if he himself abides in hearing the Gospel. Insofar as he listens to it, he will be able to be a messenger, he will be able to give the voice of God to others: "This is my beloved Son, listen to him."

The reading continues: "He called us ... not in virtue of our works but in virtue of his own purpose and [his] grace" (2 Tim 1:9). This verse may at first discourage us. If we imagined that our qualities, our merits and suitability were what singled us out, then we learn: No. No man on his own is proportioned to God's word and great enough to be able to convey it. But precisely this fact that humbles us also gives us courage. For if we were to look at our own stature, then we would lose heart over and over again, we would have to start asking, "Lord, why me, of all people? There are, after all, much better suited individuals." Then we would all necessarily be in the situation of Elijah—and of Jeremiah—in which we say: "Lord, that's enough for me. Let me go! I want nothing more to do with such a commission!" Our own stature is never enough. But precisely for this reason we can attempt it full of confidence, because *He* wanted us and because He leads us. The humility to which he brings us in this way gives courage; for it means that we no longer need to look around. I do not need to worry what will become of me. Instead, light-heartedly leaving ourselves behind, we can walk in confidence in him who wanted us and who knows us as we are.

I would like to highlight another sentence from this reading, like the first: "Take your share of suffering for the gospel" (2 Tim 1:8). Clerical ministry is not a job in which you can remain personally aloof. It is not some kind of care-giving profession in which you put in your hours and then become a private person and let the annoyances of the profession roll off your back and step out of it. It is a profession that calls on us in the most personal way, that wants us as persons, that demands of us nothing less than the willingness to take this Gospel and its service into our inmost being and to find it worth suffering for. And only someone who has personally accepted the suffering can also understand the suffering of others, can truly console and heal. Only the crucified Redeemer, the one who had suffered himself, could become the Savior of the suffering of this world.

The second major service of the deacon is charity: the service that is dedicated to this world's suffering and need in the love of Jesus Christ. In the ancient Church, the ministry of the chalice, of the Blood of Jesus Christ, was assigned to the deacon in the Eucharist as a sign of this dedication to suffering out of suffering and the transforming love of Jesus Christ. Being called to the charity of Christ means, on the one hand, being anchored in the deepest mystery of the Eucharist in the center of the Christian liturgy, and precisely from this perspective it means the ability and the willingness to accept with the Lord the neediness of the world and to address it by consoling, healing, and loving compassionately. The person is part of the definition of the diaconate, along with the willingness to suffer personally also for the Gospel; to accept it into the depths of one's own life. And that is why it is profoundly meaningful that the Church has joined to the diaconate, as a step toward the priesthood, the promise of celibacy as the expression of the willingness to stake everything—along with one's whole life—on the Gospel. We know how much this arrangement is criticized today. We know how many serious and, more than anything else, practical-pragmatic questions are raised about it in view of the priest shortage in our time; but I think that it is tremendously great and bold for the Church to have this fearless courage of her faith, above and beyond all pragmatism, and to perform this real act of protest against a society that is wallowing in pleasure; that she holds fast to this sign of faith as an expression of our real Yes to the Gospel. And however much protest there is against it, somehow it remains a thorn in the flesh of this era that there are men who believe so much in the Gospel that they do for it something that in earthly terms is irrational and that they stand up for it with their whole lives, body and soul, and thus verify it; for without interior commitment to the Gospel, such fidelity is not possible. The more freely it is lived, the more we encounter the Lord in it; we encounter the new love that offers us the prospect of such freedom and the fulfillment that grows from fidelity.

In this reading we hear also the message that all of this was already granted from all eternity but is now revealed through the appearance of Christ (2 Tim 1:10). The Eternal is realized in time. This is the greatness of the diaconate, that it does not just carry out some transitory business but, rather, translates God's eternal will and gift into our time and accomplishes in it the appearance, the epiphany of Jesus Christ and causes to fall upon it the beam of light that the disciples saw on Mount Tabor, not in such a way that the world becomes a paradise thereby. We must go farther down into the valley, but in such a manner that in this going farther, while staying close to his word, we bring the manifest light of his goodness, which gives us a path.

The Deacon—Master of Thanksgiving

Munich, December 1978

Reading: 1 Thessalonians 5:16–24

Dear candidates for ordination,
dear brothers and sisters in the Lord!

Today, on the Third Sunday of Advent, the Church reads us an excerpt from the oldest letter of the holy apostle Paul and, thus, generally from the beginning of the written New Testament. You can practically feel the early morning joy of the beginning, the gladness about the fact that the promise is being fulfilled, that the seed of the word is bearing fruit, that it is spreading, that the tree of the Church is gradually beginning to extend its branches over the whole globe. And at the same time you sense also the increasing fatherly concern to make sure that the word takes deep root, that it is not taken away again after an initial enthusiasm but, rather, grows constantly toward the harvest. And so it ultimately says what Advent is: living on the closeness of God and toward the closeness of God.

But it also tells us something about what is happening in this very hour, for this, after all, is the peculiar thing about God's word: it is so rich that with every new hearing it is

"Der Diakon—Lehrmeister des Dankens", for the ordination of permanent deacons in the Liebfrauendom, Munich, on December 17, 1978. Previously unpublished. [B 476]

able to say something new. Let us just look at a few verses of this passage from the First Letter to the Thessalonians. It begins with the sentence: "Rejoice always." Since the earliest times, this is the chord that the Church has struck on the Third Sunday of Advent, although earlier she read this sentence from a late letter by Saint Paul, the Letter to the Philippians, which he writes in prison, facing death. But this now creates a great tension that is deeper than if we heard the message from only one letter. Paul remained faithful to himself. What stands here is not just the optimism of the beginning; it will stand again at the end, having proved itself through much suffering. "Rejoice! Rejoice always!" Actually, viewed from a merely human perspective, this sentence is an unreasonable demand. There is so much that can trample joy down: sickness that breaks into a life; the death of people who are dear to us; failure, enmity, misplaced confidence. All this is likely to discourage people, to take away their joy, to drive them into resignation or even into cynicism. And when we look around today: on how many faces do we read resignation and cynicism! And to a great extent the mass media's view of human beings is prone to ridicule as naïve anyone who dares to rejoice, to believe that life and the world are good and worthy of joy. But Paul, who pronounces this sentence, is not naïve. We have only to read the account of his life in the Second Letter to the Corinthians to see what trials he had to go through. And despite them and precisely because of them, he says: "Rejoice always!" The Christian is immersed in a joy that cannot be taken away from him. When a person receives a great love, when he is privileged to know that he is loved by someone who is good and powerful and absolutely reliable, then this is no guarantee that something terrible will not happen to him, too, and remain terrible. Nevertheless, it will not be able to destroy him, because there is something in him that all these terrors cannot touch: a light and a strength that are stronger than all that. The Christian, though, is such a person; for to him is granted the gift that he is loved by God, who is absolutely kind and powerful, whose love does not depend on any moods and whose fidelity never wavers. And therefore resignation, joylessness, sullenness, humorlessness, and cynicism do not suit one who is Christian. The spiritual doctrine of the monks of the early Church and to some extent also the medieval doctrine of virtues—and we have forgotten this much too often—depicted "acedia" as the vice of all vices, as the real repudiation of the faith: the term means sadness and sluggishness of heart that can no longer trust, no longer rejoice, and no longer love. Joylessness in this most profound sense is the repudiation of the faith, the repudiation of the God whose Yes is still the foundation of our life, whatever may happen. "Rejoice" therefore means: be believers, immersed in the certainty of what the Gospel has proclaimed to us: God loves with a love that is not fickle.

And so the passage is addressed to you, dear friends. After all, you are supposed to become deacons of the Gospel. Evangelists of Jesus Christ in this world of ours. But someone who is resigned or embittered himself cannot be a bearer of Good News. The Gospel can be proclaimed credibly only by someone who, on the one hand, has suffered, who has not evaded reality, the difficult reality of this world, and has stood fast in his faith in the love that is stronger than suffering. Only someone who is an evangelist in this way can hand on the joy that we need, which is not a surrogate, a brief anesthesia, but withstands the truth of this world.

"Rejoice always, pray constantly, pray without ceasing", the second sentence reads. This again is an unreasonable request. And of course it is not meant superficially or externally, as though we had to or would be able to pray constantly with words. But once again let us make a comparison: a person who is profoundly occupied by an idea or a passion, let us say, by a political cause, by a scientific finding, by a passion—pride, hatred, love—by a deep, burning concern, such a person can do and say all sorts of things; but when it is over, he will return again and again to that passion, which in the depths of his heart he never really left, because it profoundly occupies him. "Pray without ceasing" is supposed to mean that the depths of our soul are perpetually immersed in God, that at the bottom of our heart we always come into contact with him and are always in an exchange with him and that in this way we are truly praying with all our being. Only when we come into contact with God at this depth can it also give strength and fruitfulness to the words of our prayer. On the other hand, of course, only the struggle to put our prayer into words will bring the depth of our soul to God again and again and be able to keep it near him. I think that much too often in recent years we have forgotten that the first and foremost ministry of the deacon, the priest, and the bishop is to pray for others. The Holy Father not long ago said this very emphatically: The most important thing, he says, that you can do is prayer, even more important than Catholic Action, because without prayer it dries up. The Divine Office for those who have been ordained should be understood in this sense. Not as an additional burden, but rather as a means without which everything else falls apart. The distinctive character of our activity must proceed from the fact that we are men who pray.

A bishop from the eastern part of our fatherland [i.e., East Germany] recently told me that his main concern was that in every locality, in the midst of this enormous decline of our faith, at least two or three people should remain who pray, and then it will be different in that place if there are still people there who carry on this thread of prayer. "Pray without ceasing." This is both a task for the whole Church and also in particular a task for us, for you who are to become deacons of the Church. Masters of prayer, which you can be only if you are unceasingly learners in prayer and from prayer.

The next sentence is: "Give thanks in all circumstances." Once again such an unconditional sentence. Always rejoice, always pray, always give thanks! Again the same irrational demand, and I can hear in the background how some are saying to me: Aha, these are the virtues of the oppressed, by which they are trying to keep them down. No, they will tell me, we have to learn insubordination. Now a Christian is not a person who conveniently conforms by allowing himself to be swayed by group therapy methods and relinquishes himself to the group. We will hear this in just a moment. He can put up opposition, but the first thing is not saying No but saying Yes. Learning to give thanks in everyday events, the difficult ones as well as the happy ones. Learning to see through them to the God who loves me in this way and precisely in this way. And if we understand this, if we begin to transform everyday matters into thanksgiving, then we will see that our life changes and the world changes, that it acquires a new, positive face. Only thanksgiving is creative, the only real transformation there is in this world. It happens in the *Eucharistia*, in the thanksgiving of Jesus Christ, in which he transformed death into thanksgiving and thus turned it, so fruitfully for us all, into the bread of eternal life. The grain of wheat that has died is productive, but we will be able to celebrate the thanksgiving of Jesus Christ, the *Eucharistia*, only if we ourselves have become people who give thanks. As deacons, you have the task of being servants who lead others to the Eucharist, and essentially that will mean: masters of thanksgiving, so that our thanks become, so to speak, the vessel in which the thanksgiving of Jesus Christ can happen.

Two more sentences: "Do not quench the Spirit." Spirit needs protection; it can so easily be trampled, and we know how the rise of the Spirit is trampled nowadays by passions that are soon over. Being a deacon means taking care of the Spirit in oneself and in others, so that he can grow, work, and be strong. And finally: "Abstain from every form of evil." The unconditional openness that is so often preached is not biblical and not Pauline; in reality, it is pride and sloth at the same time. Only the passion of renunciation can purify us and make us free. In order to learn and teach it anew in a time when all sorts of insubordination are taught but renunciation—the true and most deeply purifying resistance—meets with nothing but disdain, we will have to be schoolmasters of this resistance. Knowing that when a person puts aside the Ought, nothing remains but the Must and that liberation from obligation ultimately will be liberation for compulsion.

When we take up all these imperatives, they will be turned into prayer for us in the greatness of what they exhort us to do. Prayer that the Lord will place perpetual joy into our hearts. Prayer that he will teach us to pray, that he will make us people who give thanks, that he will help us to keep the Spirit awake and to resist evil in every form. And all of us who are participating in this ordination ceremony wish to pray in this hour for you, dear brothers, that the Lord may grant you this: that he may truly make you deacons of the Gospel and his evangelists in this world.

Living on Christ's "Yes"

Munich, February 1979

Reading: 2 Corinthians 1:18–22

Dear brothers and sisters in the Lord,
dear candidates for ordination!

In this hour of your diaconal ordination resounds the wonderful saying of Saint Paul that we have just heard: Christ is not Yes and No at the same time; Christ is God's Yes, the Yes to all the promises. Paul develops from this a whole theology of liturgical action. In the Amen that we pray through Christ, we enter into it, into God's Amen, and thus into the unity of heaven and earth, of promise and fulfillment. From this perspective, we notice the connection between God, Christ, Church, the individual believer, and believers among themselves. The Letter tells us that God is the one who makes us firm in Christ, who has anointed us and, therefore, has himself appointed us as Christians, who has sealed us and has sent a share of his Spirit deep into our hearts.

Although all this is said initially about Baptism, it still takes on a special connotation in this hour, when as baptized men you place yourselves at the service of the baptized.

"Aus dem 'Ja' Christi leben", for the ordination of deacons in the Liebfrauendom, Munich, on February 18, 1979, under the title "Christus ist Gottes Ja", *Ordinariatskorrespondenz*, Munich, no. 8 (February 22, 1979). [B 493]

For this is indeed the hour in which you allow yourself to be moored in Christ and, with your life, cast anchor there and find there the home, the permanent abode, the fixed place of your life, where you have support and from which you are supposed to give support to others. This is the hour in which you are sealed in a special manner for him and by him, are provided with his ownership mark, and now are stamped by him and for him, for all the world to see, so as to be a signpost pointing to him, in order to become a bridge on which one can go to him. And this is the hour in which you receive the Spirit's mission to speak the words of God's Spirit in this world, the word of the Gospel of Jesus Christ.

I would like to select from this unfathomable text and emphasize in particular two more points that in their own way are connected with today's event. The first: Christ is not "Yo", a mixture of Yes and No, but Christ is the separation of what is mixed together indistinctly, Christ is clarity, unambiguousness, and truth. In him occurs, as it were, the parting of the waters; Yes and No separate. And a step farther: in this parting, Christ does not stand on the side of No. He is God's Yes. Being a Christian, therefore, means to live on this Yes. It means being an affirmative person who believes in the strength of the Yes, who believes that even in the midst of all the destruction of history God's creation is good and that God's gift to mankind has remained in it. The Christian believes that the world does not need destruction and denial above all else but, rather, that its salvation consists of strengthening the Yes, siding with the Yes, purifying it of denials, so that the world might become livable, so that it may truly become God's world and thus a human world.

The Christian is a man of the Yes. We witness to this in a world in which the negative dialectic had temporarily become something like the religion of the intellectual, a world in which Marcuse's grand refusal of wisdom seemed to be the last word. The idea was that we must negate this world that consists entirely of negation, in which everything goes wrong, so that from the denial of the denial the positive emerges. From there, all of history was then rewritten and the concept of man revised. Those who supported history positively suddenly seemed like the ones who were upholding the pernicious power of the powerful, as the truly "negative" ones. And only the negative people, the rebels, the naysayers, the heretics were carrying the torch of truth and goodness. Anyone who wants to be on the right side of history can side only with denial, must take the side of the heretic, for one must always assume in advance that he alone can be right. In the same way the catalogue of virtues and morality were revised from this perspective. The positive virtues appear as the support of injustice and of the powerful, and only rebellion, criticism, destruction, and nay-saying are the real virtues that usher in a better world. Accordingly, Christ, too, was seen in a new way as the rebel who takes a stand against the traditions and the faith of the fathers and who accomplished on the Cross the great act of rebellion, of refusal, and of No.

Paul knows better: Jesus Christ is the Yes. He lived out his Yes to the Father. And his whole life was this "Yes, Father." The Cross is not an act of rebellion but, rather, the final great Yes of obedience that he endured. Christ became obedient even unto death, death on a Cross. And this Yes that he endured in the midst of the darkness of the world, *that* is what redeems. The door was opened for him through the Yes of the woman who said: "Yes, be it done to me according to your word." Christ dwells in the Yes. And becoming his servants means adopting Mary's attitude, through our Yes opening the door to his Yes.

And that means that we dare the Yes of love, that we live on it, on its affirmation, and hence practice the virtues that have been branded as heretical: obedience, humility, meekness, kindness, and trust. I would go so far as to say that a Christian is recognized by the fact that he harbors no bitterness, that he lives on the Yes and cleanses himself from the bitter element in the negations and thus can say Yes himself, lead people to the Yes, and give them God's joy. Celibacy, too, which you will now promise, can and must never become the expression of contempt or disdain. In that case it should not be practiced and it would not be Christian. It has to be the greater Yes of trust in the creating, redeeming God; a Yes that dares it with him and knows that even in this act of reaching out to him fully the world remains a Yes and precisely in this way becomes a new Yes.

This brings us to the second point. The unambiguousness of Jesus Christ implies at the same time his constancy, reliability, and fidelity. Man's freedom does not consist in being able to invent something else for himself each day and to do something else. Freedom is precisely the ability to act definitively, the capacity for eternity, as Karl Rahner once put it. Freedom as the divine element in man consists of the fact that man can find, not some thing, but himself, that he can become definitive, that he can find his truth, with which he can abide. Of course, one can only abide with something that itself abides and is worth abiding with. But that is describing truth and love alone. Someone who walks away from the truth does not become free but sinks again into the cycle of necessity and compulsion. That is why Christ never needed to take anything back; that is why he is the eternally Reliable, Faithful One, because he stands in the truth, in love, yes, because he himself is the Truth. That is why in him an abode opens up for us in which we are at home, in which we are our-selves, in which we are free. Walking away from him does not liberate but makes life empty and enslaves it. Man is reliable and faithful only if he sincerely does not mean his Yes merely for the moment, but stands by it tomorrow and the day after tomorrow, too, perhaps through storms, if he does not blend it in with a "Yo", if he does not become a reed tossed about in the wind. The truth demands not only the moment but all the time and patience of our life. And so it becomes evident that the truth is not our instru-ment on which we play, but, rather, this Yes stands above us: the truth is our mistress who takes us in hand, trains and leads us. And of course it is also true that if the Yes was not worth keeping, if it was based on untruth, then it would naturally become an enslavement for our life. But if the true Yes exists, if there is the truth, the Yes of Jesus Christ, then there is a truth by which we can and must stand, which we can take as our mistress and in whose discipline we are not destroyed but, rather, find ourselves. The more we stand by it in the storms, in the wind and weather of this life, the more evident the depth and wealth of his Yes become, along with the brevity and ultimate futility of anything that stands against it. Being a deacon means sur-rendering oneself into the Yes of Jesus Christ, and thus it means giving people courage again to say Yes, courage to be faithful, courage to trust, to love—something that we need so much in a world that is full of mistrust because it fears there is no truth at all. And that is actually a sign that we must set up. And again: being a deacon means entering into a relationship of service; it means entrusting oneself to someone and entrusting oneself forever. We can entrust ourselves to him because he is everlasting fidelity, from which proceed the courage to be faithful and the right to fidelity as well as to love in this world.

Another look at the Gospel, at this ever moving story of the men who climbed up on the roof and uncovered it so as to lay their friend at Jesus' feet so that he might find healing. It seems to me that this story actually depicts the priestly and diaconal ministry. Ultimately we can do absolutely nothing other than just this: lift people up and, by whatever paths, bring them to Jesus' feet so that he may heal them. And then, of course, what happens here in the Gospel will always occur again, that Jesus answers a question we did not ask at all, fulfills a wish we did not recognize at all, that nevertheless, in precisely this way, he makes our center free and gives us what we truly needed to be able to walk, to become free, to be grateful, and to be able to transform the world.

In a few moments now you will lie here at the feet of Jesus Christ. Together with all the saints whom we invoke on your behalf, we all want to pray that what was granted to this man might happen to you, that the Lord might give you an answer that surpasses all your questions and yearnings, so that you can take up the burden of your life again and again, become free and walk, and that the world might thus find an occasion to praise God, to say Yes, to be glad in the God who is the great Yes.

Faithfully Awaiting

Munich, December 1979

Reading: Philippians 4:4–7; Gospel: Luke 3:10–18

Dear candidates for ordination,
dear brothers and sisters in the Lord!

We are performing this diaconal ordination at the climax of the Church's celebration of Advent. These two things are profoundly and intrinsically correlated, for the diaconate is an Advent-like ministry, the translation of the spirit and mentality of Advent into the service and the attitude of a whole life. The meaning of Advent was expressed precisely in a single sentence by Saint Paul in today's reading: "The Lord is near." But what it means when this perception of the Lord's nearness strikes the heart of a person, is accepted by it, is experienced by it as reality, and is responded to can be expressed only in the many refractions of human destinies, feelings, and mentalities in which men throughout history break this great light of the Lord's nearness into the multiplicity of its colors. We hear something of it in the Church's prayers for the season of Advent, which are indeed this response of the believing heart to being touched by the Lord's nearness. Thus we

"Getreulich in der Erwartung stehen—Der Diakon im Dienst der Kirche", for the ordination of permanent deacons in the Liebfrauendom, Munich, on December 16, 1979. Previously unpublished. [B 538]

read in the Church's prayer that Advent is *fideliter exspectare*: "to await faithfully", and thus an interior correspondence to the psalm verse: "I wait on your word." Advent means not descending from the observation peak that gave us a view of what is to come, of the One who is to come. Advent is dynamism and fidelity at the same time. It means standing fast by what has been found and, precisely by this abiding, to go out, to press on to meet it, and thus to go forward and to change oneself and the world toward it. *Fideliter exspectare*—to keep watch faithfully.

The Church's prayer on Friday expresses it even more vividly when it says: Advent is expecting him with the utmost vigilance. It means hastening with a watchful heart toward the encounter with him. It is therefore, first of all, vigilance, waking up from sleep, which detains us with things that are superficial and illusory. Becoming aware of the fact that the hidden one already stands in our midst. And Advent is haste. This means: through it our life has acquired a task, an urgency that is all-demanding, that is important at every moment. In contrast to the haste of many people, which often represents only the will to forget insignificance and the feeling of meaninglessness, here we have the incursion of a real urgency concerning what our life and what the world demand. We are to hasten toward him as watchful people who no longer allow the appearances of this world to drive from our ears and from our eyes one fact that the world tries to make us forget: that he is the real center, that he is in our midst. To live in the spirit of Advent means to live as someone who has been awakened, and then this also includes the responsibility of someone who is keeping watch to awaken others, to point out to others what gives our life importance, because it is the truly important thing. And so the diaconate means an Advent-like service: doing what John the Baptist did.

Pointing a finger toward the one who already stands hidden in our midst. Making clear that the Savior whom we await does exist and that he is not here or there but is named Jesus Christ. The diaconate is the ministry of a baptizer, and precisely therein it is a Christological ministry, speaking about the one who ultimately matters in our life, giving witness to him who is the true light of the world and of our life.

The various individual services of the diaconate then follow from this essential center. Someone who wakes up and perceives Christ, the immense fact that the Son of God is here and looks at us, is frightened at first. His situation is like that of the people in today's Gospel; he must ask: What should I do? However, because one cannot learn to do by speaking but only by doing, the diaconate originated precisely and in a special way as a ministry of "showing how to do". When the apostles called the seven men from whose efforts the Church's diaconal ministry developed, they did so in order to entrust to them the ministry of charity in the Church, so as to be free again as apostles for the ministry of the word. Since then charitable work, showing how to believe and to love, has always remained a defining feature of the diaconal ministry. Our Lord himself not only spoke words and performed signs but also carried out his message with the reality of his life, even unto death on the Cross; therefore doing, or charity, the carrying out of the mind of Jesus Christ in everyday life, is never just an incidental, additional activity for the Church that she conducts so as to have a say somewhere in the world. Rather, showing how to love as Christ did is part of the sacrament of Christ, at the heart of the act by which the Church herself comes about. It is a part of the properly ordained ministry that keeps the priestly and diaconal ministry of Jesus Christ present down through the ages. A Church that neglected this demonstration of charity, of social and human concern, and the actualization of Jesus Christ's goodness in practical matters would neglect an essential part of her mission.

Therefore it was also profoundly meaningful and necessary that, precisely in this era, which has become so much an era of words in which the cry for love is so often unanswered and the need for love in this world is so overwhelming, the diaconal ministry, the ministry of showing how to do, was recreated and reestablished in the center of ecclesial life. This is related to the fact that in the reading Saint Paul prepares the way for the sentence, "The Lord is at hand", by saying: "Let all men know your [goodness]." The goodness of Christians is the space in which the Lord's nearness can be achieved. The goodness of Christians is the translation of the nearness of Jesus Christ into the being and life of Christians. The term for "forbearance" or "goodness" in the Greek text is τὸ ἐπιεικὲς ὑμῶν. This is an expression from Stoic legal and moral philosophy, and it means: let your integrity, your honesty be known to all. This refers to what the Romans then call *aequitas*—justice or fairness; the attitude that knows no partiality and, precisely because it favors no one but sees in everyone a brother or a sister of Jesus Christ, treats people, not with a false egalitarianism, but rather unequally, just as they themselves are unequal. This is the disposition of creative goodness that recognizes what is unique in each individual person and approaches him as this unique person. It is the disposition of the seeing heart, which cannot be replaced by any institutional structures, because a man will always be a unique, new person. It is an attitude that not only gives alms but wants what is just for the other and really accepts him as another subject of rights just like myself, an attitude that nevertheless goes beyond mere justice by purifying and deepening it in a creative goodness. This is the disposition in which justice and love are fused and what is universal and permanent in moral standards combines with what is unique and unrepeatable, which however can be discovered only by a heart that is touched and illuminated by belief in the nearness of the Lord.

With that, the reading leads directly to the Gospel, with the message of the Baptist who tells the people in various walks of life what they should do to correspond to the nearness of the Lord. Here a second aspect of diaconal ministry becomes visible: showing-how-to-do remains mute unless it is interpreted in an explanatory proclamation, in the message that commands the deeds in the first place. This is why this catechesis of the Baptist, which was supposed to make people capable of the Lord's nearness, was always quite naturally read by the Church also as her baptismal catechesis, for she knew that she, too, owes people moral instruction and especially social, ethical instruction, for this alone opens up the space in which Advent, the encounter with the approaching Lord, can be accomplished. Again and again it impresses me to reflect that Saint Ambrose starts the conclusion of his baptismal catechesis with the words: "Day after day we have spoken about moral matters. Now the season admonishes us to speak about the mystery." The fact that the collection of moral guidelines that Jesus Sirach collected in the late Old Testament period received the title *Ecclesiasticus*—the Church book—points in the same direction. The mystery, the secret center of all our faith and being, can live only if our daily bread continues to be our moral struggle to correspond correctly to the nearness of the Lord. One of these decisively diaconal ministries is to carry out this mission of the Baptist, which is a perpetual, Christological mission. To actualize the *cottidianus sermo*, the daily word, the daily bread of this interior direction, of doing, feeling, and living in the footsteps of the Lord. I think that the Church must venture much more to do this again, and I ask you, dear brothers, to conduct this catechesis which provides the human prerequisites for being a Christian, which we really lack today, to reawaken and to consolidate the basic human virtues—Paul calls them the "Stoic" virtues—that open up the space in which we can find the true man, the God-man Jesus Christ, and contact one another with him.

Someone who becomes aware of the Lord's nearness is frightened; he notices how little his life corresponds to it and asks: What should I do? But anyone who stands firm for a while in this proximity will hear a second word, too. Not only: "Let all men know your goodness", but also the call: "Rejoice in the Lord always. Again I will say, rejoice." The nearness of the Lord is joy, for it means to discover and perceive that I am accepted, I am needed; there is someone who wants me, who loves me. And all the futile moments of my life are undergirded by the fact that my life is willed and needed. Antoine de Saint-Exupéry, in his *Little Prince*, said: "If you knew that on one of the stars there is a flower that wants to be tended by you, the whole sky would be different for you."

Dear brothers and sisters, this flower exists; the Lord is there on that star of ours, and the whole sky is different because we are expected. And because our human loving and failing is also supported by this will that is good to us and needs us. To discover the Lord means to discover joy. And then proclaiming Christ means not only preparing human virtues, becoming a man so that we might be the God-man with him. It means proclaiming joy, being an evangelist. And the wonderful words of the prophet Isaiah that we hear in Advent are true of the deacon: "How beautiful are the feet of those who proclaim peace, who bring good tidings of joy." We would be able to proclaim the message even more compellingly if we ourselves interiorly were more moved by this joy that causes the heart to tremble because he is the one who gives meaning and goodness to everything. "The Lord is near! Let all men know your goodness. Rejoice always." This triad of biblical sayings from today's liturgy expresses the essence of the diaconate, its spiritual face, and thus your face, dear brothers. And in this hour we all wish to pray with one accord that you will be touched more and more by the experience of the Lord's nearness. That more and more of your lives will be translated into the good that transforms the world. And that in this way your life will be increasingly illuminated and permeated by the joy that he himself is.

Called to Nuptial Service

Munich, January 1980

Gospel: John 2:1–11

Dear candidates for ordination!
Dear brothers and sisters in the Lord!

The evangelist John himself, in the first words of today's Gospel, provides us with the key to the mysterious account of the wedding feast in Cana. For it begins with the words: It happened "on the third day". Experts on the Holy Land tell us that there, according to an old custom that may go back as far as the time of Jesus, the third day of the week, Tuesday, was the usual day for weddings, just as Saturday generally is for us. And so this note at the beginning would initially say something quite commonplace; as usual, there was a wedding on the third day.

But in John's Gospel, even the usual, merely human things are transparent and give us an insight into something greater, the mystery of God and Jesus Christ. And so this commonplace remark about the third day shines first backward into the Old Covenant, where particularly in the Sinai accounts the third day is the day of theophany, of God's appearance, of the entrance of his glory into the world of men. And it shines forward into the Paschal

"Gerufen zum hochzeitlichen Dienst", for the ordination of deacons in the Liebfrauendom, Munich, on January 20, 1980. Previously unpublished. [B 549]

Mystery, which Christendom has professed since the days
of the early Church with the words: "On the third day he
rose again from the dead." Christendom is convinced that
only with this Paschal Mystery did the real, the essential
theophany of God occur in this world, the entrance of
his power and glory: on Good Friday, with the humility of his self-effacing and self-surrendering love, and on
Easter Sunday, with the power of this love which throws
open the gates of death and thus invalidates the primal law
of this world, the law of "die and become", through the
power of life that is not doomed to death. Jesus' first miracle points toward this Paschal Mystery. It points toward
his real sign, which at the same time is his new reality that
transforms the world.

Thus John presents to us in an event and in the image
of this event what Mark condenses into one sentence at
the beginning of his Gospel when he says: "The kingdom
of God is at hand; repent, and [do penance]" (Mk 1:14f.).
Wedding, feast, and wine are symbols of the Paschal Mystery and thereby signs of the kingdom of God. Wedding
and feast mean that the world becomes festive, the leaden
everyday routine vanishes, and a love enters that opens up
the borders between men: a new freedom, a new togetherness. And wine means, as it were, the lifting of restrictive
human limits generally speaking, the opening of the border between man and the world; it symbolizes the wealth
and the delightfulness of God's gifts. All of this makes clear
what God's festival with this world will be someday.

Another detail in the description of the event in today's
Gospel is important: the superabundance. According to
the measures that John notes, Jesus provided between 110
and 160 gallons of wine, much more than could still be
needed at that late hour. But this makes God's law, the law
of love, evident: namely, the superabundance that does

not count or reckon or ask whether that is enough now, but lavishes unquestioningly and thus proclaims the greatness, the festive freedom of love. Superabundance is God's law, the law of love and that of the New Covenant. Only with the start of a mentality that no longer looks around, counts, or weighs, "What more do I have to do for it to be enough?", does the New Covenant begin.

Jesus' first sign, the wedding on the third day, points ahead to his last and most characteristic sign, to the Paschal Mystery, to the kingdom of God. But in order to interpret this passage completely, we must now reflect also on several striking details in the story. Indeed, Mary meets at first with a quite brusque refusal of her request. "What have you to do with me? My hour has not yet come." Jesus' hour is the Cross. Yes, only with the Cross can the reawakening begin, can Easter begin, and, with Easter, the New Covenant. He cannot simply bring about or produce this hour; he himself cannot make the Cross; the way to it must be walked. He is standing just at the start of his journey; his work has scarcely begun. And therefore the only thing that counts in this hour is the Father's will and not the Mother's will. But then again, we find something strange: after this refusal, Mary continues as though nothing at all had happened. She gives the servants advice, instructions to do what Jesus tells them to—and in fact he performs the miracle. It is true that he cannot create his hour himself, it has to arrive; the way must be walked, the Father's will must be fulfilled. And nevertheless the Mother's request does not remain unanswered. He anticipates the mystery of his hour. He makes it present in the sign of this gift of wine.

Mary stands here—as always in the Gospel of John— for the Church. The Church stands in the affliction of this era, in which mankind runs out of wine again and again, indeed, often runs out of water, too, so that we think the story can no longer continue. And out of this affliction she cries to him after his hour: Thy kingdom come! Although we cannot force the hour to arrive, nevertheless the cry does not remain unanswered. Even though the hour has not yet come, he already gives us now the mystery of his love; even now the thing that constitutes his kingdom, in the sacrament of the Church and in the nuptial sacrament of the Eucharist. He gives himself to us, and in doing so, he makes his love shine forth into the world, a love that gives us the strength to keep on going, to withstand the times again and again, and to lead them to him.

Mary stands for the Church. Beside her, quite close to her and at the same time quite close to Christ, stand the servants in this Gospel, whom the Greek text twice calls *diakonoi*—deacons. Thus the Gospel speaks now directly to us, it addresses us. These deacons heed Mary's call. They stand ready to do her bidding. She herself, however, tells them to do the bidding of Jesus Christ. Jesus orders them to draw water, to provide the elements for his miracle. Basically, they must first of all quite simply help him to do a human kindness, to offer the routine yet unfortunately all-too-uncommon help that would assist these people at the moment when their feast threatens to run aground and to turn into sadness. But by serving Jesus' goodness, they serve to make his hour present. This goodness in which they collaborate becomes for them the sacrament of the kingdom.

Finally, there is something else here that is remarkable and important. The chief steward, we read, did not know where the wine came from. The servants, the deacons, though, knew. In their collaboration, they were sharers in charity. And as collaborators and sharers in charity, they had become sharers in knowledge. The specialist could not perceive it, but collaboration and sharing in charity had opened their eyes and given them knowledge. And as sharers in knowledge, they were called to become believers and, thus, again loving witnesses to the love of Jesus Christ.

This narrative arc, which depicts the participation of the deacons in the mystery of Cana, actually describes as a whole what the ministry of the deacon signifies. It means, first: being ready for the Church's call. To be available to do her bidding. The Church, however, leads to the bidding and instruction of Jesus Christ. And the Word of Jesus Christ requires us to become servants of his mercies. Servants in the great mystery of his kingdom and, then, servants in the everyday mission of his love.

Since the most ancient times, the deacon's ministry in the Church has been associated particularly with the chalice. The chalice embodies the inmost mystery of the Eucharist, the Blood that Jesus shed for us. Consequently, it points right to the most practical mystery of the faith, to the process of becoming transparent for the love of Jesus Christ in our life. When this sign is not given, the mystery, the sacrament remains mute, also. In all this, we are called to become sharers in charity, sharers in suffering, and thus more and more sharers in knowledge with the Lord.

Allow me, dear candidates for ordination, to add a very personal note. As deacons, we are servants of God's mysteries. But at the same time, we are and indeed we also remain very ordinary guests at table or perhaps hosts, as the bride and groom at Cana were. And everyone who serves in this way as host will someday have the same experience as this bride and groom: their own wine ran out. Whatever knowledge, resolutions, experience, willpower, or wine of our own we may have prepared for the company at the feast that we want to celebrate as a step toward the Lord, it is not enough. It may happen, then, that some will go away full of resentment and become accusers of the Church. But it may also happen that in precisely this way we will really encounter the hour of Jesus Christ for the first time and have the privilege of experiencing its presence even now. That is, if we have Mary's patience and humility. After all, she actually made no request of Jesus. She only told him what the situation was and commended it to him and knew: since it is in his hands, then all is well, even though his answer will be different from what I expect; even though I cannot figure out this answer in advance. Even refusal does not lead to discouragement, but there is peaceful, faithfully trusting knowledge that even his refusal is still love. And so through this failure and this refusal, she has the privilege of reaching the presence of his hour, the paradox: although the Father's will has not yet called for this hour, the Mother's request is accepted. If we continue in this way in patience and confidence, then we, too, may be certain that the Lord always touches us with his hour, gives us the new wine that far surpasses our imagination and all that we were able to prepare. And so in this hour we all want to pray for each other and especially for you, that the Lord might grant us the humility, the patience, and the cheerfulness that allow us truly to become the servants of his hour.

Joy in Christu

Munich, December 1980

Entrance Antiphon: Philippians 4:4–5
Reading: Isaiah 35:1–6a, 10; Gospel: Matthew 11:2–11

Introductory Remarks

Dear brothers and sisters,

The motto that the Church has assigned to the Third Sunday of Advent from the earliest times was written by Paul from prison to the Christians in Philippi: "Rejoice in the Lord always; again I will say, Rejoice.... The Lord is at hand." We rejoice in this hour because we have the privilege of sensing something of the nearness of the Lord, who again has called a group of men to become deacons of the Gospel, servants of his joy among the people. We wish to ask him to allow these men, who today set out on the path of his service, to experience always and ever more the power of his nearness and to lead us all more and more into his nearness and, thus, to enlighten the darkness and to grant us his joy.

"Freude in Christus", for the ordination of permanent deacons in the Liebfrauendom, Munich, on December 14, 1980, in *Priester aus innerstem Herzen* (Munich, 2007), 168–73; previously in *KlBl* 61 (1981): 4–5; under the title "Diener der Freude des Herrn unter den Menschen und Träger des göttlichen Erbarmens in der Welt", *Ordinariatskorrespondenz*, Munich, no. 42 (December 22, 1980). [B 589]

Homily

Dear candidates for ordination,
dear brothers in the episcopal and priestly ministry,
dear brothers and sisters in the Lord!

"Among you stands one whom you do not know, and I myself did not know him." We are reminded of these words of the Baptist from the Fourth Gospel by the incident about which we heard in today's Gospel. For a long time the Lord has stood in our midst, and yet the question arises again and again: Are you the one, or must we wait for another? He stands among us, and nevertheless it happens again and again: we do not know him, and I myself did not know him. John recognized him when the dove of the Holy Spirit halted over him. At that moment he proclaimed him as the Lamb of God who takes away the sins of the world. Dove and Lamb reveal the mystery of the Redeemer. This means: John recognized him when he stopped looking for the Redeemer with his own eyes and stopped seeking him according to his own criteria of judgment, when he started to look with the eyes of the Holy Spirit and to subject himself to his standards. Then he saw: this man, the hidden one, the apparently insignificant one, the Lamb is the Redeemer.

God comes as a lamb and not as a lion or a wolf or a bull. That was the way people had expected him to be, the primordial power that lifts the structures of this world off their hinges and creates brand new ones instead, that brings the day of God's wrath of which today's reading from the prophet speaks. But he does not come as a lion—the symbol that the kings of the earth repeatedly use for themselves. Nor does redemption come through the she-wolf that was the symbol of ancient Rome, which with its peacekeeping force offered itself as the rescuer and redeemer of the world. Redemption does not come through the big, strong animals that are symbols of the powers and forces of this world. God comes as a lamb, in the power of defenseless love, and this is his might. And the moment you see the dove and recognize this, you also become aware that deep down we were waiting for the Lamb, for the greater power of defenseless love that overcomes the noisy, violent powers of this world, that does not destroy but heals. God comes as the Lamb; this is the redemption of the world.

Today's Gospel says nothing different. On a first, superficial reading, one might think that all the emphasis here is on the extraordinary and the miraculous: the deaf hear, the blind see, the dead are raised up. But if you listen more carefully to this text, you see that, quite the contrary, it intends to defend the inconspicuousness of Jesus, his littleness of which the last sentence of the Gospel speaks, for Jesus Christ is the least one in the kingdom of God. And precisely in this littleness of God comes the new greatness, in comparison to which all the greatness of this world is merely ridiculous and ultimately insignificant and miserable. By giving this answer, Jesus means to say: If you are unwilling to accept me and recognize me, if instead you expect the big explosion that turns everything upside down, then read the prophets once again, and see whether this is not precisely what was foretold.

The deeds of Jesus Christ, his true signs, and his authentication by the prophets are reduced to two in this prophetic saying that he quotes: the Good News is proclaimed to the poor—evangelization is the one sign. The blind see, the lame walk, the lepers are made clean, the dead arise— mercy from God's mercy, that is the other sign. The deeds of Jesus, his true signs, the signs of the Lamb, are these two: the Gospel and mercy—the word and love. And

that is why these two are still the standard, also, for all
Christian discipleship and the standard for all service in
the Church, for all service to the Gospel of Jesus Christ.
And that is also why it is no surprise that they agree exactly
with the description of the diaconate that Church tradition
has given and gives: it is the service of the Gospel and the
service of the love of Jesus Christ for God's poor, to those
who await the sign of his mercy. When this service is performed, the sign of Jesus Christ is thereby made present
again, the words of the prophets are fulfilled, and the way
is shown to him who stands unknown in our midst.

Therefore, you should become evangelists first, heralds
of the Good News. A renowned thinker of our time said
that this age is characterized by the inability to mourn. I
think that we must say, even before that and even more,
it is characterized by the inability to rejoice. Joy appears to
be something almost amoral, an attack on righteousness in
this world, where so many are tortured, where so many
go hungry, where so many are robbed of their freedom,
where so many suffer unbearably. Are we really allowed
then to rejoice? Or is not joy the expression of dullness,
indifference, or even cynicism, which itself becomes
oppression of those who suffer? And, in fact, when we
look at the world as it is, we see some cause for joy but
much, much more that is terrifying. And this is why today
we see so many faces lined with sorrow, anger, or indig-
nation, on which joylessness and anger are written like a
spiteful creed.

When we snuff out the light of joy, when we renounce
joy, then the world just becomes darker, sadder, and more
discouraging. Eugene Ionesco once said: One can love men
only if they carry God within them. I would like to add:
One can love the world only if it is willed by God, if it
carries God within it. But this is precisely what faith shows

us. And then there is a new factor that is stronger than all the terrifying things that we may record, then there is, nevertheless, a reason to be glad. This is why the believer is a man of joy, and he will be so all the more, the more he is a believer, and the joy that faith arouses is a power that changes the world. We owe a debt to the world and to men if we let this joy be snuffed out. We do not improve it, but, rather, we deprive ourselves of the task that was assigned to us.

This, after all, was the moving thing about the papal visit, the thing that thrilled people: that we could rejoice again, could experience again the fact that faith is joy and agreement. In fact, the Christian faith is not an endless grim debate. It is not perpetual suspicion, which is then ultimately denial. Faith is quintessentially agreement. It is Yes. It is joy. And it comes from God's Yes, from the Yes that, as Saint Paul puts it, Jesus Christ himself is. It is God's Yes in us and to us. Because during the recent days of the papal visit we had the privilege to experience the faith again in this way, as the right to agreement, as an invitation to joy, the faith also dawned on us anew. Only in the power of the Yes can we overcome the world's denials. And only the great Yes of God that is Jesus Christ can become for us the power by which to overcome the denials.

Therefore you are supposed to be evangelists. And the world is looking for evangelists, even if it does not know it or even disputes it. You are supposed to be evangelists in many different ways. Often it can be just a simple word, a kind gesture, a greeting. But the most important part of being an evangelist is proclaiming the message of Jesus Christ. Proclaim it calmly, joyfully, in all its simplicity and directness. Indeed, today we often hide it under a thousand apologies. So often it disappears in the convolutions

of our methods. But we have no reason to apologize for
the Gospel. We must apologize for hiding it. Let us say it
as plainly, as directly, and as simply as it is, in the power
of its Yes. Let us not hesitate to proclaim: God the Father,
who created the world and loves us, every one of us;
Christ, who redeemed us and suffered for every one of
us; the Holy Spirit, who even today accompanies the
Church; the sacraments through which he sanctifies and
guides us; the promise of eternal life. If we do this, then
we may also live to see again and again how the prophetic
words are fulfilled. How the blind gain their sight—how a
light goes on for a person who no longer found anything
in this world comprehensible, how life becomes bright
again for him. How the lame learn to walk—in a pathless
life a new way arises. How the lepers are made clean—
the disgust of an unfortunate life falls away, replaced by a
new openness. How the dead arise—how a life that had
long since sunk into non-living or the opposite of living is
reawakened and once again becomes Yes.

Every pastoral worker who proclaims the Gospel can
report how, to his great joy, he has experienced profoundly
over and over again the truth of the promises, how the
Gospel is God's mercy and heals the poor, the sick, and
the suffering and works God's miracles even today. And he
will see that the Gospel is not only word but is also mercy,
love. Yes, there is no mercy and no development in the
world without the word of light, without the word of the
Gospel. And conversely, where the Gospel is proclaimed
properly, there is mercy, there it is and becomes deed.

With that we have arrived at the second point: you are
supposed to be bearers of the divine mercy in this world.
Just like joy, mercy, too, is disparaged today. They tell
us: No, not mercy, do not have mercy on the individual;
that just solidifies the deceitful situation of this world. We

must change the structures so that we no longer need any mercy. This was probably the view of the priest and the Levite, too, who walked past the victim of robbery on the road from Jerusalem to Jericho and left him lying there. They, too, were of the opinion that individual mercy does not help, since such things happen ten times a day. The only thing that helps here is to change the situation. And perhaps they even went to a committee meeting where structural changes were discussed. But this refusal to show mercy is a rejection of the merciful Samaritan, who ultimately is Jesus Christ himself.

The world needs mercy. The Holy Father told us this again in his recent encyclical with great forcefulness, based on his own experience of a merciless so-called justice. Where justice is separated from mercy, justice becomes cruel and unjust. Only mercy can keep justice fair. And where there is mercy, righteousness is built up, too. Be such men of mercy: for the elderly, for the sick, for the children, for the young people who so often lack the experience of loving parents and siblings—men of mercy for God's poor! And do not forget that rich people can be very poor, too. If the word of mercy has never reached them, has never touched their hearts, then it becomes evident that true wealth is not ownership but mercy, love, the light that proceeds from God's love.

Finally, among the words of the Lord in today's Gospel there is another odd sentence: "Blessed is he who takes no offense at me." This recalls the first sermon of Jesus in his native town of Nazareth. There he quotes the same prophetic words about the blind seeing, about the good news for the poor, and says: Today this has been fulfilled. But very soon the townspeople of Nazareth contradict him. They find it ridiculous for him to make this claim, since they know him, the son of the carpenter, whose relatives live there, whom they have dealt with over the years. And finally they whip themselves into such a fury that they drive him out of the synagogue, throw him out of the town, and try to stone him. This incident at the beginning of Jesus' public life is only a foreshadowing of his whole career. For his whole career is a representation of the prophets, of the Good News for the poor, of God's mercies. And this entire career ends with people throwing him out, getting into a rage, and crucifying him.

Those who expected God to come as a lion or as a bull or as a wolf cannot accept the one who comes as a lamb. Those who are themselves lions, wolves, or tigers do not like the God who comes as a lamb. They want to pounce on the lamb to tear it to pieces. This being the case, another part of the mystery of Jesus Christ is the Cross. We oversimplify, indeed, we distort the figure of Christ if we leave out this reality, if we just say his words and forget that he backed up those words with his life. We oversimplify the figure if we make Jesus out to be just the ever-tolerant teacher who is always acceptance and unconditional affirmation and considers everything all right and says Yes to everyone and may even provide an ideology for all occasions. The real Jesus is different. The fact that he is lamb implies at the same time his Cross. That is why only someone who goes so far as to accept that point, too, really stands by him. That is why part of being a Christian, the center of being a Christian, is participation in the Eucharist, in which his Cross is made present, the Cross on which he transformed men's anger into mercy and in his mercy became a sacrificial victim for us. That is why another part of being a Christian is the courage of the Cross and the patience of the prophet, which we heard about in today's reading from the Letter of James. Jesus is not looking for reeds, weathervanes turning with the spirit of the age, or men in soft garments. He is looking for steadfast men, men with the patience of the Cross.

This steadfastness which withstands the contradiction of the spirit of the world can of course be maintained only by someone who deep down is united with the crucified and risen Lord. For he knows that nothing can separate us from the love of Jesus Christ: neither past nor future, neither height nor depth, neither life nor death. He is the one who upholds us. And fear of the contradiction of the spirit of the age is ultimately anxiety about losing love, anxiety about loneliness. But he is with us, the one who has the greater love, who no longer calls us servants but friends. And this love is the force that sustains us, that is stronger than any other force imaginable.

So at this hour I would like to wish for you that you may ever more profoundly be able to live close to him, that you may encounter him more and more, be united with him, and thus be ever more deeply rooted in the force of this love which is indestructible joy; so that in this way the motto of this day might come true more and more in your life: "Rejoice! And again I say, rejoice!"

Your Place in the Liturgy Is the Gospel!

Munich, December 1981

Entrance Antiphon: Philippians 4:4–5
Reading: 1 Thessalonians 5:16–24
Gospel: John 1:6, 8, 19–28

Dear candidates for ordination,
dear brothers in the episcopal and priestly ministry,
dear brothers and sisters in the Lord!

"Rejoice always", this verse which the choir has just sung for us, repeating the first sentence from today's reading, since the earliest times has struck the basic chord of the Third Sunday in Advent. It is the basic chord also of the entire Pauline message. Paul wrote it down here in his first and oldest letter (1 Thess 5:16), at the beginning of his missionary career and yet at the same time in the midst of many hardships, knowing that the joy that he had to proclaim is much stronger than those hardships. Then this word joy occurs again at the high point of his work in the Letter to the Romans (cf. Rom 14:17) and in the Second Letter to the Corinthians (cf. 2 Cor 1:24) and finally, as he is already facing martyrdom, when he says in the Letter to the Philippians: "Even if I am to be poured as a libation

"Euer Ort in der Liturgie ist das Evangelium", for the ordination of permanent deacons in the Liebfrauendom, Munich, on December 13, 1981, *Diakon Anianus*, no. 39 (July 2005): 34–36. [B 648]

upon the sacrificial offering of your faith, I am glad" (Phil 2:17). In prison, facing death, he writes to the Christian community in Philippi: "Rejoice in the Lord always; again I will say, Rejoice" (Phil 4:4). This word of joy is not about Saint Paul's personal temperament; it is light that he has kindled by the light of Jesus Christ; it is simply the expression of the message that he received on the road to Damascus; it is the expression of the Gospel, which in the deepest sense says nothing other than this: Rejoice, there is reason to be glad! So this message makes its way through time. It started with this, for the beginning of the Gospel takes place in the angel's greeting to Mary: "Rejoice, O full of grace" (Lk 1:28; cf. Zeph 3:14–15). When it enters the world publicly for the first time, on that Holy Night, the angels again begin their proclamation of the message with the words: "I bring you good news of a great joy.... For to you is born this day in the city of David a Savior, who is Christ the Lord" (Lk 2:10–11). Finally, the height of the Gospel is reached on Easter morning with the message: "The Lord has risen!" (Mt 28:6; cf. Lk 24:34); with the news that the sorrow of Good Friday— and, most profoundly, all the sorrow of the world—ends and is transformed. When Paul says, "Rejoice", he is simply proclaiming the message that comes from the Lord, for he is the evangelist of Jesus Christ.

And with that, dear candidates for ordination, we have arrived at this hour, for from now on this is your calling and the beautiful thing about your calling: the fact that you are evangelists of Jesus Christ. You are commissioned to proclaim the Gospel in the liturgy. Again and again at Midnight Mass you have the privilege of being the angel with the message for people "this day" and telling them today in all the darkness of these times: "I bring you good news of a great joy. To you is born Christ the Lord!"

Then the high point and center of the diaconal ministry is at the Easter Vigil to reverence the Paschal candle, which is for us the symbol of the new light of the Resurrection, symbol of the risen Jesus Christ, and then in the *Exsultet* to invite heaven and earth to rejoice, to sing, and to exult with us. You are evangelists. Your place in the Church's liturgy is the Gospel. And this is not a random, mechanical assignment of roles, just so that everyone has something to do; it is the summary, center, and interpretation of what you are undertaking with this ministry in the first place. This is the point of departure in which it is gathered and from which everything else is continually derived. You are called to this; this is your state in life: to go to the people and to bring them joy. What more beautiful calling could there be than to be on the way with joy, giving people joy. You have the privilege of telling them: You are regarded with eyes of love, for that is what Christmas means. And also: Love is stronger than death, for that is the meaning of Easter.

You are first and finally evangelists. When we look now at today's Gospel, in the titles of the precursor of Jesus Christ, we encounter the two further tasks of the deacon, which are nothing more than the interpretation of this central task. These titles are: witness and baptizer. Both make it evident how this can happen—how you can be an evangelist and bring the joy of Jesus Christ here into the world today. One can proclaim the joy of that Holy Night and the joy of that Easter morning only if he is a witness who has recognized the truth of this message himself and has been filled with it. That is why you can become an evangelist only if the light of that Holy Night has shone into your heart. That is why a deacon of Jesus Christ must be someone who has had the experience of Mary in that Easter morning hour, who heard Jesus say her name and, as she was called by name, recognized the one whom she had earlier mistaken for the gardener (cf. Jn 20:11–18). In order to be a deacon, you must somehow like Thomas have placed your hands in the side of Jesus Christ and have recognized: Yes, he suffered for us, and he lives. The love that these wounds express is alive, it is present, and it is here. In order to be an evangelist, one must be a witness, one must know Jesus, his voice, the sound of his words, his way. That is why I ask you with all my heart to listen again and again to Sacred Scripture, to accept the message that Pope Gregory IX wrote to Saint Elizabeth [of Hungary]: "Like Mary in Bethany, gladly stay at the Lord's feet. Listen to him. Do not go away until the warm south wind of his mercies wafts through the senses of your garden." Staying with the Lord, listening, getting to know him!

In this connection something once said by the great nineteenth-century theologian of Tübingen and Munich, Johann Adam Möhler, occurs to me: "If we did not have Sacred Scripture, we would not know how Jesus spoke, and I think that I would no longer want to live if I no longer heard his voice." At any rate he adds: "If we did not have the Church's tradition, we would not know who spoke then, and immediately that would extinguish our joy over how he spoke." Love Sacred Scripture, be at home in it, read it in the midst of the Church's living faith, so as always to know at the same time who is speaking and so as to hear how his voice calls to us.

On the morning of the day on which I was ordained a lector, according to the old rite, to do the readings in church, one of my fellow students left me a slip of paper on my desk on which were written the words that Dostoyevsky has the Monk Zosima say: "Read Sacred Scripture, read it to people, but make no great theories, no great words about it. Let the word itself penetrate your heart again and again with few explanations and have no fear that people might not understand it. The faithful heart understands everything." I think that it is extremely important that we do not proclaim theories about Sacred Scripture but again and again let Scripture itself speak. Scripture itself, as it stands, just as it was given to us by the Church through the power of the Holy Spirit. It is important for us not to proclaim an assortment-Jesus as he is reconstructed in sources that may or that are said to have been behind it, but rather to proclaim the Jesus who meets us there, the whole, living, real Jesus, so that that way we hear him and let him speak to us. Remaining at the feet of Jesus so as to become a witness. Part of this is listening to him and looking at him anew, over and over again. Part of this is answering him and speaking with him. Praying the Liturgy of the Hours, to which in a moment you will commit yourselves, is not some external add-on to the diaconal ministry. It is the inner center of this task of being a witness. Joy can remain only in a man who receives, and only someone who perseveres in prayer can receive. Keep in prayer your ministry, your congregations, the people who are entrusted to you, and believe that such prayer is the inmost power of all pastoral activity. The Church does not live primarily through theory and organization but through the power of the Holy Spirit, which we invoke in prayer. And if in today's reading we find the sentence: "Do not quench the Spirit", this also means above all: Trust God. Trust prayer. And be doers based on your prayer, so that the Holy Spirit can act in our time.

Above all, though, being a witness also means bringing oneself in. A witness is more than a reporter. The witness vouches for the word with his own life. And so being a witness means not only proclaiming the Gospel with words but putting it into action. That is why the service of charity to our neighbor and the works of corporal mercy have from earliest times been the core of the diaconal task. This is not a social supplement that we do in order to justify the Church in this age but, rather, the most essential, necessary fruit of the Gospel. No one can proclaim joy as credibly as someone who brings joy, who does joy, who does charity.

And finally the other title of the Baptist: just so, he baptizes. This, too, is by no means a merely ritual activity that is now assigned to you along with the Gospel, along with charity. It is again the message of the joy of Jesus Christ. About the Baptist Scripture tells us, on the one hand, that he preached in the desert and, on the other hand, that he stood by the stream and gave people the water of purification, the living water. These two things are only apparently a contradiction; the two belong together. In the wilderness, he finds the people, and he directs them to the stream, and so he prepares ways for God and ways for the people themselves. Desert means solitude, isolation, space in which there is no other, in which being alone becomes at the same time a space of death and of sterility. How much desert there is today in the middle of our major cities! A pastor recently told me that in his parish more and more dead people have to be brought from their residence by the police or the fire department. They die alone. No one knows them; no one gives them a final kind word in the hour of their departure. The locked doors have to be opened by force. How much desert, how much isolation, how much pathlessness there is!

Baptizing means not just performing a rite; it means leading people out of the desert to the stream; it means leading them to purification. Today we have an almost ritually exaggerated external hygiene, which may also be a substitute rite for the deeply felt lack of the inner hygiene

that man cannot give himself but only God can give him.
Bring people to the waters of purification and, thus, to
the waters of refreshment, to the waters of life, and in that
way be what John wanted to be, what the deacon must be:
people who build roads by preparing paths for God; paths
that lead to each other and at the same time overcome the
wilderness, reinstate living fruitfulness, a togetherness that
only the love and the mercy of the Redeemer can give.

Rejoice always! To bring the joy of the Gospel, one
must be filled with it himself, one must receive the Gospel
himself. This is the Church's prayer for you, our prayer for
you, dear deacons, dear candidates for ordination, in this
hour: that the joy of the Gospel may accompany you all
the days of your life, so that you, while giving joy, might
receive it yourselves ever more deeply. We pray for this
with great confidence, according to the truth with which
today's reading concludes: God is faithful. He began it, and
he will also bring it to completion.

To Enter with Him into
the Ministry of Life

Munich, February 1982

Reading: Leviticus 13:1–2, 45–46; Gospel: Mark 1:40–45

Dear candidates for ordination!
Dear brothers in the episcopal and priestly ministry!
Dear brothers and sisters in the Lord!

The urgent petition in the prayers of today's Mass is the call for a new, clean heart, for purification and renewal. At first glance, this seems to us far removed from the questions and needs that concern today's world and us here in this country and at this time. But if we go a little deeper into it, we can tell that this very same call characterizes all times, ours no less than the ones before it. Our knowledge about history has grown more and more. Under the X-ray vision of Marxist analysis, all the terrible, frightening, and negative things in this history have passed even more garishly before our eyes. The yearning for liberation from this guilt, from this deformation of mankind has grown ever greater. The yearning to shake off this tainted existence, to begin anew, to break with the past and emerge from it,

"In den Dienst des Lebens mit Ihm treten", for the ordination of deacons in the Liebfrauendom, Munich, on February 14, 1982. Previously unpublished. [B 667]

really to build a new world with new men, is stronger and more urgent today than ever before.

Right now in our time, therefore, this yearning is alive. Certainly there is the other side, too: the experience of futility, the recognition that just when we try to shake all these things off, we get entangled with them again; and then, as a result, flirting with impurity, pleasure taken in filth, which nevertheless is something like a cry for help. God, if you exist, then look at how dirty we are! Then you will not be able to tolerate it any more, then you will have to create new, pure men, then you will have to bring about renewal and create a new world!

In today's readings this question comes up in the form of the leper. In the ancient world, a leper was viewed as a carrier of death who bears death and corruption on his living body and brings death to others. The leper [*Der Aussätzige*] is someone who above all must be cut off from God, because God is life and has nothing in common with death. But because he is alienated from God, he must also be cut off from men. He is set apart [*ausgesetzt*], so that the power of death that he carries within him may be expelled from their midst. That is the meaning of "unclean", *ausgesetzt*: because he carries a life-destroying ailment, he is rightly driven out into the zone of death. Coexistence with men and coexistence with God are taken away from him, and thereby he is truly handed over to death; for a man lives by being with others, and in solitude he is driven out of the setting that gives him life.

The Old Testament could recognize this situation and also pinpoint it, but it could not respond to it or change it. I think that it seemed rather curious to all of us a moment ago after the reading that in response to these disturbing instructions—"he shall dwell alone outside the camp"—we were supposed to say: "Thanks be to God!" We can, nevertheless, say "Thanks be to God" now—even when confronted with these horrors of the world—because the Old Testament no longer has the last word, because we read it in the New and with the New Testament, and Jesus Christ is now able to say the word that the Old Testament could not pronounce, a word that no revolutionary movements or innovators of this age can say, either: "I will; be clean." The leper, who must cry "Unclean" to keep people away from him, goes up to him, and Jesus does not turn away, as he ought to have done according to the Law. For him, this man is not an untouchable who brings the power of death into life. He touches him, and he can do this because he is the Son and because God, who reveals himself in him, does not need to fear death. He can touch him because in him the power of life and the contagion of life are stronger than the contagion of death.

So this little scene from the Gospel offers Christians an image for the entire mission of Jesus Christ. He came to say: "I will; be clean." He came to bring the contagion of life. He came to give purity and newness. He came as the servant of life, so that they might have life and have it abundantly, as Saint John put it (Jn 10:10).

Becoming a deacon of Jesus Christ means entering into the service of life with him; it means being enlisted in this service of purification and renewal. Jesus Christ gives us this gift. According to the Gospel, this purification and renewal which he accomplishes happens in three stages, and we certainly can see therein parallels to the three dimensions of the diaconal ministry. First, the account tells us that Jesus had *pity* on him. That is not yet anything supernatural or theological, but something quite human. He does not turn away, he does not hide, he does not pass him by, he is not cold and self-contained, he is a man. He sees this terrible power of death, the destructive force of

being driven out, and the human fear of death; he sees
and is moved with compassion. In the Greek text, this is
expressed much more strongly and dramatically; it adopts
the nuance of the Hebrew when it writes: σπλαγχνισθείς—
"he felt bowels of pity." The whole human being, a body-
soul composite, is disturbed by such misery. Jesus is human.
And precisely in this humanity, God can be incarnate and
grant himself. Saint Bernard of Clairvaux coined the wonderful phrase: "Deus est impassibilis, sed non incompassi-
bilis" (*In Cant*. Serm. 26, 5). Although God cannot suffer,
he can experience compassion. And the Holy Father, in
his encyclical *Dives in misericordia*, revealed God's mercy to
us as the core of our image of God and as the core of the
new image of man that is derived from this God. Humanity is indeed a component of the service of Jesus Christ.
Because man is an integral whole, the supernatural and the
new cannot exist without the natural and the human in
which it comes to pass. Christianity today is endangered
precisely by the fact that human virtues threaten to crum-
ble and humanity is on the verge of a collapse. If we want
to be deacons of Jesus Christ, we must try to cultivate in
ourselves this humanity that was manifested anew in the
incarnate God and to develop in ourselves the virtues of
humanity, of being human. Because this is true, one component of the diaconal ministry, which does lead to the
priesthood yet does not stop there but, rather, remains
indispensably in it, has been from the very beginning the
dimension of charity, that is, of service to one's fellow-
men, which presupposes an eye for people and a heart for
people. And so I ask you, dear candidates for ordination,
first to keep trying to learn this humanity of Jesus anew,
to strive to have a human eye and a human heart so as to
awaken them in others, too. To find meaning and joy
in being a man for men, to discern the desire for good

in children and to respond to it, and likewise with the elderly, the poor, and the abandoned.

Today—thank God—in our region the leprosy described here in the Bible does not exist. But there is so much that is similar: so much interior decay within a living body, so much presence of death in the midst of life, so much being driven out into solitude, so much longing for someone to dare to see it, to place his finger on it, to be a human being with the outcast and in the kindness of humanity to reveal to him a new trust in God, in the first place, and the possibility of belief. Jesus had pity on him. Humanity is a primordial dimension of Christian life and, consequently, of the sacrament, of ordained ministry.

But human solidarity, in and of itself, is not enough. It becomes horizontality. And that leaves us in the middle of time, just as it is. Then the blind lead the blind, and the dead bury their dead. The humanity of Jesus was a critical turning point in world history because in it the power of God dwells and because on the basis of this power he can touch and does touch the suffering person with the contagion of life. Jesus *touches him*. This is the second dimension of our service. The Fathers viewed this touch of Jesus as the symbol for the whole sacramental dimension of the Church. In the sacraments he is still here and corporeally walks shoulder to shoulder with us, touches our body with his body in a bodily way and so causes us even now to sense that it is true: σπλαγχνισθείς—"his bowels were moved with pity" (Mk 1:41). With his body he rescues and delivers our body. As deacons, you, too, are servants of this sacramental touch, inasmuch as he touches us and we have the privilege of passing his touch along to our time. Jesus touches him. The sacrament, however, is not magic, and, therefore, touching Jesus in the sacrament means touching him as a person. This is why it is so decisive for servants of Jesus Christ really to touch him, person to person: like Thomas, to place our hand again and again into his open side. This is the great significance of the Liturgy of the Hours. To have time for Jesus, above and beyond mere human solidarity, which by itself can remain empty; to go forth and to get in touch with him. To get to know him, to learn to hear his voice, as he says about those who are his own. And this is the second request: that you never let go of this touch of Jesus and never view it as something secondary that can also be put off till tomorrow. Without this touch, everything else becomes empty. Stay with him! Seek to become ever better acquainted with him; ever more practically to hold this hand which guides us, which alone has the contagion of life within it. And in this touch, celibacy, too, can be lived out meaningfully and fruitfully. Not as a denial and refusal, but rather as: "Yes, Lord, you need me, you take me, so that by your power I can testify that you are the strength that supports a life, that the great contagion of life, its newness, and its purity proceed from you."

Here then is the third point. Jesus touched him and said: I will; be clean. The *word of Jesus is added*. The Fathers saw in this once again an expression for the force of the sacramental word. "I will; be clean." Only in the authority of Jesus Christ can one say to a person something that no psychotherapy is capable of doing: not only discussing the past and ruminating on it, but really taking it away. I will; be clean. But at the same time, the whole dimension of the word of God is hidden in it. One component of Christianity is God's humanity, another is the sacramental touch, and still another is the word of God that speaks to our mind, to our understanding, and to our question about meaning. God encountered us in the word and wants us to make him comprehensible again and to learn to understand ourselves in that word. Love for the word of God, and on the basis of that love—understanding, and on the basis of that understanding—proclamation: again and again the Lord seeks men for this, and you, dear candidates for ordination, are saying Yes to it in this hour. Love the word of God, frequent it regularly, learn to grasp it with your mind and with your heart and in this way to interpret it in turn for other minds and hearts.

And something else about this is very important: Christianity is not just signs, it is not magic; it has words, which means that it reveals truth. This word is not arbitrarily replaceable, an add-on, so to speak, because you have to say something when you do something. The Christian faith consists of content, too, and not just of meaning well; the knowledge and the acknowledgment that cannot be manipulated arbitrarily but constitutes the intrinsic spiritual and understood unity of the faith. And yet another thing emerges if we read farther in the Gospel. Jesus forbids this man to appear in public as a Jesus-propagandist. He even does so with a trace of anger: obviously because he sees that there is no compliance with this rule and that neither will there be any down through the centuries. He orders him to do something quite different: Go to the priests, present the offering, and in this way belong again to the People of Israel. He does not order him to make private propaganda for a powerful man and his agenda but, rather, commands him to enter into the sacrificial faith community of the People of God, into the common history of God, in which he created for men this With and this We that is life, because life is based on communion and the loss of the latter is, in fact, the death sentence of the outcast, who is truly healed only when he has entered into this great, sheltering With of the prayer and faith community created by God, into the whole achievement of general salvation history and of his word. That is Jesus' call to us, too. Not to make private Jesus–propaganda, which only divides and fractures and passes by the deepest mystery of Jesus, but, rather, to enter into the With that he has given us, into the With of his Body, the Church. However weak and frail and afflicted it may appear, it is nevertheless the place in which he who did not hesitate to touch weakness touches us again and again in the coexistence of the history of faith and saves us.

In the concluding prayer of today's Mass, the petition for renewal and cleansing found in the collect prayer and the offertory chant is brought to its fulfillment. The Latin text, which is unfortunately somewhat blurred in the German translation, contains two points: First, thanks that in the Eucharist God has let us experience his joy and then, consequently, the petition that in the power of this joy we might always be on the way to him by whom men truly live: to his truth, to his love, to Jesus Christ himself. This is my wish for you, dear candidates for ordination, at this hour, that you might again and again have the privilege of experiencing God's joy, that this joy of God in you might be again and again the force that shows you the way to the one by whom we truly live, the force that helps you to point out that way to others, so that they might have life and have it abundantly.

FIRST MASS

Fishers of Men

For Franz Niegel

Berchtesgaden, 1954

Gospel: Luke 5:1–11

Today's Gospel, which the deacon just proclaimed for us, captures a bit of the charm of the Holy Land.

It is almost as though you could hear for a moment the rushing of the lake over which the Lord traveled so often with his disciples, as though you could see the brilliant gleam of the southern sky vaulting cloudlessly over it or the welcome of the meadows around the sea, with their flowers that the Lord praised in his parables. The Lord incorporated something of the rushing of the lake in his homeland and of the fragrance of its flowers into his message about the eternal kingdom, and we rejoice, because we joyfully recognize the kinship with the beauty of our own homeland.

But all that has just been said is merely the external context in which the greater and more important thing takes place: the early morning hour of a human life in which a

"Menschenfischer", for Franz Niegel in Berchtesgaden on July 4, 1954, *MIPB* 2 (2009): 21–25; previously in *PrKat* 98 (1959): 361–66. [B 3]

man receives the call and mission of his existence. Once again this Simon, who for many years has sailed on the sea as a fisherman, sets out as before in order to catch fish. But when he hauls ashore the heavy, miraculous freight that is not his doing this time, something new begins: "Henceforth you will be catching men", the Lord tells him.

Now the net can be left there with the boat, and others can worry about it. You are now to cast God's nets into the sea of the world. You are to haul home to the shore of eternity the people there who resist and barricade themselves in the false appearance of their supposed happiness. You are to do this through the dejected night of many failures. You are to do it cheerfully and without grumbling even in the bitterest hours of the day, in which everything seems useless to you and the work of your life wasted.

That was then, almost two thousand years ago: the early morning hour of a human life. But it was not merely a thing of the past. It is: even now, here and today.

For what else happens in priestly ordination and at a First Mass than this: that Christ again comes up to a few young men and takes out of their hands the boats and the nets to which they have attached so many dreams of their youth and says to them: Now you are to be fishers of men. You are to sail out on the sea of the world and cast God's net with undaunted courage in an era that seems to be quite intent on escaping the holy hunter God.

Hence it is like an echo from the Lake of Gennesaret when at the beginning of the priestly ordination ceremony the bishop tells the young deacons who are standing before him their future tasks: objectively, soberly, and succinctly, as the language of the Roman rulers of the world once put it.

The priest must sacrifice, bless, preside, preach, and baptize. Succinct but weighty words on which our newly ordained priests pondered for many an hour during the days of their retreat before priestly ordination, for encapsulated in these words is the whole content of their future life.

To sacrifice, bless, preside, preach, baptize: I would like to pick just a few lights out of the fullness of light that is concealed in these words, so that we can get a glimpse of what sort of a day in the life of a priest is supposed to unfold from this early morning hour of being sent. First there is preaching.

If I may relate briefly a personal memory: how often as a student I looked forward to the opportunity to preach someday, to be able to proclaim the word of God to people who in the perplexity of an often godforsaken daily routine must be waiting for this word. I looked forward to it particularly when a new insight into a passage of Scripture, a connection with the doctrine of our faith, had occurred to me and had made me glad. But how disappointed I was when the reality proved to be quite different, when people obviously were waiting, not for the word of sermon, but rather for the end of it.

Today God's word is not one of those fashionable items in great demand for which people line up. On the contrary: it is fashionable to know better and to arrive only when the sermon is over, "since it will not be of much use anyway".

So to tell the truth, preaching today has become a tiresome part of the priest's trade of catching fish. And yet precisely in preaching, as well as in religious instruction, which actually is only another form of preaching, he does one of the greatest things that the Church has ever been commanded to do. The Roman theologian Hippolytus, who died in the year of the Lord 235, once said: "The birth of Christ is not yet over. Christ the Lord is still being born in this world. The Church bears this Christ by teaching all nations and preaching to them."

The Church dares, even now, in a world in which lies, dissimulation, and sensationalism routinely carry the day, to speak God's word infallibly, and she thereby makes a place for God in the midst of this world.

The world would become infinitely poor if those who, regardless of the latest sensation and regardless of the wind that blows in these times, take a stand for the one, unsensational, and perhaps useless-seeming truth of God and proclaim it were to remain silent instead. With every word of this sort, God is brought into our world again; shelter is given to the God who even now is seeking shelter and even now is homeless: Christ is born once more.

It would be a good outcome of this sermon if we resolved to reawaken in ourselves the humility to hear. The humility to hear and, along with it, of course, the courage to speak, which Christians today need more than past generations. Now only priests preach at the pulpits in our churches. But alongside them stands the pulpit of daily life, at which everyone can and must become a priest and a preacher. For it may become necessary, at one's workplace, in the office, or somewhere else to profess what one believes and loves as a Christian and to speak a word of faith into a world of disbelief. Someone who does this basically accomplishes the same task as preachers do in church: he makes room in this world for the homeless God who is seeking shelter.

Christ is born once more.

Besides the task of preaching, there is the task of blessing. Especially in these weeks after the First Mass, this is indeed the task that is most evident: the newly ordained priest brings his first blessing from house to house, and he is welcomed with great joy and cordial confidence. You believe that you sense even more vividly and refreshingly the power of the Holy Spirit who anointed these hands than you do with a priest who has been in the service of blessing for a long time already. Yet the priest's vocation always remains a service of blessing. He is always commissioned to bless in a world that perhaps curses or only calculates.

The priest blesses the children in the school, he blesses the faithful at Holy Mass, he blesses the hikers who go up into the mountains or the travelers who journey to a distant land, he blesses the sick and the dying in their hours of need and in their final abandonment, into which only God's kindly hand can make its way. He blesses at the graveside with a final blessing to send the soul off into eternity.

Yes, basically all the sacraments that the priest administers are nothing but a blessing with heightened effectiveness. If we wanted to translate roughly what "blessing" really means, we could say: It means approximately "Best wishes from God, in the name of God." If that is the case, though, then every blessing is an acknowledgment of the fact that machines and money are not the only things controlling the world.

By the very fact that we men wish each other happiness on many days, we admit that happiness and success do not lie in such commercial matters alone but, rather, depend more on the inner goodness of people, on the fact that it is good to be with each other and for each other.

When we acknowledge God's blessing, that is, his best wishes, we say even more thereby: we thereby profess that our happiness and our success ultimately depend on the love of the eternal God. That ultimately the world and our lives are regulated, not only by the calculations of commerce, but by God's deliberation and, therefore, by the eternal love "that moves the sun and stars" (Dante).

When the priest extends his hand over us in blessing, we bow and stop for a moment, because we know that God's finger, the finger of the love that moves the world, comes into closer contact with our life for a moment, because we know that our fate lies in the hands of him who now wishes us happiness and who alone has the power not only to wish happiness but also to give it.

Perhaps at one time or another it has struck you as odd that a blessing is given with the sign of the cross, of all things. With a sign that reminds us of the final distress of the God-man Jesus Christ and, in general, of the secret distress that is hidden at the bottom of all things. But it must be that way. It reminds us of the hard and yet inescapable fact that all blessing comes from sacrifice. That all divine blessing comes from the Cross of Jesus Christ. From his sacrifice. This is why the third and highest duty of the priest is to offer sacrifice.

This means, first of all, the celebration of the Holy Eucharist, in which the sacrifice of Jesus Christ on the Cross is once again made present. But the priest's personal sacrifice always has to stand behind it; day after day he gives away his own love, the yearning for distinction and happiness in his own life, so as to be completely at God's disposal.

Many things could be said about this, but perhaps it is better for us, without talking a lot, to make an honest effort to put ourselves wholeheartedly into this first holy sacrifice, in which our newly ordained priest performs the sublime service of offering sacrifice, and to pray to the eternal God from our hearts that he will grant him to live more and more by the strength of this sacrifice, so that he can receive from it more and more the fullness of blessing for himself and the strength to bless others.

All blessing comes from the Cross: this brings us again to today's Gospel, from which we started. For that shining morning hour of vocation was followed three years later by the hour of the definitive mission, as reported in the Gospel on the vigil of the day of priestly ordination. Many things had happened in the meantime: between one and the other came denial, Cross, and Resurrection.

And now the Lord, who is about to depart, stands once again in front of Simon on the shores of the same Lake of Gennesaret on which he had once called him to discipleship for the first time and gives him the order: "Feed my lambs ... feed my sheep" (Jn 21:15–17). But in farewell he adds a serious remark: "When you were young, you fastened your own belt and walked where you would; but when you are old, you will stretch out your hands, and another will fasten your belt for you and carry you where you do not wish to go" (Jn 21:18).

Again it is like an echo of this event when in the hour of priestly ordination the anointed hands of the priest are tied together tightly and then with these bound hands he touches the chalice in which he will soon offer the redeeming Blood of the Lord to the eternal Father.

His hands are tied and will never again belong to him. His whole being is bound for God. Those times of hopeful dreams, in which all paths seemed open and all possibilities seemed to beckon, are past: he has placed his hands, bound, into God's hand forever. God now determines the path and the possibility, he alone.

But with radiant certainty of victory the Entrance Antiphon of today's Mass speaks of the confidence that our own hands are safe in God's hand, when it says: "The Lord is my light and my salvation; whom shall I fear?" Someone who has given his weak human hands into God's strong fatherly hand has placed them in the bosom of eternal love.

And despite all the storms that may come, he can serenely sail the sea of this world, for with him for all days is the one who said about himself: "Be of good cheer, I have overcome the world" (Jn 16:33).

The Priest: A Man Who Blesses

For Franz Niedermayer

Kirchanschöring, 1955

Every year it is truly a great day, not only for the cathedral in Freising, but also for our whole vast diocese, when on June 29 the bishop comes up to his young deacons in order to impose his hand on them for Holy Orders and to send them out into God's field that awaits its harvesters. The question that the bishop once again asks his archdeacon just before this sounds weighty and serious: *Scis illos dignos esse?* Do you know that they are worthy? All of the responsibility of this hour trembles in this question. And once again, when the archdeacon has replied Yes, the bishop turns to all the people and asks them all whether they agree that these young men should be ordained priests in the Church. For all the people are affected by what is happening. And only if no one raises an objection can the sacred ceremony begin. In the Litany of the Saints the whole congregation of the saints, so to speak, is called to help; we practically see them in our mind's eye as they take their places around the altar, the glorious company of the apostles, the praiseworthy army of martyrs, the

"Der Priester—ein segnender Mensch", for Franz Niedermayer in Kirchanschöring on July 10, 1955, *MIPB* 2 (2009): 25–30.

holy virgins and widows—they are all asked to come and help in this holy hour. And then (when, as it were, the plenary assembly of Holy Church has been convened) the bishop goes over to each man and silently imposes his hands on him for a while. According to the teaching of Holy Church, this is the actual moment of ordination, in which a man becomes a priest forever, an unforgettable moment for each one who has had the privilege of experiencing it! The moment when the bishop's hand lies on his head, this hand that now no longer really belongs to a man at all but rather is the symbol and instrument of God's fatherly hand reaching out to a man, of the "Finger of God", the Holy Spirit, who is now sent out upon a man. And the one kneeling there knows: "With the bishop's hand the hand of God is laid upon me. God has laid his hand on me; I no longer belong to myself at all. He has taken me from myself and confiscated me; I am his property. I am at his disposal." After the bishop, all the other priests present may also impose their hands and, as it were, co-ordain the men who from now on are to collaborate with them.

And if I may now make a very personal remark: it was an unforgettable and moving moment for me when I, too, had the privilege of imposing my hand on my dear friend, our reverend celebrant of this First Mass. We had gone to secondary school together, had survived the *Luftwaffe* and labor service together, until in January 1945 our ways parted: God had another difficult, troublesome detour planned for him: he was called up to a unit that was stationed in the East; he was subsequently wounded and spent two and a half hard years in Russian captivity. When he finally came home in December 1947, he found his father seriously ill, and it is a miracle that the latter, although almost completely blind, now is able to kneel with us at the altar of this First Mass. And we want to thank God for that in this Holy Sacrifice; we also want to pray to the eternal God for his father and for his dear mother, that many more happy years may be granted to them from God's goodness.—Somehow I was aware of all this in the moment of the imposition of hands, as though finally now the door to the sanctuary was opened for him, too, the door that had remained closed for so long but had always remained his sure, unwavering goal. After the imposition of hands, all the priests then stand there for a while with hand outstretched, and I like to think that this very thing is one of the most profound symbols of what a priest is and is supposed to be in the first place: a man who blesses, one whose hand does not exist to curse and to strike, or for technology and business, but rather to bless. (And that is more than all the rest.) And so, dear Reverend Father, as you celebrate your First Mass, we can now ask you to make use of your power and to extend your hands over us in blessing and to bless this whole congregation with your first blessing . . .

Devout Christians! I have just tried to say with one expression what a priest really is: a man who blesses. This is precisely his task in the world: He exists to bring blessings, and I think that we must regain a sense of the fact that this is a truly necessary task, that the builders who are rebuilding our people and our land build in vain unless God, the Lord, builds with them. And the history of the last fifty years has indeed shown us that all of men's building, however industrious it may be, leads to chaos if God is not present as the master builder. And again we must acknowledge that in a village like this, too, people work and toil in vain unless the church remains the heart of the village and unless the life that is transmitted to us by the priest lives in this church.

And we see, especially in these years when the weather fools us again and again, how helpless men still are, despite all their technology, how little ultimately we can do if God does not say Yes to our plans and to our will. The priest is a man who blesses; we tried to recognize that in the example of the hands outstretched during priestly ordination. I would like to add two more very brief images in which we can look again from a different angle at what the priest actually is and why he exists.

The first of these images comes from this Sunday's Gospel, from the story about the miraculous multiplication of loaves that I just read to you. This event, though, was preceded by another incident that is recounted by Mark in chapter 6, I will have to summarize briefly for you. The Lord Jesus had worked tirelessly for several days before that. People came and went, and Sacred Scripture tells us that they did not even leave him time to eat. Then Jesus decides to stand up and go away and to seek solitude. He takes a boat and travels across the lake. But the people notice it and go on foot along the shore of the lake, and even before Jesus can arrive with his boat, they, too, are on the other shore. When he arrives, he finds there the very same people from whom he has just intended to flee. And now something marvelous happens: he does not get angry, he does not scold, as a man would probably do, but he looks at them and has pity on them. He sees their deep, inner helplessness that prompts them to run after him, that would most likely prompt them tomorrow to run after someone else if he were to promise them something more and seemingly better. Then we read in Mark the wonderful verse: "He had compassion on them, because they were like sheep without a shepherd" (Mk 6:34).

This is like a snapshot of mankind in general. If someone from another planet landed on earth today and could survey it thoroughly, in one glance, so to speak, he could probably not describe mankind better than with the sentence: they are like sheep without a shepherd. Mankind today no longer knows what is right and what is wrong, what a person may do or not do, what will actually work and what is impossible for a man. In a village, the situation is probably still somewhat better, but when a young person is thrown into the city today, into a business, into a job somewhere, then he very soon notices that all common convictions have broken down there, that there is no propriety left that people follow and are simply bound by; he notices that everyone now takes himself as his standard and does whatever he thinks is right. Such behavior in turn ends in chaos; we can actually see evidence of this every day in the newspaper reports about national politics as well as in the local news reports. Man has lost his bearings; otherwise, it would not be possible today for every soothsayer, astrologist, and doctor touting a miracle cure to find his docile public; otherwise, it would not be possible for every faction leader to gather any number of followers. "They are like sheep without a shepherd." The Lord sees this; he sees it first in the few Palestinians standing on the shores of the Lake of Gennesaret, but he looks through them down the millennia, to today's mankind, and he sees our contemporary mankind, too, and has pity on it; for he is the shepherd, the only true shepherd, the Good Shepherd.

Now I think that you already see what this actually has to do with the priestly vocation: to be a priest means to be a witness and servant of the Good Shepherd Christ Jesus; to be a priest means to be a shepherd with Christ, the Lord, and to share in the Lord's pastoral concern and pastoral duty—and Christ himself said what this means for a man in another passage of the Gospel that reads: "The

good shepherd lays down his life for the sheep" (Jn 10:11).
To be a shepherd with Christ means to participate in Jesus
Christ's surrender of his life; to be a shepherd with Christ
means to be a man of dedication, someone who wants
nothing more for himself, but everything for God and
for his neighbor for God's sake. One becomes a priest,
not for oneself, but for others; one does not become a
priest in order to have many extra graces, so to speak, in
order to hold a preferential position with the dear Lord;
and priestly ordination is not a reservation for an especially
good place in heaven. No, a man who becomes a priest
does so in order to become a servant of others, servant of
the servants of God ...

Think of the magnificent Gospel for Holy Thursday, in
which the Lord stands up in the midst of his disciples, and
he, the Son of God, girds himself and washes their feet.
Saint Augustine tells us that this is a perfect example for
what the priest has to do: indeed, he has to listen almost
every day in the confessional to the filth of humanity;
through the grace of God, he has the privilege of washing,
so to speak, the dirty feet of this world and of these people
again and again. He is a servant of the servants of God at
other times in his daily routine, too; for everyone who has
a trouble or a sorrow may and should come to the priest
with it. And even in his most sublime duty, in celebrating the Holy Eucharist, the priest is really not a privileged
person, but, rather, he celebrates Holy Mass in order to
be your waiter. He is like God's waiter who sets for you
the table of the divine meal. Yes, I think that we must
say that the priest does not get to heaven any more easily
than others do, but, rather, it is more difficult for him; for
no one can get there alone, least of all a priest. He will be
asked about the others, about all those who were entrusted
to his pastoral care and his pastoral love. The priest is a

man who blesses; the priest is also, however, a shepherd with Christ the Shepherd, and that means he must share in Jesus Christ's surrender of his life. Although earlier, after the first part, I asked our dear Reverend Father who is celebrating his First Mass to make use of his power to bless and to bless us; now, after this second part, I have a request for you: being a priest means being a shepherd with Christ; it means sharing in his surrender of his life, and that is a very, very difficult task, a task that, viewed outwardly, is almost too difficult for a man, and no one could presume on his own to assume this duty unless God called him, unless he knew that all the others were helping him to carry this burden, that he had the care of the whole crowd of the faithful behind him. And so I would like to tell you the concluding words of the well-known saying that a priest wrote down a few hundred years ago in the Salzburg dialect. It begins with the words: "A priest must be quite big and quite little ..." and ends with the request: "... unlike me; pray for me!" Yes, pray for the priest celebrating today his First Mass, and pray for all your priests.

I would like to add a third image: It was in April of the year 1207, in sunny southern Italy. It was the month in which Saint Francis of Assisi was disinherited and repudiated by his father. He had no belongings left now, not even the cowl that he wore on his body belonged to him personally, and yet he had something that no one could take away from him, namely, the love of God, to whom he could now say "Father" in an entirely new way. And he knew that that is much more than all the possessions in the world; and so his heart was full of great joy, and he went on his way singing through the forests of Umbria. But near Gubbio, the foliage rustled and a pair of robbers jumped out and ran toward him; surprised by his strange appearance, they called to him: Who *are* you? He answered: I am the herald of a great king. Francis of Assisi was not a priest but, rather, remained a deacon his whole life, but what he said then is also a profound description of what a priest is and should be: he is the herald of the great king, God, he is herald and preacher of God's kingdom, which is supposed to spread in the heart of the individual and throughout the world. Such a herald will not always go his way singing, although occasionally he will, of course; for again and again the good Lord gives every priest moments in which he recognizes with amazement and joy what a great task God has given him. But robbers, so to speak, still rebel against this herald because they do not like his message. First, there are the indifferent people who never have time for God; it always occurs to them right when he calls them that they actually have something else to do, that they have so much work. Then there are those who say that housing should be built first, not churches; yet they do not care at all if all sorts of movie theaters and recreational facilities go up then. To these people, the priest must announce again and again the often inconvenient fact that man does not live by bread alone, but also and even more by the word of God. And the fact that man does not live by bread alone but on more than that is, I think, quite evident today. After all, there will always be people who have everything they want, who have enough money, who can dress and eat however they like, and yet one day put an end to their life and say: I cannot live any more, I cannot go on like this, it no longer has any meaning. Then we see that a man needs more than bread, that a deeper hunger is concealed in him, the hunger for God, which ought to be satisfied by the word of God. I think that today, during this sermon and during this First Mass, we can all reflect a little on whether we, too, do not belong in one form or another to these indifferent people who by their criticism, by

coming late or not at all, make the priest's task more difficult and unpleasant.

Then there are the hostile ones who suspect some sort
of clericalism behind every priest, a power against which
they must protect themselves; and I certainly do not
have to tell you the sorts of words and ideas that are
circulating these days; for you all know as well as I do,
and I think that we all see, not only that the harvest in
your fields is brought in by the sweat of your brow, but
also that the harvest of the kingdom of God again and
again demands the sweat of those whom God sent as his
harvesters into his field, where thistles and thorns grow,
too, just like on the fields of this world. And despite all the
contradictions, the priest will have to proclaim again and
again this message about God's kingdom, which is meant
to spread in this world, for he is the herald of the great
king, God, a voice crying in the wilderness of time or, as
theologians put it more simply and soberly: He now shares
not only in the pastoral ministry of Jesus Christ but also in
his teaching ministry; he is sent not only to administer the
sacraments, but also to proclaim the word of God.

Dear Christians! What I have been able to say now in
this sermon gives only a few small, minor details from the
full picture of priestly life. But in the presence of the great
realities of God, everyone is actually just like a stammering child, and even the greatest man can really not tell
very much more than a few minor details. In conclusion,
I would like to repeat once more the request that I made
of you earlier; before the newly ordained priest becomes
now in the Canon of the Mass the servant of the miracle of transubstantiation, he will turn around to you again
and say to you: "Orate fratres", "Pray, brethren, that my
sacrifice and yours may be acceptable to God the Lord."
And then please do not take it as a phrase, as a sentence

from the Missal that the priest has to say just because he now comes to it, but rather take it as a real request that he addresses to all of you. For perhaps a priest today needs nothing so much as for people to pray for him a lot, and it is infinitely comforting for him to know that people care about him in the presence of God, that they pray for him. It is as if a kind hand were to hold on to him on a steep path, so that he knows, "I can go on safely, for I am upheld by the kindness of those who are with me." And every time in the future when one of you goes to Mass and hears "Orate fratres", "Pray, brethren", then take it as an admonition and as a genuine, living request of you: Pray, brethren, that the sacrifice of the life of this priest and of all priests may be acceptable to God the Lord.

Meditation on the Day of a First Mass

In the Rhineland, 1962

First Reading: 1 Samuel 3:1–10
Second Reading: 1 Peter 5:1–4
Gospel: Matthew 20:25–28

Even now, the day on which a young man has the privilege of transforming the bread of this earth into the Lord's Body for the first time is a great feast day. We still experience the first blessing that he can impart with his consecrated hands as a precious gift. The priesthood is still a gift for which we wait and for which we joyfully give thanks. But we know also that the festive joy of this day occurs against a gloomy background: our major seminaries, which not long ago were completed and expanded, are almost empty; fewer and fewer dare to take the final step to the altar, and more and more come to doubt afterward the meaning of their vocation and look around for another way. The shadows are becoming longer, the loneliness—more profound, and the question of those who remain—more difficult: What sort of a future do they face? Does it still make sense to become a priest in a world in which only technological and social progress

"Betrachtung am Primiztag", in *Dogma und Verkündigung* (Munich, 1973), 431–37; 3rd ed. (Munich, 1977), 425–31; 4th ed. (Donauwörth, 2005), 435–31. [B 180]

matters now? Does faith have a future? Is it worthwhile
to stake one's whole life on this card? Is priesthood not an
outdated relic from the past that no one needs anymore,
whereas all our efforts should be applied to eradicating
poverty and furthering progress?

But is all that really the case? Or is mankind, by running
the machine of progress faster and faster, not at the same
time rushing into suicidal insanity? The famous French avi-
ator Antoine de Saint-Exupéry once wrote in a letter to a
general: "There is only one problem in the world. How
can we restore to man a spiritual significance, a spiritual
discontent; let something descend upon them like the dew
of a Gregorian chant. Don't you see, we cannot live any
longer on refrigerators, politics, balance sheets, and cross-
word puzzles. We just cannot." And in his book *The Little
Prince*, he says: How uncomprehending the world of adults,
of clever people is. By now we understand only machines,
geography, and politics. But the really important things, the
light, the clouds, heaven and its stars, we no longer understand. And the great Russian author Solzhenitsyn records
the cry of distress of a Communist who landed in Stalin's
prisons: We could use cathedrals in Russia again and men
whose pure life makes these cathedrals alive and turns them
into a space for the soul. Indeed, man does not live by
refrigerators and balance sheets alone. The more he tries to
do that, the more desperate he becomes, the emptier his life
is. We need even today, and today more than ever, people
who do not sell luxury items and do not make political
propaganda but, rather, ask about the soul of a man and
help him not to lose his soul in the tumult of everyday routine. The scarcer priests become in the world of business
and politics, the more we need them.

But what really is the task of the priest? For what purpose
is he ordained? The two passages from the New Testament

that we just heard (I Pet 5:1–4; Mt 20:25–28) describe his task in a word: he must be a shepherd. He must be a servant. Shepherd—in the background stands the image of Jesus Christ, the true Shepherd. In the ancient Near East, kings were referred to with the word shepherd. In this way they expressed all the disdain they had for their people and all the claim to power they let themselves determine: the people were only sheep to them, and like shepherds they disposed of them as they pleased. Jesus, the Son of God, is the true Shepherd to whom the sheep belong because they are his creatures. And because they belong to him, he loves them, he wants what is best for them. He pastures them by laying down his own life. Without imagery, this means: through his word he showed men how to live. He showed them the truth, which man needs as much as daily bread if he is not to waste away. He gave them the love that they need as much as daily water if they are not to die of thirst.

And since his word was not enough, he gave himself: he backed his word with the currency of his own lifeblood.

Like Christ, the priest should be a shepherd. But how can he do that? First, this means that the priest is not primarily a bureaucrat who pores over files and makes administrative decisions. Certainly he will frequently have to do that, too, but it should be peripheral. It is not his essential duty. Others can and should help him with it. Being shepherds in the service of Jesus Christ means more. It means leading people to Jesus Christ and, thus, leading them to the truth and the love, to the meaning that they need even today. For even today man does not live by bread alone and not by money alone. Leading people to Jesus Christ, leading them to the truth that is meaning—this happens by handing on the word of Jesus Christ and by administering the sacraments, in which the Lord continues to give us his life.

Word and sacrament, the two main tasks of the priest—that sounds very sober, very ordinary, but it includes a wealth of things that truly can fill a life. To begin with, there is the *word*. At first we are inclined to say: But what is that, the word? Only facts matter. Words are nothing. But if you reflect more carefully, you hit on the power of the word that creates facts: one single false word can destroy a man's whole life and tarnish his name irrevocably. One single kind word can transform a person when nothing else can help. So it ought to become clear to us how important it is for mankind to talk not only about money and war, about power and utility; that there be not just the gossip of the day, but that there be talk about God and about us, about what makes a man human. A world in which that no longer happens becomes infinitely boring and empty. It becomes inconsolable. And it becomes motionless. We are witnessing today how life becomes ennui and absurdity for people, although they have everything for which they could wish. They no longer know what they are supposed to make of themselves. What man is actually supposed to do and not to do. Man becomes a meaningless entity, unbearable to himself. He must always invent himself first and yet in doing so is constantly overwhelmed; he discovers nothing but boredom and misery. Thus we can begin to understand again what it means for our children not only to learn to count and to do arithmetic but also to learn to live. All arithmetic and writing is of no use to them if they do not know the purpose for which they are living and, from that knowledge, obtain freedom, gladness, and goodness.

The word of God occurs not only in preaching; it occurs in instruction in the school. It occurs in conversation with the elderly, with the abandoned, with the sick, with people for whom no one else has time, for whom life has become gloomy and difficult. How much we need

today people who can listen. Who are there for someone who is in doubt or struggling. Who can speak with a
sick person in the twilight of life and give him hope and
meaning, while the lights of this world are going out. The
word of God—we really need it as we need daily bread.
And we need people who are there for this word precisely
because it has become so strange to us. We should reflect
on all this when we complain about the homily, when it
is too boring or too unimportant for us. It is difficult to
proclaim God's word today in a world that is supersatu-
rated with every sort of sensation. It is difficult to proclaim God's word today in a world where even the priest
has to grope laboriously in the dark to reach it and faces
the choice of either saying something that no one understands or else very hesitantly and insufficiently translating
into our world something that is so far removed from our
daily routine. The service of the word has become difficult. Sometimes the priest today is like the prophet Jeremiah, whose prophetic proclamation caused him nothing
but trouble and who often rebelled passionately against
his task as a prophet: You deceived me, God, he cries out
in his despair; leave me in peace. He would like most of
all to get rid of the word that has made him a lonely fool,
a marked man with whom no one wants anything to do.
But he must carry the burden of the word. And in precisely that way, he serves the people who are unwilling
to understand him. We should reflect on all this when we
groan about the inadequacy of the preaching. Instead of
scolding, we would do better to pray for one another: that
God might give to the listeners the gift of listening well,
to the speakers the grace of speech, and to all of us lots of
patience with each other; that by all these means he might
preserve his word for us, the bread of truth for which our
soul hungers, too, even if we do not understand it.

Alongside the ministry of the word stands the ministry of the *sacraments*, which intend to encompass all of life and to place it visibly in the hands of Holy Mother Church, in the hands of the Lord himself. Once Goethe almost wistfully depicted how the Church's sacraments encompass and transform all the major hours of life, from birth to the difficult hour of the final departure. Precisely in terms of sacrament, the priest becomes someone who accompanies the whole journey of life, of the major fundamental human decisions that ultimately can be made correctly only if God lends us a hand.

Let us look at just two sacraments that above all define the priestly routine: the sacrament of Penance and the sacrament of the altar. The reception of the sacrament of Penance has become less frequent. But that changes nothing of the fact that sin exists even today and that we need forgiveness even today. What does it mean if we know that man can repent. That now and then in the course of the year he is obliged, not to shift blame onto others, but to reflect on himself. To accuse himself. To see and confess his sin. To acknowledge that he is guilty. That he has made mistakes. And what does it mean to know that there is forgiveness. That I can make a new beginning. That there is an authority that can say: Go, your sins are forgiven. From God's forgiveness, however, we ourselves should learn again and again to forgive, for a world without forgiveness could only become a world of mutual destruction. The privilege of pronouncing the word of forgiveness is one of the most difficult and most beautiful tasks of the priest: often it is oppressive to be the place where all the filth of mankind is laid down. And, nevertheless, it is at the same time an activity full of hope: to know that everything can be transformed, that a person is allowing himself to be transformed.

The daily high point of priestly life is the sacrament of the altar, the mysterious intimate connection between heaven and earth that it furnishes. God invites us to his table. He wants us to be his guests. He gives himself to us. God's gift is God himself. The Eucharist is the holy feast that God himself gives us, however wretched the external conditions may be: here something breaks through the threshold of everyday routine; God celebrates with us. And this celebration of God is worth more than all our free time, which becomes empty when the celebration that we ourselves cannot make no longer exists. But let us reflect here on one thing: the celebration comes from sacrifice. Only the grain of wheat that has died bears fruit. The center of priestly life is the sacrifice of Jesus Christ. But this sacrifice cannot be celebrated without us. Without our own accompanying sacrifice. For the priest, this means that, without sacrifice, without the toil of slowly learned self-renunciation, he cannot truly perform Christ's ministry. In the Gospel we just heard this. To follow Christ means to follow the one who came to serve and to give himself. That is the greatness and the difficulty of the priestly task. He will never be fully successful: the servant is not above the Master. And in any event, the priest can be successful only if he is supported by others who carry the burden, believe, and pray with him: all of us, too, live as Christians only in dependence on one another, and every celebration of the Eucharist is meant to call us anew into this mutual existence.

In conclusion, let us listen again to God's word, as it encountered us in the Old Testament reading of this First Mass (1 Sam 3:1–10). It is night. Eli, the high priest, is old and is starting to go blind. All this is at the same time an image of the hour in which Samuel was called. Israel lives in the night, as though blind in God's sight. Life has become routine, the days go by, and God seems far away. Daily routine has hidden him; it is as though he no longer existed, and in a time of calm and material comfort, no one asks about him, either. Nevertheless, God's lamp has not gone out, and the Lord's voice calls this youth, whose heart is pure and whose soul is open. God allows himself to be heard again in the midst of human indifference. He pursues people, even when they are in danger of forgetting him. He remains. But he is able to call only because in the middle of the night in Israel there is one person who can hear. Whose life is not stuffed with the rubbish of his own concerns and interests. Samuel hears. From hearing comes vocation, and from the vocation a burden that must be endured in the toil of a long life. But out of the burden comes grace, for himself, who in the midst of the difficulty of his service finds fulfillment, and for the people, who slowly become reacquainted with God and, thereby, also with themselves. How stirring this story is for us in the dark hour, in the hour of blindness in which we live. Let us pray to God that his lamp may not go out today, either! Let us pray that he will call men today, too! That even today he will awaken people who can hear. And let us thank him in this hour that again he is sending a young man out with his word. Let us commend the journey that begins today into his good hands: Lord Jesus Christ, O Good Shepherd, bless this beginning. Bring to completion what you have begun.

So that God's Word Might Remain

On the Burden and the Joy of the Prophet

For Karl Besler

Traunstein, 1973

First Reading: Ezekiel 2:2–5; Second Reading:
  2 Corinthians 12:7–10
Gospel: Mark 6:1–6a

Reverend Father,
dear brothers and sisters!

The stern seriousness of the three readings that we have just
heard contrasts oddly with the joy of the First Mass that is
being celebrated. All three speak about the strangeness of
the prophet in this world, about distress under the burden
of God's word on account of men's contradiction, while
the cheerful brightness of our parish church in Traunstein
and the festive beauty of the Mozart Mass setting cause us
to experience Catholicism as a religion of joy.

"Damit das Wort Gottes bleibt: Von der Last und von der Freude des
Propheten", for Karl Besler in St. Oswald, Traunstein, July 8, 1973. Previously
unpublished. [B 678]

This contrast reminds me of the same day in July in the year 1951, on which a First Mass was likewise celebrated here in this church, and in a very similar way, in the midst of the joy of the day, the Gospel for the Eighth Sunday after Pentecost was intoned, the Gospel about the unjust steward (Lk 16:1–9), which must have branded a warning onto the souls of the two priests who were celebrating their First Mass that day. They had not become masters on that day, but stewards who are measured by their fidelity. One who works "with you for your joy", Saint Paul calls the apostle of Jesus Christ (2 Cor 1:24). He does so in the same letter in which we just heard the admission of his weakness and of his distress under the word of God. How do these two things go together? What is actually happening here? Which ministry is it that starts in the hour of the First Mass? Today's liturgy depicts the figure of which we are speaking by means of three persons: the prophet Ezekiel, the apostle Paul, and Jesus Christ himself. They only seem to disappear in the twilight of the distant past or in the height of an inaccessible holiness. In reality what is common and continuous in all divine callings is made clear very nicely in these examples.

At the age of twenty-five, at precisely the moment when he was supposed to begin his service as priest at the Temple in Jerusalem, Ezekiel was swept up in the wave of national misfortune and deported to Babylon with the educated and wealthy individuals of his nation. Instead of his priestly ministry, he now had to build canals in the damp climate of the Euphrates lowlands, the compulsory labor performed by the conquered. The plan for his life seemed to be ruined, his homeland—a bitter dream. Could anything be expected now from a God who had not protected him, the priest in the Temple, and had delivered him to a foreign nation?

And yet, precisely at this moment of outward collapse, this Ezekiel rediscovered his priesthood and for the first time truly found out what it meant. He recognized that the God in whom he believed was not only the God of Jerusalem and the God of the Temple but was also the God of heaven and earth. And he recognized that priesthood does not just mean celebrating the liturgy in the Temple, but that it most fully asserted its claims in that hour and demanded that he give people new meaning and new support based on God's word. We know from his writings that these deportees from Israel had lost their faith. That in their view God had been defeated with their nation. That they no longer accepted any God or any idols, but relied now only on themselves and on the little happiness of the moment, that they had become hardhearted, distrustful, and hostile and had renounced all ties. In this hour he had to show them that God was not dead, that his commandments applied even if no clan and no neighbors observed them, that even in a foreign land God's word remained and that even there his heart beat for mankind. We know today that this ministry of the man of God in exile very realistically became the prerequisite for Israel's survival as a nation, for if it had not maintained its distinctive features, it would necessarily have dissolved into the other nation, as is the fate of all immigrants. This was the trick of Babylonian policy: destroying nations by uprooting them. Israel survived, whereas the oppressed and the oppressors perished. It survived because it found in the word of God a new home that supported them in the midst of their outward homelessness.

In reality that brings us back to our own time. We Catholics gathered here are not deportees, and the wounds of the deportation in 1945 are slowly beginning to heal. Nevertheless, in the spiritual realm, something very similar has been happening in the upheaval in recent years, a spiritual destruction of the Temple, a crumbling of what had been our spiritual home. The world and the times are becoming so different that all that went before has suddenly become a thing of the past; nothing holds and supports any more. "God is dead," they tell us, "for we have learned meanwhile the laws by which the world functions, and we know the ways in which life developed." The commandments [Ge-bote] of yore no longer hold. They are the expression of domineering authorities that demean men who have come of age, and the prohibitions [Verbote] are nothing but ridiculous taboos. In this world in which all that formerly held mankind together is supposedly no longer true, in which the ground is swaying under our feet, we encounter also the crisis of the uprooting of priestly vocations, because they tell us: "We no longer need such medieval, outmoded things today." "Today we face entirely different tasks and obligations." There are no temples in the new world. And, nevertheless, some young men who celebrate today the Holy Sacrifice for the first time have had an experience like Ezekiel's; they have recognized that God is necessary right now if men are to survive; that priests are necessary right now if the word of God is to remain alive. We are all beginning to recognize more and more that mere utilitarianism does not save mankind, that cities in which man plans for and thinks about only himself become unbearable, that they need the breath of the Eternal in order to be inhabitable by men, too; that people must learn again to recognize God's reflected glory in each other and in creation, so that they can put up with each other, so that they can enjoy their life again, so that they can recognize again what love actually is. We need more than engineers and new machines; what we need most of all in this crumbling of the former world is servants of humanity who care about people. And the only way this can happen is from God.

Let us turn to a second perspective: in the reading that we just heard, Ezekiel is addressed as "son of man". This brings up the figure of Jesus Christ, who preferred to be called "Son of man" and, thereby, aligned himself with Ezekiel. In the language of the Old Testament, this is an expression of man's weakness. "What is man that you are mindful of him, and the son of man that you care for him?" Psalm 8 says, and with that the psalmist expresses his alarm that the immense God should care about this worm, that nevertheless man is in truth compared with the greatness of the universe. And this is precisely how the title is meant here, too, for the closer the word of God comes to man, the stranger and more incredible it becomes that God should attend to him. God speaks to me? How can that be? What then am I? A little man, nothing more. And so excuses and protests spring up in this regard. Paul—we just heard in the Second Letter to the Corinthians—hears again and again: "That Paul, that sickly, inhibited man—is *he* supposed to be the bearer of a message that is greater than all the wisdom of the Greeks and the learning of the Jewish scholars of the Law?" "And Jesus, well, we know him," the people say, "he is the carpenter's son. We do not have to worry at all about his message. After all, we know who he is." All this has not changed since then. On both sides: the priest himself is alarmed about the unreasonable demand that he should really deal with God, for he knows all too well his own weaknesses. And perhaps the most awesome thing that is enjoined on him is that he should have to utter constantly the greatest words in the human language, which we can dare to touch only reluctantly: justice, truth, fidelity, purity, love, unselfishness—words that judge and accuse him, too. We have to understand from this perspective, I think, the fact that there are so many priests today who simply can no longer admit this themselves, who want to break with this unearthly responsibility and to regard their business as just another job and nothing more, as something that anyone else does anywhere. And of course on the other side protests develop, so that people have many good reasons for saying: "You preach to us, but take a look at yourself first!" "And this Church, with all the scandals and the wretchedness that we know about, claims to be the bearer of a divine message? No, we are not going to comply with that!" God speaks through the children of men. He wants some of them to dare to take his word on their lips, so that it might be in the world, and he wants the others to accept it, precisely through that weak creature. I think that we can see here something of the common task of all believers in the Church. What it can mean for a young priest if he sees that he is supported by the people in a congregation! If he recognizes that they accept his weakness and his inability also, that precisely thereby they support him as the messenger of something greater that does not come from himself. That they help him to believe personally the word that is given to both. And what destruction there can be if he runs into a wall of skepticism, if people see him alone and do not help him to carry on the greater cause. Today everybody talks about the rights of the laity, so that often one cannot see at all why we still need priests. Nevertheless, I think: *this* is where these great rights and duties of the lay people in fact lie. It is their duty and their right to compel the priest, as it were, against his own timidity, to be what he is called to be, to want him as their priest, and to help him keep the word of God alive in this world. All of us together must carry this call, must struggle for it and make sure that its authority remains present.

The frailty of the human vessel: by that, of course, God meant something even deeper. Ambrose once said: God did not call philosophers but fishermen. Had philosophers been the ones to carry Christ's message through the world, then people could have said: They thought that up for themselves, and we have had enough traveling preachers who think up their own ideas. People would have discussed it just as they discussed all the many sorts of practical wisdom of that time. But fishermen came, stammering a message that infinitely surpassed them. The very weakness of the messengers confirmed the truth of the message. For it testified to the fact that this message was not the invention of those men but that it came from somewhere else, that someone else had given it to them. Maybe this is also the reason why God again and again allows unworthy servants and unworthy priests, so that it remains clear that human wits and human capabilities do not sustain the Church; rather, she is upheld by a completely different force. Of course, the true human significance of the fact that God calls the weak is found elsewhere. It is supposed to lead the servant of the word to unselfishness, so that he learns not to proclaim himself but, rather, the Church's faith, which is the property of us all. Paul says somewhere: I must not water down God's word the way they water down wine. I must pass it on as it was given to me. And this ought to be the lasting confirmation of the message and of the messenger: the unselfishness with which he steps back behind the greater cause.

Naturally this raises the question that we hear so often today: Is that a reasonable and meaningful task for a man today? How is he supposed to find his identity, then, if he is never allowed to be himself? Selma Lagerlöff tells in one of her legends about a medieval knight, a brutal, hardhearted, egotistical man who one day got the idea of bringing a

burning flame intact from the Holy Land back to his home
in Northern Italy. And through his selfless service to this
flame, which is now the sole law of his journey, he himself
becomes a different man. For he can no longer consider
what becomes of him; the flame alone is the substance of
his journey and of his life. In this service to another, he
becomes free of himself, he becomes whole, he becomes
mature, he becomes kind, he becomes warm, and for the
first time he develops his true potential. It seems to me that
this can be a very profound image for a true priestly vocation. He is not there to care for himself, to earn as much as
possible, to achieve the highest possible status, but to carry
the flame and in this selfless service to become free and
pure and mature right in his selflessness.

With that we have returned to our initial question:
What sort of a ministry is it really that is beginning here,
what is the task of the priest in the world? The usual
answer that occurs to a man of routine, who experiences
things only superficially, is to say: "Well, the priest is there
to say Mass." And then a further reflection automatically
occurs to him, to say: "But that cannot fulfill a life. You
can do that on the side." But that is a profound mistake
about the scope of the task. It is about more. It is about
keeping the word of God in this world. And slowly, in
places where we see that mankind is getting bored in its
wealth, that it is destroying itself thereby, we begin to recognize that this is the greatest wealth in the world and that
mankind would become infinitely poor if this light were
to be extinguished. He is there to keep the word of God
here, and he is there in order to care for people in terms
of God's word. Having the care of souls means to make
sure that they do not become soulless, that the soul in
them does not die, that they do not become likenesses of
their machines, as is happening to a great extent, but rather

remain likenesses of God. And only in this context can the Eucharist be celebrated. The first Eucharist, the sacrifice of Jesus Christ on the Cross, cost the death and the life of the Son of God; it does not get any less expensive. The feast does not come out of thin air; it requires the spiritual context in which it can live. In order for Mozart Masses to remain more than a concert and in order for church buildings to remain more than museums, there must be people who live the Church. The museum is a storeroom of the past, however precious it may be. When you leave it, it leaves you with the oppressive melancholy of what is dead and gone forever. Churches, however, are spaces of life and of the living. In them yesterday has its today, and in them the future is present. But they can be and continue to be this only if they themselves are lived, if a man is there who keeps them alive.

In this connection I am often overcome by a depressing vision: today in Freising four priests are being ordained for a diocese of more than two million Catholics. Last year there were five. And the trend will continue this way. You can calculate statistically the day on which there will be no more priests for the magnificent churches of our homeland. And then more will have disappeared than a bit of folklore, the way other customs die out. This will be a landslide of a completely different sort. A desertification of the spiritual landscape that can horrify even someone who has little use for faith and religion.

We are servants of your joy. We all love celebration and joy, but it is not to be taken for granted, and it is not free; it can exist only at the cost of a life that is there for it. And so the beginning and the end are linked together, and it is clear once again that this is a concern for all of us, because one cannot try to pick the fruit of celebration quickly at just any moment and otherwise let it be. What

would remain then would just be empty displays, with all
the poverty of what is gone forever. All this concerns us,
and the question arises: What can we do to avoid that
landslide? Management does not help much here. For if
that could solve everything, then our century would necessarily be a more glorious example than any other before
it. Not even the bishops and the priests alone can accom-
plish this. In Saint Luke's Acts of the Apostles, there is an
answer that is still valid. The first call in the Church—he
tells us—occurred when the Church was of one accord
and when she prayed (Acts 1:14–26). When the Church is
of one accord and when she prays, then she does not have
to worry a lot about advertising, then she can be certain of
the Lord's answer.

Today, though, is a day of joy and thanksgiving. Of
thanksgiving for the fact that our churches are still alive,
that our liturgy is still a celebration, that today a young
man has again dared to say his Yes. This thanksgiving to
God is in itself a petition that this journey which is beginning here might be blessed. That the call might continue,
so that the praise that glorifies God and saves man may not
be silenced.

JUBILEE HOMILIES

A Guide Directed by Jesus Christ

Fortieth Jubilee of Episcopal Consecration
of Bishop Paul Rusch

Innsbruck, 1978

Entrance Antiphon: Revelation 5:12; 1:6; Reading:
  Ezekiel 34:11–12, 15–17
Responsorial Psalm: Psalm 23; Gospel: Matthew
  25:31–46

Your Excellency, dear Bishop Rusch,
dear brothers in the episcopal and priestly ministry,
dear brothers and sisters in the Lord!

Forty years have passed since Paul Rusch was consecrated
a bishop, so as to serve the People of God, first as apostolic administrator and then since 1964 as diocesan bishop
here in the region of Northern Tyrol, which had been
cut off from its mother diocese of Brixen by the border
drawn in 1918. It was a difficult time when Bishop Rusch
had to take the shepherd's staff in hand. Austria had been
incorporated into Hitler's dictatorship, in which there was

"Wegweiser aus der Weisung Jesu Christi", for the fortieth jubilee of the
episcopal consecration of Bishop Dr. Paul Rusch, in the Innsbruck Cathedral
on the Feast of Christ the King, November 26, 1978. Previously unpublished.
[B 470]

supposed to be only one will, one power, and one mind left, the mind of a man who had declared himself *Führer*, the Leader. Long before that, this land had been placed under the protection of the Sacred Heart of Jesus, thus professing allegiance to the One by whom every power in this world must be measured. Devotion to the Sacred Heart and the Feast of Christ the King are in close harmony with each other, for both are concerned with the God-given freedom and dignity of man. That human freedom which is based on his moral dignity is guaranteed only when no one can simply do what he wants, only when everyone ultimately is responsible to the standard that binds us all. And this moral dignity in turn is founded on the fact that man was created by God and is loved by him even unto the death of his Son. Therefore it is not surprising that devotion to the Sacred Heart and profession of faith in Christ the King became the antithesis of the regime at that time, that the bishop drew down on himself the hatred of those who did not want to place themselves under the Lord's dominion. Therefore, however, it is also profoundly meaningful that we celebrate this jubilee on the Feast of Christ the King, that we celebrate it by reflecting on what the kingship of Christ the King means.

Today's reading and Gospel, as we just heard, interpret the kingship of Jesus Christ from the perspective of the shepherd. "Shepherd" was the title by which the rulers of the ancient Middle East were designated, in order to express their unconditional power over the peoples, which for them were only sheep. And in fact, again and again they treated them like sheep, and they also let them be slaughtered like sheep. Because Israel knew that in truth there is only one Lord of the world, it transferred this title of authority to its God. And because Jesus Christ is the Son of this living God, he is the true Shepherd of all mankind. Now when this true Shepherd appears, the image of the shepherd of course changes fundamentally. For the true Shepherd does not slaughter his sheep but, rather, loves them. He pastures them, not with violence, but with love; moreover: the true Shepherd manifested himself by becoming a lamb himself, the Lamb that was slain. And consequently the Church begins today's liturgy with the Entrance Antiphon from the Book of Revelation: "Worthy is the Lamb who was slain, to receive honor and power and might forever."

But what does that signify now, what does that look like, what does it mean: The Lamb is the true Shepherd, the true Shepherd is the Lamb? What the reading and the Gospel together say about it in today's liturgy, along different lines, is connected by the Responsorial Psalm, Psalm 23, which is one of the most beautiful prayers not only of the Old Covenant but of mankind in general, in which the figure of Jesus Christ immediately shines forth. The Old Covenant becomes transparent to the new: "The LORD is my shepherd," this psalm says, "I shall not want; he makes me lie down in green pastures. He leads me beside still waters.... Even though I walk through the valley of the shadow of death, I fear no evil; for you are with me; your rod and your staff, they comfort me. You prepare a table before me.... You anoint my head with oil, my cup overflows." In this song, the message of the reading and the Gospel is taken up meditatively, as it were, and sung into our hearts. In this song, at the same time, above and beyond the ancient Middle Eastern title for a ruler, another background for the image of the shepherd and of the mystery of Christ's kingship becomes visible. Since around 300 B.C. in the Mediterranean region, pastoral poetry had developed, an expression of a late culture, in which people experiencing the stress, tumult, alienation,

and agitation of the major cities longed for a simple, pure,
primitive life, for something of a world that was whole.
"Arcadia", the land of the shepherds, became the image
of paradise. In a world of inner strife, people longed for
primordial wholeness. Jesus Christ speaks to this longing
of his era, of every era—because ours is indeed all too similar to the one then—when he says: This Arcadia that you
dream about really exists. And the good shepherd that
you seek exists, for I am he! But how does he prove this?
How can we become aware of this? He proves it by doing
what people expect of such a life, of such a shepherd. And
what do they really expect? Now, it says here: "Even
though I must walk in the shadow of death, you are with
me!" What all of us dream about deep down, what no
one can stop expecting, is security, in which he no longer
needs to be anxious or afraid, in which his life is kept safe
in a love, in an unconditional Yes. We yearn for security.
Of course, not the security of a slave who does not fear
because he has nothing to lose, but, rather, the security
of complete freedom, the security of a real love. On a
seventeenth-century painting of a shepherd (by Giovanni
Francesco Barbieri, 1616–1620), the viewer sees, clashing
with the pastoral theme, a death's head and, beneath it,
the inscription: "Et in arcadia ego", "Even in the land
of the shepherds I am there", death, as it is everywhere!
But then it is no longer a real paradise, then the last essential fear has not been taken away from us. The real shepherd would have to be the one who has power even over
death. General De Gaulle once related that Stalin had told
him ominously: "In the end only death counts ...": the
acknowledgment of an unscrupulous dictator who tacitly
admits his powerlessness.

Only a man who has power to throw himself into the
jaws of death, who can banish even this final fear, could be

the shepherd whom we need. Jesus Christ did this; in the Cross he set up the tree of everlasting life. An acknowledgment of the kingship of Jesus Christ is therefore first and foremost an acknowledgment of him who has the power to give us eternal life. Faith in eternal life is the only thing that can be redemptive for man. This day is supposed to remind us first of this: that we stand by the man who has power that extends beyond death, which proves him to be the true shepherd.

Yet the Good Shepherd possesses not only power, the ultimate power. We expect him not only to keep death away, but also to make life abundant, to preserve the fullness of knowledge and love, or, as the psalm puts it: "You prepare a table before me; my cup overflows." The Fathers of the Church saw in the background of this verse the mystery of the Most Holy Eucharist: the festive meal in which the Lord lowers the barriers between [himself and] men and makes them members of his Body, in which he gives us the great, free, unrestricted life in which the barrier between us and creation, the barrier between us and the living God, is overcome in the great fullness of his life. Or to put it differently: Jesus Christ is king as priest, and his kingdom consists of the fact that he performs priestly ministry for us, that he makes divine worship possible for us.

There was a time, and not so long ago, when people would have smiled at the words "priestly ministry" and regarded it as something old-fashioned. But we need not be surprised, either, that right away, in its place, quack doctors of the soul appeared, sectarian preachers, heralds of all sorts of salvation, from whose arcane spiritual pharmacies people now draw abundantly. And if we hear about terrible experiences, as in this past week, which basically are only the tip of the iceberg, even then we need not be surprised. Man cannot live unless it is revealed to him that he is called beyond earthly, calculable things. Communicating this calling is an essential part of the priestly ministry. And so we should cheerfully profess our allegiance to Christ, who is Priest and gives the priestly ministry to the Church.

Finally, today's Gospel points out to us a third aspect of the kingship of Jesus Christ: this King is a king because one day he will also be our judge. One day we will be before him, naked and without distortions, with the sum total of our lives. One day we will have to give an accounting of our lives in his presence, and our eternal destiny will depend on his sentence. The Fathers of the Church again saw hints of this in the psalm, when it speaks about his rod and staff that guide us. The true shepherd also possesses a shepherd's crook, the staff that guides and corrects. Once again, this does not really fit into our idea of emancipated Christianity. Actually, we think instead that this shepherd should be glad if we walk a few steps toward him now and then. But this shepherd's cross is, after all, not an expression of arbitrariness. His staff is the Cross, with which he leads us out of the valley of death into the land of resurrection. And anyone who sought a freedom in opposition to the guidance of the truth would ultimately think his way into futility. Any freedom that contradicts the truth could never itself be love.

And this brings us back to our starting point, to the era that did not want the standard of Jesus Christ and therefore fell into extravagance and led us all to the brink of the abyss. Since then a lot of time has passed. In these four decades in which Bishop Rusch has served the People of God as a priest, there were many mountains and many valleys to walk through. After the privations of the war: the great spiritual awakening that came then, the longing to live again in its fullness a firmly rooted Christianity that is nourished by the purest waters of faith; an awakening into a Christian life that was supposed to be a perpetual bulwark against the sorts of events that we had experienced; joy in the new liveliness, breadth, and greatness of the sources of the faith, which then led to the years of the council. At it Bishop Rusch took decisive steps so that the great ideas of the faith, which had been formulated right here in Innsbruck by Josef Andreas Jungmann, by Karl and Hugo Rahner and others, could find a place and become fruitful throughout the Church. And to tell the truth this was not, as it seems to many people now, an effort to cheapen the faith, to water it down, but, rather, an effort to give it plenty of the pure water of its origin. Because he had stood up in this way at the council, afterward, without having to change, he could remain in all sobriety for his diocese a guide directed by Jesus Christ and draw with the shepherd's staff entrusted to him the dividing line between Spirit and the evil spirit, between true and false renewal. For all this we thank him today with all our heart. His diocese thanks him for this, and so do I as the bishop of the neighboring Diocese of Munich and Freising. At the same time I would like to thank him in the name of the whole Church. We thank him by giving thanks to God for him and by asking God to grant him many more years of health and strength. Together with him, we all wish to pray that this beautiful land of Tyrol might remain a land of the Sacred Heart, a land of Christ the King, a land of faith, peace, and freedom.

"Peace" as One of the Names
of the Eucharist

Seventieth Birthday of Auxiliary
Bishop Ernst Tewes

Munich, 1978

Dear Confrere, Bishop Tewes,
dear brothers and sisters in the Lord!

The liturgy opens the new Church year with Saint Paul's
greeting to the Church of God in Corinth, which we now
recognize also as the initial greeting of the revised liturgy
of the Mass: Grace be with you and peace from God our
Father and the Lord Jesus Christ (cf. 1 Cor 1:3–9). These
words are characteristic of the Advent season. The light of
the Lord's grace and peace is brought into time, and we
are called to this light in keeping with the psalm verse that
introduces Advent: "To you, O LORD, I lift up my soul"
(Ps 25:1). At the same time, however, these words of the

"'Friede' als einer der Namen der Eucharistie", for the seventieth birthday
of Auxiliary Bishop Ernst Tewes in the Liebfrauendom, Munich, on December 3, 1978, under the title "Zum 70. Geburtstag von Bischof Tewes", *Ordinariatskorrespondenz*, Munich, no. 40 (December 7, 1978); excerpt under the
title "'Friede' als einer der Namen des eucharistischen Sakraments", in *Gott ist
uns nah: Eucharistie: Mitte des Lebens*, 2d ed. (2001; Augsburg, 2002). Paperback
edition: 1st and 2d ed. (2005); 3d ed. (2006): 123–24. [B 473]

apostle highlight the most profound core of the apostolic ministry, which continues in the ministry of priests and bishops. And so at the same time, it resounds also in the particular circumstances of this hour and of this day, on which we celebrate the birthday and the jubilee of Bishop Tewes, to whom the care of the Church of God in this our city of Munich has been entrusted in a special way for ten years.

Grace and peace from God our Father and from Christ. This is the task of the priest and of the bishop: again and again to call down the Lord's grace and peace into this time. First, it is a thoroughly human appeal, that we among ourselves might be people of grace and peace, people who do not perpetually have to calculate, who can just draw the bottom line and do not have to settle scores, who do not let the poison of resentment proliferate in them but can get over it and make a new beginning. The Greek word for grace, *charis*, comes from the word joy and means at the same time gladness, joy, and also beauty, delight, sympathy. When there is this ability to set something aside that we could still perhaps demand; to make a new beginning; to practice the heartfelt generosity that does not harbor grudges in a corner of the memory for later occasions— then joy grows, then beauty comes about, then goodness shines upon the world, and there is peace. Of course, these human intentions and deeds of ours are never enough, ultimately. And the priest, too, is never just a preacher of morality. He proclaims what we cannot give to people: the new reality that comes to us from God in Christ and is more than a word or a resolution. Behind the term *peace*, the ancient Church heard the mystery of the Eucharist. Peace very soon became one of the names of the Eucharistic sacrament, for in it, after all, God comes to us, makes us free, and, although we are sinners in his sight, takes us into

his arms and gives himself to us. And by leading us into the
communion of his Body, into the same space of his love,
and by nourishing us with the same bread, he also gives us
to each other as brothers and sisters. Eucharist is peace that
comes from the Lord.

Behind the word *peace*, the Church saw the mystery of
Baptism and of the sacrament of Penance: forgiveness, the
grace that God grants us. Of course, these have become
almost foreign words to us. Sin is something from another
world, and that is why God's forgiveness and grace do not
seem to us to be something that could really play a role
in our life—just theological phrases without real practical
value. By chance I recently read the account in which
the great French author Julien Green describes how he
converted. He relates that he was living in the period
between the world wars just as a man lives today, with all
the concessions that he makes for himself, no better and
no worse, shackled to pleasures that are against God's will,
so that, on the one hand, he needs them in order to make
life bearable and yet, at the same time, finds this same life
unbearable after all. He looks for some way of escaping,
strikes up relationships here and there. He goes to the
great theologian Henri Brémond, but it remains just an
academic discussion, theoretical hair-splitting that does
not help him make headway. He becomes acquainted
with two great philosophers, the married couple Jacques
and Raïssa Maritain. Raïssa Maritain refers him to a Polish Dominican. He goes to him and again describes to
him this fragmented life. The priest says to him: And
do you approve of living this way? No, of course not!
You would like to live differently, then; you regret it?
Yes! And then something unexpected happens: the priest
says to him: Kneel down. *Ego te absolvo a peccatis tuis*—I
absolve you. Julien Green writes: Then I noticed that

deep down I had always waited for this moment, had always been waiting for there to be someone, sometime, who would say to me: Kneel down, I absolve you. I went back home, I was not a different man; no, I had finally become myself again.

If we are honest and investigate this story from within, we will recognize that ultimately this expectation is in all of us, that our deepest being cries out for there to be someone who says: Kneel down. *Ego te absolvo!*

Some time ago a well-known Lutheran-Evangelical theologian said: The parable of the prodigal son ought to be told today in a new way as the parable of the lost father. And, indeed, this son's forlorn character is due precisely to the fact that he has lost his father, that he does not want to see him at all. But we are this lost son. His misery is the misery of our time, which boasts of being a fatherless society. In the footsteps of Freud, we have believed that the father is the nightmare of the superego that interferes with our freedom and therefore we must shake him off. And now that that has happened, we recognize that we have thereby emancipated ourselves from love and have amputated what enables us to live. With that, however, the innermost aspect of the episcopal and priestly task once again becomes visible simultaneously: the privilege of representing the Father, the true Father of us all, whom we need in order to be able to live as men. The bishop or the priest has the privilege of making him present by putting into effect his peace, his grace, by carrying out the transforming word of absolution.

I think that at this hour we should thank Bishop Tewes from our hearts that he did indeed make the true Father present in our age and for the good of us all. In the "Church without a waiting room", he gave us here in Munich the space where this very thing is said: Kneel down. I absolve you! And his concern was always to make sure that the peace of Christ that the Eucharist gives us might be celebrated in a lively, fruitful, great, and profound way among us.

A second task of the priestly ministry closely interwoven with this becomes evident when Paul says in the next verse: "You were enriched in him with all speech and all knowledge." Let us take this as an examination of conscience. Of course we are very rich in speech and also rich in knowledge. But are we really rich in the word that is knowledge and directs us in the fullness of speech? Or have we not become very poor in that respect? Once again Julien Green. He relates how his Anglican mother practically immersed him in Sacred Scripture from his childhood. To be able to recite all 150 psalms by heart is something that he has taken for granted to this day. Scripture formed the atmosphere of life. And he says: My mother taught me to understand it as a book of love. And she filled me deeply with the thought that from one end of Scripture to the other only love speaks. My whole being wanted nothing else but to love. A man who has received such a foundation can ultimately not be lost.

How about us? Would we not have to begin all over again to make room for this word, in which love envelops us from one end to the other, to make it the atmosphere of our houses and of our daily routine? There is no insurance against many things going wrong in life. But there is one final supporting force that will lead us home again and again, that will make us rich in true knowledge.

And again we have Bishop Tewes to thank for doing so much to make this word of life and love present among us. Think of the meditations "Five after Five" and of the forum at Saint Michael's Church, and of many other things. Let us allow them to speak to us. Let us recognize again that in our speech we need the richness of knowledge, the word that is nothing but present love.

And finally there is another, third point: Paul says that he is grateful that "you are not lacking in any spiritual gift." With this sentence I almost see before my eyes a bit of Saint Paul's facial expression as he smiles cryptically with gentle irony. For a few pages later he will point his finger and indict the Corinthians, because they are virtually addicted to charisms. He does not take back this remark; it is not mere flattery. No, all charisms, all the gifts of grace are there. But they are in danger of losing all sense of proportion because they are concerned only about special things, because each one would like to outdo the other, and so they lose sight of the fact that all charisms, all gifts have only one purpose: to lead us into charity and, thus, to build up the living Body of Jesus Christ. But I think also of Saint Philip Neri, whose Oratory Tewes entered as a young priest, the saint who with unfailing humor and immense faith transformed Rome in the second half of the sixteenth century back into a city in which the light of Jesus Christ stood on the lampstand and Christians could take it as a standard. He gathered young people, who read Scripture with him and went into the treasures of Church history; for them it went without saying that someone who drinks in this word must share afterward, must go to the sick in the nearby Ospedale dello Spirito Santo, to the suffering and the poor in Rome. Such admirable men as Cesare Baroni, the great Church historian, and many others grew up in this school of charisms; in them gifts were awakened; in them, without any particular office or vocation, the power of God's word came alive and drew men into its service, and finally all this was always gathered toward the center that is called love, faith, hope. And again a word of thanks that Tewes tirelessly and in ever new and imaginative ways tried and succeeded in awakening gifts that make possible something new in the Church, which nevertheless all flow back into the common center of our faith.

In conclusion, my glance falls on the saying of Saint Paul: I thank God always for you. I think that it would be the finest birthday and jubilee gift to Bishop Tewes if he could say this about the Church of God here in our city of Munich. And it would be the finest fruit of this hour if from our midst could rise up as a heartfelt proclamation, so to speak, the tribute that our faith and life here in the Church of God in Munich should be such that the bishop who cares for this city can say joyfully: I give thanks to God always for you. Then conversely we can respond to him with the concluding words of today's reading with the full assurance of faith in the steadfastly reliable word of God: "God is faithful, by whom you were called into the fellowship of his Son, Jesus Christ our Lord" (1 Cor 1:9).

On the Way to the Depths of
the Mystery of Christ

Fortieth Priestly Jubilee of the
Ordination Class of 1939

Freising, 1979

Gospel: Luke 5:1–11

Dear confreres in the priestly ministry,
dear brothers and sisters in the Lord!

There is something dawn-like about the Gospel that we
have just heard, an element of hope, joy, and spiritual
awakening that may remind us of the hour forty years ago
when Cardinal Faulhaber imposed his hand on you to
ordain you priests and you heard the word of the Lord: Set
out into the deep sea, and you said with Peter, "At your
word, Lord, I will try it!" It was a great hour, when fifty-
one young men were ready, in the middle of a difficult era,
to place themselves at the service of the Gospel message,
and the great crowd that enlisted in this service was itself a
special sign of hope and confidence. Of course we know
that at the same time the darkness of that era loomed over

"Unterwegs zur Tiefe des Geheimnisses Christi", for the fortieth priestly
jubilee of the ordination class of 1939 in St. Mary's Cathedral, Freising, June 25,
1979. Previously unpublished. [B 516]

the day: the harassment of the Third Reich that you all certainly experienced at your First Mass; and soon afterward the outbreak of the Second World War, from which seven of you did not come back alive. Then new hope in this awakening to the faith that followed the collapse of the anti-Christian regime, and then again times that became more and more difficult, in which each of you so often found yourself in Peter's situation and had to say to the Lord, or at least struggled with the desire to tell him: To what purpose, really? After all, we have worked the whole night with nothing to show for it, the faith is declining, the Church is becoming more and more wretched, more and more divided, more and more dubious. And nevertheless: like Peter, you too again and again let the Lord encourage you and give you the confidence to say: At your word, I will go on. And no one in your class was unfaithful to his priestly ministry! For this sign of fidelity that you had the privilege of giving by God's grace, we want to thank the Lord especially in this hour. And as bishop I would like to say cordially to each and every one of you who spent these four decades beneath the yoke and the grace of the Lord, May God reward you!

So in retrospect after these forty years, the passage will not look the same as it did at the beginning. Indeed, this is the richness of the biblical word, the fact that it journeys with us and has something new to say in all stages of life. One observation in particular impressed me, namely, the change in the titles for Christ before and after the miraculous catch of fish. Before it, Peter says to Jesus: "Master", in Greek, *epistáta*, which means approximately "Teacher" or "Rabbi". He still sees Jesus as the great preacher of Israel, the one who knows how to teach Scripture and, consequently, can teach life. The rabbi is a man, a teacher in Israel, albeit more than a mere professor who conveys intellectual knowledge. He is a master of life. And this is why Peter, at his word, does something that by conventional everyday standards, according to his own rational calculation, would be senseless. He bets on the man who is master not only of the word but also of reality. Trusting that that man is capable of giving instruction from the fullness of God's word that applies to our experience, he takes the step. When he returns, he addresses him, no longer as "Master", but rather as *Kyrios*: Lord! This is the divine title. He has recognized in what happened that not only was he sent by a great teacher of Israel, but that he is now standing in the presence of the power of the living God. And so between these two stops there is not only an excursion of a few miles, but an interior journey of life, a journey into the mystery of Jesus Christ that reveals in all its depth what he was, what he is. Only because Peter dared to take the first step can this excursion become a journey into the depth of the truth that transforms him and will transform the world. And in this new recognition of Jesus Christ, he also recognizes himself anew. What happens next is not simply what one would normally expect, sheer joy at success—a great catch!—but rather alarm about himself, the realization of his own truth, shrinking back from the greatness of God's mystery and from the sinfulness and misery of his own being. But just as he rediscovered Christ and in doing so recognized himself in a new way, so too he receives himself back in a new way. Corresponding to the new title of Christ is the fact that he, too, receives a new name. Simon becomes Peter: the name by which the Lord now calls him, by which he is more than he could be on his own. Because he has abandoned himself and his own calculations and has sailed into God's word, into the Lord's call, therefore he receives himself back and more than he himself is: the whole power of Jesus Christ's calling.

These forty years fill the intervening space, so to speak, between these two calls. Like Peter, you dared to sail out onto the ocean of vocation, into the world that closes itself off from Christ and, nevertheless, is called by Christ into the immense mystery of God's word. On a journey like this, there are hours of darkness, hours of alarm at oneself, in which we dread the greatness of the mystery and the helplessness of our activity. But there is also the dawning of the insight that Christ's power is greater than our helplessness, his mercy is greater than our failure. If we look back correctly today, all of us can probably say that precisely in this adventure with the Word, in this act of setting out into what appears almost nonsensical—they used to tell us then: there will be no need for priests in the new Reich—we were given to ourselves anew, the Lord calls us with a new name, and we can perceive his greatness again and again in a new way.

And so, going back to the beginning, I would like to say again a word of heartfelt thanks for the faithfulness and patience of these forty years. How much has changed! How often you have had to start over, as it were, to dare to begin again, to say "Yes, at your word", despite all the probabilities, in an era that was becoming dark, in a faith community that was becoming more dubious, to give him your hand calmly and coolly again and again in the knowledge that his call does not deceive. May God reward you for all this. Filled with gratitude, we lay everything that was granted in those years into his hands, just as we commend to him our failure. We know that in the future, too, his grace will be stronger than all the powers that oppose it. And in this consoling certainty, we wish to leave this hour, joyful that we have the privilege of being his servants and that we can thereby do the greatest thing that is possible: be possessed by eternal salvation, by the kingdom of God.

Being There for God's Mercy

Thirtieth Priestly Jubilee of the Ordination Class of 1951

Freising, 1981

Reading: Exodus 3:1–6, 9–12
Gospel: Matthew 11:25–30

Dear confreres,
dear sisters and brothers!

This day invites us to reminisce, to a kind of reminiscence of course that leads not simply backward but, rather, into the depths and, thus, onward and upward. It was thirty years ago that we lay prostrate here and the Litany of the Saints was prayed and we were wrapped, as it were, in the mantle of prayer. They were to accompany us, and we were supposed to know that we are never alone on this path and never walk alone; rather, the whole believing, praying Church of all centuries always walks with us and supports us, and being carried is the only way in which we ourselves can come to help carry. We were supposed to receive the great confidence of this breath of the centuries,

"Da-sein für die Barmherzigkeit Gottes", for the thirtieth priestly jubilee of the ordination class of 1951 in St. Mary's Cathedral, Freising, on July 15, 1981. Previously unpublished. [B 626]

inasmuch as we know that the Church is not something that we produce today; she strides down the centuries and carries within her the strength of the Lord. Of course, this also means again and again that it is true: one sows and another reaps, that is, often enough we will be prevented from seeing *our* successes. Yet at the same time we know that the *Lord's* success, which is different from ours, does come about and that his seed, as we heard in the Gospel for last Sunday (Mt 13:1–23), sprouts in the midst of all difficulties and that his people continue to walk.

Here the hand was imposed on us. We all probably still see before our mind's eye the image of how the elderly Cardinal Faulhaber stretched out his hand motionless over us all: a sign of God's fatherly hand, of the roof of his protecting hand that stands over us. A sign of this hand that was laid on us and tells us: I have placed my hand on you, you are mine! A sign of this demanding and often difficult claim of God, that we should be dispossessed of ourselves and emerge from a merely private life into one that is dedicated to him, a life that we did not plan or devise and that we cannot bring to its conclusion. But also a sign of this kindly hand that says: "I have written your name on my hand. You stay in my hands." A sign of this immense trust in a hand that never lets us fall.

This was where we took the chalice into our hand as the central task of proclaiming the Lord's death and the resulting salvation of the world. This was where we were told: I no longer call you slaves but friends, because you know what I am doing. Since then we have often experienced the burden of this friendship, of knowing what the Lord is doing; the burden of knowing God's secrets, his weakness in this world, the abysses of misery, godlessness, and hostility toward the Word. But again and again we have experienced also the grace of this friendship which, precisely in this common knowledge with its burden and in the help we offer to carry this burden, makes us recognize the reconciling power of his kindly forgiveness, which bridges all the abysses of this world.

Here the story we just heard in the reading came true for us. Here we recognized the flame of the Lord's presence: the flame that burns and yet does not consume. And it was here that our name was called, that we knew that not just anyone was reading it aloud, but that the Lord knows it and calls us. It was here that we gave Moses' answer: Yes, here I am! *Adsum*, we read in the Latin Bible. I am here. We stood up and gave this answer and went forward. This was forever after the most important step of our life, pacing off the space of this *Adsum*, "Here I am." One of our theologians recently told me how some time ago this word became for him a strange experience. He was walking along the Ludwigstrasse in Munich; as usual there was a large crowd, and suddenly he heard someone behind him say: "Is there nobody here?" He turned around and saw a blind man who was trying in vain to get his bearings with his cane. The street was full of people, but there was someone who had to say: "Is nobody there?" Many were there, and nobody was there. All of them were caught up in their own plans and thoughts and schedules, and it was difficult for him, too, to be there now, to turn around and say: Somebody is here. It seems almost like an image for this world: so many are there, and often it seems that no one is *there*. And the Lord calls us to say: Yes, I am here! It is often very uncomfortable to answer in this way: I am here. Because it snatches us out of our own concerns, and yet only by answering in this way are we really *there*, inasmuch as we are there no longer only for ourselves but for the one who calls.

Although it is left out of the reading, it should occur to us that God himself answers Moses by giving his name,

and his name is: "I am", "I am the One-who-is-here."
He is the one who on the Cross is the "I-am-here", who
is the "I-am-here" in the Eucharist, in which he is constantly exposed to our indifference, our incomprehension,
yet again and again allows himself to be placed into our
hands and into our heart. To say "I am here" therefore
means: to translate his reality into human life. That is the
commission that we accepted, in which again and again
he has led us anew. Moses then says: Leave me; why do you
want to send me, of all people, to Pharaoh? How often
we have been tempted to say or actually have said to God:
You want to send me to Pharaoh; leave me in peace! God
answers such questioning by saying: I am with you. *Dominus tecum*, as we so often say. This is the grace that in the
requirement of the *Adsum* answers us from then on. "I am
with you." It may often become very dark for us, and nevertheless we would not be standing there at this moment
if it had not been granted to us repeatedly to hear this
answer: I am with you. I think that in this hour we ought
to thank God above all for the fact that he has caused us
to receive this answer time and again, sometimes softly,
sometimes more audibly. That he has led us through the
confusion of these turbulent thirty years. That he has so
many times pulled us out of the gutter again or held us
when were in danger of slipping. That repeatedly he has
made it vividly clear to us: I am with you. We thank him
first, and we thank each other for helping to carry the burden; we thank the faithful who have supported us, often
far more than we were able to support them. Indeed, they
above all have made us experience this again and again:
Yes, the Lord is here even today! Often enough the humble or courageous faith that we encounter in our timidity
may in turn become an answer, and we all live on the
fact that in this answer of faith, in our longing for him,

in the Yes to him, in the patience and bravery with which the faith is lived out, we ourselves hear again: I am with you! We want to offer him our thanks in this hour for all this—and everyone has different people to thank, different people through whom the Lord has said to him: I am with you. And as the one whose responsibility it is to lead this Church of Munich and Freising as its bishop, I can, as it were, speak to you, dear confreres, the Church's thanks for you, that you let yourself be lifted up again and again, that you heard this voice again and again and accepted it and said Yes again and again: *Adsum*, I am here! We wish to pray to the Lord that he will let us hear this voice of his again and again.

Let me add a few sentences about the Gospel: This prayer of praise by Jesus Christ was certainly pronounced when the disciples recounted what they had achieved. But even more than that, it was a situation in which the outward defeat of Jesus Christ was foreshadowed, in which there were signs that Israel would not follow, signs that his way would end in outward failure. That those who had carried the inheritance of Abraham's faith down through the centuries rejected in this hour the call of the God of Israel from the mouth of Jesus Christ. And in this hour of defeat, he praises God: "that you have hidden these things from the wise and understanding and revealed them to infants". He praises God's mysterious will, the will of God in which he recognizes how God's compassion is capable of creating a new miracle of mercy out of his defeat. God, who thus is not accepted by those who had, so to speak, been cherished by him, so as to keep the way clear for him, is recognized by the little ones, by those who have the mind of the Son. The attitude that can say "Father" and can say Yes and therefore recognizes the mystery of the Father. I think that we should learn from the Lord this confidence that out of his defeats he is able to create over and over again the unexpected, other victory of his love. We should entrust ourselves to him in this way and ask him to help us and to give us the simplicity, the freedom, and the sincerity of heart that can say Yes and that learns from it again and again the confidence and the joy of faith.

Being Close to the People

Twenty-Fifth Priestly Jubilee of the Ordination Class of 1957

Freising, 1982

Gospel: John 21:15–19

Twenty-five years ago your names were mentioned individually here in the cathedral. And they could be mentioned because each one of you had personally heard the Lord call his name, because each one had experienced the fact that the Lord knows him and wants him and that it is good to comply when he says "Follow me." In God's sight, we are not a crowd; rather, he knows us by name and calls us as we are. And each individual gave his answer, the ancient answer of Abraham, Samuel, and the prophets: *Adsum*, "Here I am", and went forward, just as Isaiah went forward when he heard the Lord's call: "Whom shall I send?" (Is 6:8). The twenty-five years since then are actually like an entrance into this *Adsum*, a continuation of this

"Den Menschen nahe sein", for the twenty-fifth priestly jubilee of the ordination class of 1957 in St. Mary's Cathedral, Freising, on June 28, 1982, in *Der Prediger und Katechet*, ed. Konrad Baumgartner and Ludwig Müdl, special issue: *Kasualpredigten* 4 (Munich, 1988): 108–11; previously in *Ordinariatskorrespondenz*, Munich, no. 29 (July 15, 1982). [B 675]

going forward, the pacing off of what was meant by this "Here I am."

Thanksgiving and Joy

When we look back now, what feelings come over us? Surely each one, depending on his own story, feels something special that belongs to him alone. But I think that common to all of us—judging by myself—there is a twofold sentiment. On the one hand, thanksgiving and joy. For when one enters into this *Adsum*, one finds, the farther one takes upon oneself the risk of this journey, that following the Lord is something beautiful, that it is not only a psalm verse that we just sang: "Blessed are those who dwell in your house, ever singing your praise!" (Ps 84:4), but rather that one recognizes it to the extent that one really dwells with him and praises him.

Probably we have all sensed that basically there is no finer profession than being there with the people for what is essential to their humanity, not just having to do something or other and afterward living your human existence, but being there for the essential thing, for humanity itself, and thereby being close to the people, and again, not as a specialist, but for the whole spectrum of life, starting from the children, through questions of maturation and life decisions until the hour of sickness and death. Being privileged to encounter the whole wealth of human life and being able to stand by people at the crossroads of human life and to give them more than we ourselves could ever give—this leads to thanksgiving and joy, despite all the trouble, despite all the conflict and the irritation. This leads to the truth of what the Lord said to Peter, who could not leave behind all that much yet had left something and said: "What will we get for it?" (cf. Mk 10:28). And the Lord not only gave him the prospect of heaven but also told him that even now they would receive a hundredfold—albeit with hardship—of what their family and all their possessions on earth may have been, namely, the great new family of those among whom and for whom we have the privilege of performing the Lord's service.

This joy of not having to live past life but of giving what is essential, of serving the essential, the privilege of really being for the people, as the Letter to the Hebrews puts it (Heb 5:1), at God's behest, that is certainly the one great emotion that moves and should move us on such a day, when we look through the clouds and the mist of the moment. For we need the memory of thanksgiving so that we can withstand the onset of the mist, relying on the lamp of the light that is nourished in the hours of good.

Discouragement

But then there is this other thing that the Lord also says quite clearly to Peter: You will receive a hundredfold even now with hardship, *meta diogmon* (Mk 10:30). This experience is present to us, too, and if we look back, maybe one or another distressing thing stands out. Besides thanksgiving and joy, there is also this sense that it is really odd to have to say great things all the time about love, about truth, about God, and about the Cross—things that we fall infinitely short of, so that we always have to fear that such words may become a lie on our lips and someone can say right away, "What are you saying, there?" and can judge us by it. How dangerous it can become that the great things wear thin as a result, as Saint Dominic said about the vocation of Albert the Great, who in fact came from the faculty of law, from which students were flocking to the Order, whereas no theologians entered, and he said that this is very easy to understand: When someone has always drunk water only and suddenly gets fiery wine, then he is intoxicated by it. But you know of course, if there is a sacristan who has to deal with the Most Blessed Sacrament every day, he soon no longer genuflects, because he finds it too commonplace. We all sense this danger: that the great thing may overwhelm us and then wear thin and that we will no longer hear or sense its greatness or will be overworked and be afraid of it and feel oppressed by it.

And surely there is this other problem, not only discouragement on account of the Too Much that is unreasonably expected of us qualitatively and the Too Great that is always more than our own, but today also discouragement about the quantitative Too Much: in an era when, so to speak, no one or only a few can tell how splendid this wine is. Then the saying about the few laborers falls heavily on those who have placed themselves at the Lord's service. And then the question arises: "What happens next? Will this not end somehow? Have we not entered into a lost hour?" And all the everyday stress can become a nightmare.

Personal Love

The two get mixed up together, and, as I have already said, I think it is good that we have hours in which we emerge from the stress of everyday routine and open ourselves again to the gift of grace that we do experience, too, and only too easily forget. The response to both experiences, I think, is found in today's Gospel (Jn 21:15–19). What should we do in times of joy and in times of discouragement? In the hour of his definitive calling, the Lord asks Simon, who was once so discouraged that he feared a maid and was ashamed to be mentioned in connection with Jesus. Now he asks him, "Do you love me?" and he sinks the feeding of the flock deep into this question, for if love is there, then the gate for the Lord is there, and he feeds the flock through us (cf. Jn 21:17).

The decisive thing, day by day, is that the Lord really is present to us, that we like him (if I can put it so trivially), that we are interiorly with him and love him—and basically loving and believing are the same thing—that we really and deeply believe in him and, by believing, then truly love him; then all the rest will follow. For if it is true that he sent us, that he loved us even unto death, that he awaits us at the threshold of our own death, that he carries and builds up the world so that it becomes his Body—if this is true, then we can surely walk with him, then we can calmly leave as it is the blank check for the unknown future that we wrote out for him then, even if he leads us where we do not want to go, because we know that his guidance is better than our preferences and leads us to better things than what we wanted, even if it goes through the dark valley of Psalm 23. I think that ultimately the quite simple and all-decisive answer is that we never let go of this personal bond with him. And after the hours of discouragement, when we go before him again and let him ask us, "Do you love me?" and say "Yes", then we can always walk farther and also see light again and again. For then we know that what matters is not measurable success but that we calmly place everything in the Lord's hands and that there everything is and remains fruitful. Then the seemingly discouraging word that he said to the apostles in advance for such hours: "One sows and another reaps" (Jn 4:37), becomes a cause for great serenity, because we do not need to measure how much the wheat has already grown, but know that everything is constantly in his hands and that what he has sown is ripening, even if others harvest it, that the Church will live and that our service dissolves and enters into eternal love.

The Great Venture of Priestly Service

Sixtieth Priestly Jubilee of G. R. Vinzenz Irger

Munich, 1983

Reading: Galatians 3:26–29
Responsorial Psalm: Psalm 63:2–9
Gospel: John 15:9–17

With today's reading and Gospel, we speak about the mystery of Jesus Christ. He is the Son of the eternal Father, who has come to call us his friends, indeed, to make us his brothers and sisters, so that with him, designated by the same Spirit, we might say to his Father: Abba, Father!

In these readings, the center of our faith is set before us: the mystery of the living God, who lives, not far away somewhere in the heavens, but right in our midst, who selects men, seeks out men to be his friends and one with him. According to the new Missal, these texts in the liturgy for this Sunday are connected with a psalm in which, so to speak, the old People of God, Israel, goes to meet the Lord who is coming, stretches out its hands toward him, and opens the door to him.

"Das große Wagnis priesterlichen Dienens", for the sixtieth priestly jubilee of G. R. Vinzenz Irger in the parish church of the Heart of Jesus in Munich on June 19, 1983, in *Der Prediger und Katechet*, ed. Konrad Baumgartner and Ludwig Mödl, special issue: *Kasualpredigten* 4 (Munich, 1988): 124–30; previously in *Ordinariatskorrespondenz*, Munich, no. 22 (June 23, 1983). [B 674 = B 701]

You, Monsignor [*Herr Geistlicher Rat*, an honorific title for a retired pastor] Irger, in the sixty years of your priestly life, have not only had the privilege of speaking the words of consecration day after day, but also have recited week by week the whole Psalter, Israel's prayer book, the prayer of the new People of God, the prayer of the Church of all ages. For you the psalms have become like the road of your life leading to Christ. In the psalms, the appeal of revelation is carried over into human life. In them we can make our own the answer that Christ himself places on our lips and in our hearts. So I think that this Responsorial Psalm, which was constantly your personal response also, can help us to understand the special character of this hour:

> O God, you are my God, I seek you,
>> my soul thirsts for you;
> my flesh faints for you,
>> as in a dry and weary land where no water is.
> So I have looked upon you in the sanctuary,
>> beholding your power and glory.
> Because your merciful love is better than life,
>> my lips will praise you.
> So I will bless you as long as I live;
>> I will lift up my hands and call on your name.
>
> My soul is feasted as with marrow and fat,
>> and my mouth praises you with joyful lips,
> when I think of you upon my bed,
>> and meditate on you in the watches of the night;
> for you have been my help,
>> and in the shadow of your wings I sing for joy.
> My soul clings to you;
>> your right hand upholds me. (Ps 63:2–9)

The Psalm reflects the rhythm of a day from sunrise through high noon to nightfall and at the same time suggests the rhythm of human life. In the morning of life, there is the new awakening, the longing for what is great, unknown, fulfilling. The morning is yearning for the light, for the waters of life. Also the awakening to the great mystery and the great venture of priestly service—which cannot occur without a vocation and is possible only as a response to a call—can get underway only if the kind of yearning is there that makes a man keep watch and listen. Only if the yearning for the light, the thirst for God, has dawned can the call be heard, too, and accepted.

The Morning

Our Holy Father John Paul II relates in one of his books a little incident in which these connections become surprisingly clear. It was in the year 1945. The Red Army was occupying Kraków, and a Russian soldier knocked on the door of the major seminary. By chance the young Wojtyła answered, who as a late vocation had come to the priesthood adventurously and at the risk of his life. He asked the young Russian what he wanted. His answer was: "I would like to enter the major seminary here." And so a conversation unfolded between the two men, in which it became clear that this soldier had very little notion of what a major seminary is but that he had grasped the ultimate and essential thing with incredible acuity. He said, "It has been drummed into me constantly from my youth: there is no God. But I always knew that God exists. And that is why I am here now, because I would like to get to know him."

In the midst of the desert of atheism, the elementary thirst for light, the elementary thirst for the living God had blossomed. Right there in the desert of atheism, this young man had had the experience that the psalm puts into words: "Your merciful love is better than life." For life without God is not real life, it lives on substitutes, it lives right past itself. God exists; I am here to get to know him! This is ultimately the only legitimate reason for knocking on the door of a major seminary. Only out of a thirst for God, out of the desire to know him and to bring him to others, can a vocation come about; only then can it grow and stand firm.

The priest is something different from a travel agent or a social engineer. All that is not enough for a person. It may ostensibly perform useful services, but it is too little unless the genuine waters of life are opened up for him, unless some answer is given to his hunger for God. Only on that basis can such service remain alive, too.

The Russian author in exile Vladimir Maximov recently told a story about contemporary Russia that once again sheds light on this connection from another side. In Russia, he says, a little legend is told: An angel came to a farmer and told him: I have come to bring you happiness. The farmer had already heard so much about happiness that this could no longer upset him, and more politely than emotionally he replied: Thank you for the good news. The angel was astounded and said: But will you not at least look at your happiness to see whether you like it? And the farmer answered: There will be time for that. First let me take a look at God.

In a world that lives by strategies for happiness and arrogantly claims to produce happiness itself and thereby has become so immensely cruel, this word sounds shallow. It becomes all the more recognizable, though, that ultimately there is only one decisive thing that can save man: having a look at God. And Maximov adds, in the great temptation of this hour, namely, in the temptation to choose between this-worldly, social promises and God, we hope that man chooses God. Only when his look at God remains undistorted can man's humanity, can the man be saved. When you, dear Monsignor, received priestly ordination sixty years ago, our country, too, was going through a time of trials. The First World War was in the not too distant past. The collapse of the liberal world and of its prosperity that had taken place during it, the *Rätere-publik* [an attempt in April 1919 to make Bavaria a socialist republic], with its tyrannical claim to offer a better world, had ridden roughshod over this land. Meanwhile cata-strophic inflation prevailed, and soon the gangs of brown shirts tramped through Munich, who in turn promised to build a better world on the ruins of the faith. In that hour you accepted God's call, you followed the human heart's thirst for his light, for the living water, and now you have served people for sixty years in God's behalf and built up the Church of Jesus Christ.

So this is the hour for great thanksgiving, thanks first to the Lord, who does not leave this world alone, who comes again and again, calls men and says to them—we still have this saying ringing in our ears from our priestly ordination—"No longer do I call you servants, but friends" (cf. Jn 15:15). We thank the Lord that in all the deserts of history he causes this thirst to blossom again and again and in this way enters anew into this world again and again. We thank the people who made it possible for you then to receive the word of faith, who opened for you the doors to the Lord and led you to him. And we thank all the many people who as believers helped to support you during these sixty years, for we priests can support only because we ourselves are supported by the faith of the Church, the faith of the people who are entrusted to us. We also thank you personally for the fidelity and patience with which you unwaveringly placed yourself at the Lord's disposal in bright and gloomy days and thus made the call to be his "friends" a living presence.

When someone makes the Lord's call present in this way, then again and again through him the Lord's invitation to others becomes audible, then others hear this call, too. In this hour of joy, which for the Church is likewise an hour of great concern, thanksgiving must therefore also become a request that here and now in our city, in this diocese, in our homeland, in Europe, in the midst of the temptations of prosperity and this-worldly promises, the thirst for the living God will remain, with the courage to knock and to say: I want to get to know him and to share him with others, because only the look at God can ultimately be the world's happiness.

Midday

The *midday hour* is described in the psalm with three phrases: I will bless you as long as I live, I will look upon you in the sanctuary, I will lift up my hands and call on your name.

Your priestly ordination was followed by this long hour of the day, and it seems to me that these three verses genuinely shed light on the three aspects of priestly service. In the sanctuary I will look upon you. The priest must be a man who thirsts for God, not only in the morning; he must remain a man who looks upon him. I will bless you as long as I live. Saying this cannot be enough; it has to become alive within us. We must let ourselves be driven by God's Spirit. We must really let God speak to our hearts. And this is precisely what the sign of celibacy actually intends to express: that we accept God as reality into the most personal and innermost aspects of our lives, let him speak, too, dare to stake our entire lives on him, accept him as a ground on which one can stand and consequently encourage others also to regard him as a reality in this world. I will lift up my hands to you. This suggests the sacramental ministry of the priest, who has the privilege of raising his hands and, thus, copying the hands of the Lord that seek us. In the sanctuary I will look upon you. The priest must be the model of prayer for his congregation, not only outwardly, but above all else interiorly. The Gospels speak about Peter's profession of the Messiah: "You are the Messiah, the Son of the living God!" (Mt 16:16). In the Gospel of Luke, there is a remarkable introduction to it that says that Peter discovered this profession when he was, like Christ, in the wilderness praying with the Father (cf. Lk 9:18-20).

Only someone who enters into Christ's solitude with the Father can get to know him. Someone who does not go in will, like the people then, take him for a prophet, a social revolutionary, or for whatever else fits his world view. Only by entering into his inmost being by praying with him does it dawn on us who he is: the Son of the living God. Therefore part of being a priest is being someone who personally prays, who in the beautiful prayers of our tradition—the Way of the Cross and the Rosary—as it were, lets his heart be filled with God and in the Divine Office prays along with the prayer of the millennia and thereby, so to speak, becomes catholic and broadens himself into the prayer of all ages. Only in this way can he prepare to be the voice of Jesus Christ in the Mass, to speak with the I of Jesus Christ, for this is the tremendous responsibility given to us, to represent the I of Jesus Christ, to say "This is my Body." No one can do this on his own, and thank God the validity of our sacraments depends, not on our sanctity, but solely on the Lord's mercies, which are always present. And yet how could we represent him, dare to give him a voice, if we have not become close to him.

I raise my hands to you. You, dear Monsignor, have spoken to us about the center of priestly ministry, about the center of the Church, the Holy Eucharist, but the other sacraments also, to which you have devoted so much time and effort during your life, come to mind at this psalm verse: the sacrament of Penance, in which the priest's hand that blesses can represent God's right hand, whose shadow is grace for us.

A priest once related that in Russian captivity a Lutheran pastor came to him and wanted to make a confession, and he asked him, "But why do that?" And the answer was: "Because I want absolution." What we need is in fact absolution, not only analyses, considerations, opinions, but rather the grace of absolution that changes us and thereby changes the world. I think that we are all experiencing all too vividly that coping with the past is pointless if there is no absolution, that in reality it becomes the poisoning of the present and the cutting off of the future. The only thing that can help us overcome the past and thus create the present and open up the future is the word of forgiveness that makes us sons of forgiveness who can begin anew and are free because of the grace that is granted them, in which they acknowledge each other as recipients of forgiveness.

I would like to thank you very especially, dear Monsignor, for pronouncing again and again the word of forgiveness in this parish church and thereby bringing into this city of ours the renewal, the change, the overcoming of guilt that alone can heal us. And I would like to invite you all cordially, dear lay faithful, to accept this grace for which the human heart thirsts in its depths, the humility of bowing down that does lead to the grace of a new beginning and allows us to serve again in newfound freedom in this world as friends of God.

Evening

And finally the psalm speaks about the *evening hour* when it says: In the shadows of your wings I am safe. My soul clings to you. Your right hand upholds me.

You told the story about your two confreres who are in a home for the elderly and can no longer celebrate Mass. But this consoling and hopeful evening word applies to them, too: In the shadow of your wings I am safe, right in the hour of night, in the hour of my own wretchedness, for my soul has clung to you. And even if my hands lose their strength, your right hand holds me fast.

For the Christian, there is no useless or worthless life. And a priest never becomes useless and is never just utterly out of service. Even if he can no longer manage a parish, he can still, as it has been granted to you, often administer the sacraments and build up the Church in this way. If he can no longer do that, then in his suffering he can still be interiorly the one who leads the congregation in prayer and can still help support it in his prayer. And if even this is no longer possible, he remains a sign for the fact that the shadow of God's wings still covers us and his right hand upholds us when our hands have lost their strength.

I think it is important in this hour to recall for a moment how much our archdiocese owes to its elderly priests, how poor it would be if their quiet, willing, and cheerful service, if their faith and prayer, if their sacramental ministry no longer shone like sunbeams into this diocese. And when I personally think about my journey, I must say that the example of the elderly priests, the composure, the peace, the maturity, the faith, and the fidelity that came from them meant no less than the encouragement, the strength, and the words of the young priests. In this parish here everyone experiences this gratefully, and we all thank you, dear Monsignor, in this hour, that you give us this sign of an evening in God's hands that is still full of radiance.

In the Church's prayer for this Sunday, there is a word of promise that, I think, could also remain for you a memento of this day. The prayer says: "You, O Lord, keep in your hand those who have taken refuge in your love." Someone who chooses God's love as his post knows that he is held by a hand that will not let him go. He knows that he cannot fall, except into God's mercies. And this is the wish with which I would like to conclude: May you always feel the supporting hand of the merciful God! May you continue for a long time to feel and to show us that God's kindness is life! And may God's right hand thus lead you someday to the place where you have always tried to live: into eternal love!

Doing the One Thing Necessary— and Becoming Rich in God's Sight

Sixtieth Priestly Jubilee of Bishop Rudolf Graber

Plankstetten, 1986

Reading: Ecclesiastes 1:2; 2:21–23
Responsorial Psalm: Psalm 90[89]:3–4, 5–6, 12–13, 14, 17
Gospel: Luke 12:13–21

Dear Bishop Rudolf,
dear and Most Reverend Confreres in the episcopal
   ministry,
Most Reverend Abbots,
dear brothers and sisters in the Lord!

"So teach us to number our days that we may get a heart of wisdom" (Ps 90:12). With this petition from the psalm, the Church responds today on the Eighteenth Sunday in Ordinary Time to the reading from the Book of Ecclesiastes that laments the shortness of human life, which is only like a "sigh". "Teach us to number our days." We observe today the sixtieth priestly jubilee of Bishop Rudolf Graber, who here, in the Abbey Church in Plankstetten, sixty

"Das Eine Notwendige tun—und reich werden vor Gott", for the sixtieth priestly jubilee of Bishop Emeritus Rudolf Graber in the abbey church in Plankstetten on August 2, 1986. Previously unpublished. [B 782]

years ago received the imposition of hands by the bishop and was ordained a priest. Bishop Rudolf knew how to number his days: he put them on God's scale and thus filled them with the weights of the Eternal One. He numbered his days by receiving them from God's hands and giving them back into God's hands. And so, in those passing days, lasting, constant things could be realized, grow, and mature. Therefore this jubilee is not only a look back at the past, at a sigh that passes by, but thanksgiving for things that last, that grew through unity with God's life-giving breath, thanksgiving and at the same time a signpost teaching us to number our days. I would like to try to explain the guidance present in this life by juxtaposing it with three things that Jesus says in the Gospel of this Eighteenth Sunday in Ordinary Time, because it seems to me that these words of the Lord gain thereby, with this life, tremendous relevance, and, on the other hand, they make visible the supportive, cohesive, and constant qualities of this life, its message for us.

This Gospel begins with a young man, who is in a dispute about an inheritance, coming up to the Lord and saying, "Lord, tell my brother to divide the inheritance with me." The Lord responds to this seemingly very reasonable, very humane request with unusual abruptness and harshness by saying, "Man, who made me a judge or divider over you?" This answer, which at first glance is almost incomprehensible, becomes clearer when we put it into today's context. For today, too, there are so many people who go up to Christ and say: Lord, tell those others that they should hand over their goods. Lord, start redistributing the goods of the earth. There are so many people who would like to reduce Christianity to a reorganization of the social structure and of political arrangements; so many for whom the faith dissolves into a bit of sociology, economy, and politics. And then this presupposes that ownership and this new order of ownership was the real salvation of man and that the world could and should be redeemed by systems of ownership, because ultimately there *is* nothing else and nothing else matters in human life but that. Considered against this background, it becomes apparent why the Lord's answer had to be abrupt. For it becomes apparent that in reality the question is that temptation of Jesus with which his story begins and which runs through all ages. What is proposed to him here is ultimately the same as in the words: "Turn these stones into bread!" (cf. Mt 4:3), in other words, redeem men by filling their bellies and by satisfying their craving to have things. And it becomes evident, also, what the unfathomable saying from today's reading from the Letter of Saint Paul means when it says that greed is idolatry. It means: When a person takes possession and ownership and systems of ownership for the ultimate and highest thing that could redeem him, he worships the possession, something that is beneath him, and he denies the living God. Lord, divide the inheritance! How loudly this cry to Jesus reechoes today, and how busy many people are, trying to reduce the whole Gospel to this one saying! And at this point, it seems to me, we see one of the main emphases in the priestly and episcopal activity of Bishop Rudolf. Like few others, he had the courage and the gift of the discernment of spirits and the strength to resist the false spirit that makes itself out to be the Holy Spirit and in reality is only Satan's wind. Like few clerics he stood fast in the ups and downs of these past sixty years, first against the temptations of the Third Reich and then again against a Christianity that is tailored to suit sociology and politics. And in precisely this way, because he lived out of the center of the Gospel, because he stood at the core of his Yes, he was able to set the right standard and could also say No when necessary. After all, despite our openness to the world, we cannot renounce the prophetic

No that is part of our faith. The creation of the world began with the division of light from darkness, and this is still valid.

A second saying of Jesus from this Gospel: it tells the story of a rich man who successfully increased his lands, wants to build new barns, and foresees the moment when he will have everything he can think of and will take it easy. But right at that moment something unexpected happens. Jesus says: God said to him, "You fool! This very night your soul will be required of you." He is directly confronted with something that he had forgotten in all his cleverness and in his calculations, although it is the essential thing: God and the soul. How vividly this man is a parable of our era! How much we can do today! Look at all the things that technology has made possible for us—new prosperity, new communications, new capacities to build and especially to destroy, also! We seem to be able to do almost anything, to calculate almost everything; just one thing does not appear in these calculations and is vanishing more and more: the one thing necessary (Lk 10:42): God and the soul. The Lord tells us that all the cleverness in this world, however great and successful it may be, is foolishness if it overlooks and forgets the one necessary thing. And again this brings us to the priestly and episcopal ministry of Bishop Rudolf, who has always thought and lived, spoken and worked in terms of this one thing necessary, God and the soul. It becomes evident that the No that he had to say to this era again and again was only an instrument of this great Yes that brings us to the essential thing, the center without which the rest becomes meaningless. This dynamic of the essential thing explains, it seems to me, the various other emphases of his episcopal activity: he was an ecumenist long before that came into fashion: among the first who sought and found encounters with the Eastern Churches—of course not in the superficial, managerial way in which ecumenism degenerates into a sort of commercial business and ecumenism is conducted like barter, as if we ourselves could manufacture the Church as our product. He conducted it, not in search of his own success, not with the mentality of dealing and managing, but quite simply in order to hear the whole voice of tradition, so as to be able to believe more deeply and to live better, to be closer to Christ, to come closer to him who alone is our unity. And from there he found the great theocentrism of the Eastern Church. From there the encounter with the Eastern Church became immersion in its contemplative recollection and silence. From there the encounter with the Eastern Church became a rediscovery of liturgy and sacrament as the Now of the One who is to come. From there the approach to the Eastern Church became an advance toward the primacy of adoration, which must carry and guide all the rest. And because he sought ecumenism in this way, without an agenda, his efforts were successful, more than many projects set in motion with much human shrewdness. And in the midst of a crisis of ecumenical dialogue, what matured in the Regensburg Symposiums that he inspired remains a bridge of hope. And so I think in this hour we must thank you, dear Bishop Rudolf, precisely for the fact that you always led and still lead us to the center and from the center out into the wider field.

And finally, a third saying of Jesus from this Gospel: at the end, as a result of these two stories, he says: Do not gather riches in this world, but become rich for God. We become rich for God when we give wealth away. Wealth given away is a treasure for God. And if greed is idolatry, then doing without and giving is a school of becoming rich for God. But we should give not only things but also ourselves; we should learn truly to lose ourselves. For in that way we become similar to the triune God, in whom all three Persons give themselves to the others and thus are the one God. And in this way justice, purity, truth, fidelity, and goodness grow in us, things that make us like God, things that are God's treasures, true riches, which really redeem and which no one can take from us. Growing rich for God: in this regard, how can we not think of the humble handmaid of the Lord, who with her *Fiat* gave everything and received everything? In her Yes, Mary presented a gift to God himself and made him richer; she gave him human nature, human life, human words. In this way she gave humanity and the earth and the world back to him again. From the first day of his conception until the final word of Jesus on the Cross, her way then was a giving-away, a release of Jesus to the Father and to us. She gives him back; she gave us as a gift the treasure above all treasures, Jesus, the blessed fruit of her womb. And she is still rich for everybody as the woman who perpetually gives. Because in Mary the Yes of the Gospel has its living embodiment, it seems to me quite logical that a bishop who thinks and lives and acts so much in the center of the Gospel should be a Marian bishop. In the confusion, in the skepticism, in the know-it-all enlightenment of our times, Bishop Rudolf had the courage, and still has it, to make audible the humble voice of the Mother who can best tell us how we can become rich in God's sight, how we become redeemed Christians.

For all this, dear Bishop Rudolf, we thank you today with all our hearts. We thank you by thanking God for you and for what he has given us through you. We thank you by praying for you, and it seems to me that the collect for today is as though designed for this occasion and, so, should be our prayer for you in a very special way: "Be near to your servants, O Lord, and unceasingly grant them your goodness."

Being a Witness of Christ's
Helpless Power

Golden Priestly Jubilee of
Monsignor Konrad Miller

Munich, 1987

Gospel: Matthew 28:16–20

Dear Reverend Monsignor,
dear confreres in the episcopal and priestly ministry,
dear brothers and sisters in the Lord!

"All authority in heaven and on earth has been given to me" (Mt 28:18). With these words, the Lord explained what happened in the Ascension event. It is the expression and manifestation of that definitive victory which Christ won on the Cross, in his obedience and in his love. As the Book of Revelation says, he opened the seal of world history (Rev 5:5). He built a bridge over the infinite abyss between time and eternity and opened to man the door to God; he made it possible for man to be happy, for his

"Zeuge der ohnmächtigen Macht Christi sein", for the golden priestly jubilee of Monsignor Konrad Miller in the parish church of the Holy Spirit in Munich on May 28, 1987, under the title "Mir ist alle Macht gegeben im Himmel und auf Erden (Mt 28, 18)", in *Priester aus innerstem Herzen* (Munich, 2007), 239–45; previously in *KlBl* 67 (1987): 160–62. [B 800]

happiness is an eternity of love, of loving and of being loved. He cast down the strongest power in this world that no one else can withstand, death, and united his power with God's power; and this is why he can say: "All authority in heaven and on earth has been given to me." Ultimately there is no opposing power. Because this is the case, the age of the Church begins with Christ's Ascension, for the Church is nothing other than the entrance of all generations into the space of this new authority of Jesus Christ; the rise of a new people out of all the peoples of this world. And, therefore, with Christ's Ascension begins also the definitive shape of apostolic, priestly ministry, which is nothing other than service to this very same saving power of Christ; and therefore the Lord in his last words on this earth described the nature of this abiding service. He expresses this in the three words of commission that we just heard in the Gospel: "Make disciples of all men", "baptize them", "teach them to observe all that I have commanded you."

"All authority in heaven and on earth has been given to me." How insignificant, how paltry this authority seems, though, to our human eyes and according to the standards of this story! When Jesus spoke these words, he had no divisions, no weapons; no groups of terrorists or subversives, either; no brain trust of specialists in seizing power; no universities; no banks and no money; no commercial empire; not one of the things that, to our way of thinking, are the basic elements of authority in this world. He had only witnesses whom he sent like sheep among wolves (Mt 10:16).

Dear Monsignor, when fifty years ago the bishop who ordained us both, the great Cardinal Michael von Faulhaber, imposed his hands on you to ordain you a priest, the talk about sheep and wolves was actually not a metaphor at all but a palpable reality. For many of your contemporaries and, above all, for those who held authority in the state at that time, those who were being ordained—and there were many—were really sheep who had not grasped the situation. Among the wolves of that time they stood there like sheep, even if they remembered that the Lord had said that his witnesses should be not only innocent as doves but also wise as serpents (Mt 10:16). The religion of the strong was extolled and contrasted with Christianity as the religion of the weak. The goon squads of the government authority felt strong enough to put a quick end to this weak religion, even though for the time being they had to make allowances because the strength of the faith was alive and still standing in our country and was a much more effective bulwark than it probably would be today in similar straits. A man who was ordained a priest back then knew that he was not standing on the side of the temporal authorities of the day and that he could not count on worldly advantages.

But of course Jesus had rejected this offer long before on the mount of temptation. "All this"—namely, all the riches, all the advantages, all the power of this world—"I will give you, if you will fall down and worship me" (Mt 4:9). Those were Satan's words. Redemption according to Satan's design, according to the notion of the Antichrist, would consist of giving people security, perfect structures, prosperity, and the freedom to enjoy everything—which they are then supposed to mistake for freedom itself—and how nice this offer is. "Wouldn't that really be redemption?" is the question all of us ask. What more, really, should a man wish for himself than security and prosperity in all respects and the right to do everything he wants to do? And even the price, "if you will fall down and worship me", seems quite modest for such a gift, and quite appropriate, especially since this worship is depicted as quite harmless. It consists merely in regarding all this as the ultimate, sufficient goal and not inquiring beyond death and not acknowledging God as the Lord of the whole world who concerns us. Then God and religion can even be admitted again as a means to the end. A religion that becomes a means is very pleasing to the Antichrist. The only religion he cannot tolerate is one in which God is worshipped and does not become a means but, rather, remains the First and the Last. However, someone who does not answer the question about death but represses it, someone who takes God away from people and does not allow him to be Lord but makes him a means, is lying to people: because he takes truth away from them and because he invalidates the greatness of their calling.

That is why Jesus answered: "Begone, Satan!" (Mt 4:10). That is why he did not accept this redemptive authority but, rather, went to the Cross. That is where his authority comes from, all the authority of Jesus Christ. All his redemption authority is authority derived from the Cross, and, therefore, the servant of Jesus Christ must begin there again and again. Therefore, the Eucharist, communion with the crucified Lord, must be the source of the new and genuine power of the Resurrection, the central point of his life and of his service; and, consequently, this service seems very simple, very humble, but precisely therein it is a profound blessing.

It consists initially of making people his disciples. This means leading people to an acquaintance with him, so that they get to know him, he becomes familiar to them, they learn to love him, and they want to become his, his disciples, his congregation that is with him.

And how much this task, dear Monsignor, has defined your life over these fifty years: in home visitations, in meetings, in conversations, in instruction, in catechesis. Unceasingly this was your way of making people disciples, teaching them to know Jesus. This was not only about drumming certain formulas into them, conveying a system of knowledge—although knowledge, too, is important. For the faith also gives information and instructs us about reality; faith is an answer and is meant to enable us to give an answer to others. But all these formulas, these answers that it gives us, do not stand on their own; rather, they are windows that open onto him, that teach us him, the living, true answer to our questions, and thus help us to become friends with him; to receive the deepest relationship of our life, which lasts through all confusion and gives us a firm foothold. Because this is the case, "making disciples" includes speaking, thinking, and teaching, but after all it is always much more than that! It is an introduction into a personal knowledge and acquaintance with Jesus Christ.

Therefore, this first task automatically leads to the second: "Baptize them in the name of the Father and of the Son and of the Holy Spirit."

Christianity is not a philosophy, a sum total of formulas and teachings, and it is not a morality, a summons to all sorts of activism—it is life! It is a communion of life with God and, thereby, with each other; for being a disciple of Jesus Christ, following Jesus, is not simply about implementing and continuing some program that Jesus set up, carrying on his ideas. Nor is it simply about imitating his human example. All this, correctly understood, may play a part, but the decisive way of Jesus is, after all, the way leading to resurrection, the way to communion with the triune God. We follow this way in being disciples; anything else would be too little and would remain on the level of other programs. We do not follow the whole new

way of Jesus Christ until, even now in this life, we follow
this whole way that leads beyond the limit of creatureliness and all that a man can ever do by himself. This whole
way is necessary for us, because man is the being who
wants and needs the impossible. He gives it to us, and this
occurs in the sacraments, in which he leads us into this
new, greater, other reality that we ourselves cannot create.
A bit of creation—water, bread, wine, oil—has the privilege of becoming the bearer of his presence. In receiving
it, we are called into a new space, into fellowship with him
and with all the saints of heaven and earth, into communion with the living God. Therefore sacrament is adoration,
and adoration is the center of being a Christian, standing
before the living God, communion with him; but because
God is the Creator, therefore communion with the Father,
the Son, and the Holy Spirit is also communion among us
all. To adore him, to receive the sacraments, means to be
led out of our isolation and to become in the sacraments
the living communion of the Church. It means that every
individual does not just believe on his own but that all
together we become the living Body of Christ.

And again, if I may reflect on this in terms of your life,
dear Monsignor—to how many people you administered
the sacrament of Baptism; how many you reconciled with
God in the sacrament of Penance; how often, in this magnificent church, you had the privilege of celebrating the
sacrament of his Body and Blood; to how many couples
who exchanged their Yes to marriage for life you granted
fellowship with the living Lord as well!

And those were truly complicated times. This church
sank into rubble and ashes, but again and again you found a
place where, nevertheless, the Lord could be among us and
where, thanks to him, life with each other became possible
again. So, despite the improbability of it, you ventured

to rebuild after the war and, even as the demographics changed and seemed to advise against it, you did not stop giving this church back to us inhabitants of Munich, bit by bit; finally, you even restored the frescos, the silent jubilation in which the joy of the redeemed is ever present. And therefore you make sure that the resounding jubilation still has its place here, too, as we had the privilege of experiencing in this joyful Mass—music born of faith in which the voices of creation are called to proclaim God's glory to us. You made this space rise up again as a precious vessel of the sacrament of the presence of the living God among us; as a perpetual invitation to the strength of this presence, as a place in which, through his closeness, Eucharist, Cross, and Resurrection are constantly here among us.

The first period of your priestly ministry was overshadowed by the crisis of National Socialism, the war, all the destruction and the hardships that this war inflicted on our people. And, then, when the time of affliction was overcome and everything seemed to promise joyful new progress, it became evident that the erosion within had continued. So now there was a crisis of a completely different sort to cope with, which now came to us, not from outside, but from within the Church: the temptation to mistake the council of the media for the council of the bishops and, consequently, to equate renewal with unauthorized innovation and mere change. There was a rampant temptation to think that the Church that we would now make with our own expertise would be better than the Church that the Lord gave us. It seemed to many people that the real thing was only just beginning, through our achievements, as if the formulas we devised could only now give us the new and long-awaited reality. A new Church was supposed to be built that would be better and would at last take up the true ideas of Jesus.

When you began your priestly ministry, you were part of the generation that conducted pastoral work with new courage, with a new boldness of faith, with new pastoral ideas, with a new dynamic and went out to the people. You never set aside this dynamic of courageous new ventures, a new way of realizing the faith as the times march on. But precisely because you were and are supported by this dynamic, you also knew that the Lord did not say to his followers when he instituted the apostolic, priestly ministry: "Sit down together, discuss your problems, and demand your rights." You knew that he did not say, "Sit and hold meetings", but, rather, said: "Go, go forth to make people my disciples!" You remained faithful to this command; and precisely for this reason you did not overlook the third word of commission given by the glorified Lord: "Teach them to observe all that I have commanded you" (Mt 28:20).

Many think that now, quite the contrary, we no longer have to observe anything and that that is dynamism, but you did not share this opinion, because you knew that only someone who stays on course really travels, while someone who does not stay on course does not travel, either, but performs an illusion. That is why you remained faithful to the call of the Holy Spirit, in whose church you have served for forty-eight years, as pastor for forty years. The Lord said about him: "He will ... bring to your remembrance all that I have said to you" (Jn 14:26) and "He who has my commandments and keeps them, he it is who loves me" (Jn 14:21).

"All authority in heaven and on earth has been given to me." At the end the Lord transforms this saying into a promise for us. "Behold, I am with you always, to the close of the age" (Mt 28:20).

Recently I read Julien Green's memoirs of his youth, which contain much that is gloomy. He recently added a new foreword in which he says: When I look back, I cannot comprehend at all the fact that God devotes so much time to an individual, so much attention, as though he were the only person on earth.

When we look only at others, at the world as a whole, and seek to judge it, then we might think—and this can become a temptation of faith—that God has withdrawn from world history. But when we look vigilantly into our own life, then every individual can tell how wonderful it is that God devotes so much time, so much attention to him, to me, as if I were the only person he had to think about. It is true; he stays with us all our days!

So today, dear Monsignor, many people thank you for giving them an encounter with Jesus, for conveying to them the answer to life's questions. Today, in particular, Holy Spirit parish thanks you, and today I have the privilege of thanking you in the name of Holy Church for your fifty years of priestly ministry. Above and beyond all our thanks, may the Lord himself show you his gratitude by making you experience and sense constantly how true it is: "I am with you always, to the close of the age and beyond all ages—eternally."

A Spokesman of Reconciliation

Eightieth Birthday of Franz Cardinal Hengsbach

Essen, 1990

First Reading: Ezekiel 33:7–9
Second Reading: Romans 13:8–10
Gospel: Matthew 18:15–20

We are gathered for a thanksgiving celebration. We thank God for the eighty years of life that Cardinal Hengsbach is privileged to complete this month. We are grateful for his ministry, and we are grateful for all the blessings that have resulted from this ministry in this diocese and throughout the world.

But the birthday of a bishop, above and beyond thanks, is a celebration of the Church. For he lives and acts in behalf of Jesus Christ. In the early morning of his life, he responded to the Lord's call as Samuel once did: *Adsum.* Here I am, Lord, at your disposal. He allowed his hands to be bound and thus laid them in the Lord's hands, so that they would be available to him as his hands in this world.

"Ein Wortführer der Versöhnung", for the eightieth birthday of Franz Cardinal Hengsbach in the Essen cathedral on September 9, 1990, in *Zeitzeuge Kardinal Franz Hengsbach: Zum Gedenken an den Gründerbischof des Bistums Essen 1910–1991*, ed. Hans Jürgen Brandt and Klaus Hellmich (Bochum, 1991), 37–42. [B 893]

In his Yes to the episcopal ministry, he renewed this beginning and took it to a new depth and breadth. Jesus' word to the Twelve now became the motto of his life: As the Father sent me, so I send you. Dispossessed of himself, he lives as the envoy of the Lord, whose spokesman in the world he is supposed to be. And he can say with Saint Paul: We do not proclaim ourselves but Jesus Christ as Lord and us as your servants for Jesus' sake. He is the hand and mouth of Jesus Christ in the world; he leads us to Jesus and shows us Jesus. But in this way he also makes clear to us what Church is, what the missions in her are, and he helps us, each and every one of us, to recognize what our task is in this hour of history.

Today's liturgy can guide us in the reflection that is thus imposed on us by this day. The First Reading speaks about the service of the watchman in Israel. The Second Reading shows us God's commandments as a signpost leading to the one commandment of love. The Gospel speaks about the communion of the Church, about its order and its promise. In God's word to Ezekiel, which we heard in the First Reading, the Fathers of the Church saw an Old Testament prefigurement of the bishop's ministry, which acquired its full significance only in the light of Jesus Christ. The prophet is addressed here as watchman. The Greek Old Testament used the word *skopós* for this, which leads directly to the New Testament word *episkopos*, which in turn lives on in our English loanword bishop.

So we stand here at the linguistic and substantial origin of the name and task of the bishop. A *skopós* is someone who watches, who looks out for others, too. The expanded New Testament form *episkopos* designates someone who has oversight, who does not drown in the details but aims at the whole—where we are coming from and where we are going—and therefore recognizes both the dangers and the paths that lead forward and promise life. And, of course, this means, not a distant view of merely intellectual curiosity, but a view that is concern and responsibility: a view that becomes deed, helping, accompanying, and leading.

Now the Fathers of the Church ask: But how does one acquire this view, this watchfulness over everything that then can also become leadership? They say that in order to have an overview, in order to see the whole, one must stand on the height. Only then does one see more. And so the next question arises: What is the height that actually allows us to see correctly, that really gives us an overview? And the answer is: The true height of a man, where he knows himself and learns to see for others, is communion with Jesus Christ. He climbed up onto the Cross, and from there he shows us who we are and where we must go. And only by going with him do we receive the right view, the view of love that comes from God and is the only thing that makes us see correctly.

And so it already becomes clear, too, also that the height required by the office of the watchman, of the bishop, is not the height of distance, of knowing better, of considering oneself above it all, much less of arrogance and detachment, but rather this height is the height of love, which is why the Church Fathers tell us: Christ taught us that man's true ascent is accomplished when he dares to make the descent of love. Only with him does a man come to the height and become great. We do not receive the height by going away but, rather, by being with one another on behalf of Jesus Christ.

Throughout his ministry, Bishop Hengsbach always strove to ascend to the height of Jesus Christ and thus to find mankind's true height, which gives the right view of life and of others. And as a result, he received the courage to be simple, the courage to be close, the courage to be with others, always siding with people, and also the courage to accept the truth and the pain of truth. The courage to contradict, when necessary, the courage to offer fraternal correction, about which today's Gospel and also the reading speak, which comes not from arrogance and knowing better but from love.

So, in the more than thirty years in which he was responsible as pastor, again and again he worked hard to bring people together despite their oppositions, to put employers and workers, those in military service and those in civil service and many others in the communion of their one responsibility under the one standard of Jesus Christ, in which we can serve one another and together find paths. He likewise resisted cold rationality and mere pragmatism as well as mere emotionalism. He sought complementarity and the fulfillment of people in terms of Christ, and on his behalf he brought them together again and again around one table and thus, in all the problems that these thirty years brought with them in those terrible upheavals, led again and again to new solutions, too. He made it known that we can see individual things rightly and respond to them correctly only from the central perspective of Jesus Christ.

This concern for people, it seems to me, has kept him young. It was never mere pragmatism, which inevitably comes to a standstill someday, collapses someday into resignation and disappointment. Therefore it has continued to be nourished by an optimism that is ever new, because it is concern along with Jesus Christ and thus has in him the certainty that nothing we do is ever lost, that we always may and can make a new beginning with him.

Anyone who speaks about Bishop Hengsbach inevitably thinks of this pulsating land on the Rhine and Ruhr rivers. And so throughout the world he acquired the name "the Ruhr Bishop". For all the worldwide duties that he has had, he has still always remained very deliberately the pastor of this region and of the people here, and as a sign of this he included coal in his ring, the sign of this earth, of its strength, and also of its needs and problems. But even in purely commercial terms, this land here could not live if it were to become self-enclosed. It needs worldwide openness, import and export, exchange with the whole world. It would destroy its social and economic identity if it tried to deny this openness and wanted to exist only for itself. Exactly the same thing is true in the Church. A Church that now wanted to be only a congregational church or a regional church would abolish herself as Church. And a man who wants to be a bishop precisely for these people here can be one correctly only by placing them again and again in the openness and breadth of the universal Church of all places and all times.

Thus Cardinal Hengsbach, being the Ruhr Bishop, became a European bishop and a world bishop, and in his hour of history acknowledged reconciliation as the major task of a *skopós*, a watchman in the Church of Jesus Christ.

"Owe no one anything, except to love one another", in which you are always debtors; so we just heard Saint Paul say in the reading. Bishop Franz knew this. And with such a view he looked at his neighbors. He recalled again the ancient tie that Bishop Altfrid established 1,100 years ago by transferring to this place the relics of Saint Marsus of Auxerre, so that that bond might again become a living force. And in this way he showed us the saints again as the bridge between peoples and made it evident that the communion of saints is the new state and the new city in which there are no conflicts of races and classes because all stand under the same grace of Jesus Christ. And where previously there was conflict, now the border between France and Germany has become a path of brotherhood, in which we share our gifts with one another and together have the privilege of being Church.

The early years had already brought Cardinal Hengsbach together with the Polish language and the Polish people here in the Ruhr region. And as he took over the shepherd's staff, this proved to be a providential preparation for his duties: seeking reconciliation not only toward the West, but also toward the East in this sorrowful history between Germany and Poland. He became the spokesman of reconciliation, again in keeping with the verse by Paul: Owe no one anything, except to love one another. In this you are always debtors. Here the debt is never paid off. Here you can never give too much, but you must repeatedly begin anew. This was the impetus that carried him and still carries him. And as difficult as it is to understand one another and to enter fully into the brotherhood of faith, as much as this path often seems to make excessive demands on the patience on both sides, someone who knows how often all of us live on the patience of Jesus Christ—who constantly, again and again, puts up with us and knows how little patience we have in this perpetual new beginning—advances with Christ so as to foster here, too, the reconciliation in which there are no more boundaries and, therefore, no boundary questions, either, because we can all be at home everywhere.

As a spokesman for reconciliation, Cardinal Hengsbach became a European bishop. And yet he never subscribed to a narrow Eurocentrism. He was one of the first to see the great challenge that Latin America poses for us. His name is inseparably connected with the word *Adveniat* [a charitable organization canonically founded by the German Bishops' Conference for the benefit of Latin America] and, thus,

with that rich history of charity which by now is concealed behind that word. I think that it would do us good
to welcome the word itself more intensely into our ear and
our heart; after all, it introduces the petition from the Our
Father: *Adveniat regnum tuum*—Thy kingdom come. So it
tells us that we do not build the kingdom of God with
all our know-how and intelligence. God does it. And we
must ask him for it in prayer. Wherever people claim that
they could do it, they deceive themselves and all of us. All
man-made paradises have always inevitably become tyran-
nies. God alone establishes his kingdom. But if we pray for
it, then this petition must form us, that is, it demands that
we move toward that kingdom, that we become open to
it, that we accept its inner orientation. And this is a much
greater challenge than the monetary or economic one. It is
a challenge that goes down to the foundation and demands
of us a change of heart, which automatically becomes a
change of action, also. It demands that we learn to see
with the eyes of Jesus Christ and recognize the dignity
of the poor, learn to understand that they are our closest
brothers and sisters. It requires us to see that property is
always responsibility for the whole, just as not even my
"I" belongs to me; rather, my "I" was given to me as a
gift, and it can be lived out correctly only if I make it over
to a "Thou". Thus no possessions are simply mine; rather,
they were given to me so that I might be a steward for the
benefit of the whole, so that I might render an account
of them, so that there might be true communion in the
goods of the earth that God has given us. Cardinal Franz
accepted these challenges and innovatively set in motion
the Adveniat project, so that there might really be communion in the goods of the world. And in doing so, he
always knew that we give too little if we give only things,
if we no longer send people, priests, and nuns who give

themselves. If money alone is to be expected from us now, then we are giving much too little. The whole problem, not to say fiasco, of developmental aid in the last forty years, which ultimately has created the mountain of debt and the ever wider gap between north and south, is based on the fact that we wanted to pay off our debt of charity with mere economic activity. We must give more, not less. Only the cycle of love can be a cycle of life. Cardinal Hengsbach has led us again and again into this cycle, into this broader effort, into this Adveniat, into this approach to God's dominion.

Dear Cardinal Hengsbach, by your work you have led us to Christ and made us see him. For this we thank you today. And included in this gratitude is all the rest, great and small, that cannot be described here. The Church introduces this Sunday's liturgy with the psalm verse: "Deal, O Lord, with your servant according to your mercy." I would like to clothe our congratulations in this simple prayer of Israel: dear Cardinal Hengsbach, may the Lord show you his kindness all the days of your life. May he continue to accompany your work as bishop and priest all the days of your life with the fullness of his blessing.

Conversion to the Light

Fortieth Priestly Jubilee of the Ordination Class of 1951

Munich, 1991

Reading: Ephesians 1:3–14
Gospel: Mark 6:7–13

Your Eminence,
dear confreres in the priestly and episcopal ministry,
dear sisters and brothers in the Lord!

In this hour of grateful remembrance, our thoughts go first and foremost back to that great moment when our ordaining bishop, Cardinal Faulhaber, in the profound silence of the packed Cathedral of Freising thoughtfully and heavily imposed hands on each one of us and thus ordained us priests of Jesus Christ. We knew that we were touched not only by the hand of a man who was already departing from this world. We knew that he stood for someone else; the Lord laid his hand on us and said: You are mine.

To lay hands on something means, after all, to take possession of it. In the symbolism of the Old Testament liturgy, the imposition of hands is still more. It is the transfer

"Umkehr zum Licht", church service for the fortieth priestly jubilee in St. Michael's, Munich, on July 14, 1991, in *PrKat* 133 (1994): 515–19. [B 913]

of one's own identity into the other person, so that he belongs to me from within; my "I" enters into his. An exchange of being, of thought, and of will is supposed to take place. The Lord had laid his hand on us. We knew: Now I no longer belong to myself, I am needed and wanted in this world. This being needed, this being claimed, this being wanted is something more and nobler than merely standing around on one's own. We stood beneath his hands, and we knew that we would now walk our path in the shadow of these hands of his, that we belonged to him.

Thus the gesture of the imposition of hands summarizes everything that we heard in the Gospel and shapes it into an effective presence. The Lord proceeded from the Father. He descended to his creation in order to look for the wandering lost sheep of mankind and to bring it back home. He chooses men so that they might go with him and fit into this ministry of his. We had the privilege of coming and conveying something that was not of ourselves. We had the privilege of coming with a higher certainty than we had devised for ourselves. We had the privilege of saying with the certainty of his presence: God exists! And this God is not just some distant higher being, a beginning of immeasurable ages. He knows us. He cares about us. He sees each one of us. This God about whom men throughout history ask, partly anxious, partly hopeful, partly resisting him, this God exists, and he is just like Jesus Christ! If this enters our lives as truth and certainty, it automatically means conversion, as the Gospel tells us; that is, our whole life has a new orientation and finds its way. We had the privilege of bringing the Word that is reality, which is communicated as Presence in the sacrament.

In today's Gospel, this sacramental dimension of priestly ministry is expressed in a way that perhaps seems a little odd to us. The Lord sends the Twelve out; with them his

missions until the end of the ages begin; on them he con-
fers authority to drive out unclean spirits. At first we may
think that that is just something rather outdated. But if we
reflect more profoundly, everyone will have to admit that
today, too, a detoxification of souls is necessary; indeed,
we may need it more urgently than ever before. Today we
are increasingly aware of the poisoning of creation by what
we do, and we desperately ask ourselves how we can stop
it or even reverse it. We men have learned to use and
to consume things in such a way that they are irretrievably
consumed, that they emerge from the perpetual cycle of
renewal and life and become irrevocably consumed and
dead. In this we see also an image of our tendency to over-
power the world and to distort ourselves. Since we already
must seek so much and so urgently for ways to preserve
God's creation so that it does not come crashing down
into a state of death and perpetual exhaustion, we likewise
need a method of detoxifying souls, of reconciling them:
with themselves, with creation, with others.

How can we be reconciled with ourselves, with others,
with God's reality and his creation if we are not reconciled with God, if he does not reconcile us from within?
And if we start to ask what material there could be that
detoxifies souls that are poisoned by fear, hatred, and envy,
that leads them out of the vicious cycle of death and killing
onto the path of life—what else can detoxify the world but
the redeeming love of God who became man, who took
its poison into himself and in his love transformed it? We
knew that this power was given into our hands, although
we were unworthy of it.

God is not loud. He does not make headlines. In the
forty years of our priestly ministry, we have had the privilege of experiencing quietly again and again, in the silence
of God's work, who it is who in fact renews souls so that
they can emerge from the cycle of death and shine again:

reconciled, full of gratitude for being, for their own being, as creatures and as men. We went on our way in the shadow of his hands. More and more, even through all the confusion, we learned that it is a good shadow.

The fundamental gesture of the imposition of hands, in which priestly ordination is actually accomplished, is surrounded in the Church's liturgy by a wreath of ceremonies that explain it and further illustrate it. Our hands were anointed and tied together. So we took hold of the chalice. That was a way of telling us that these hands are no longer for taking or making or hitting. They are supposed to be hands that serve the Lord, that carry the chalice of his mercies into this world. For me personally, the ceremony that was most deeply engraved on my consciousness, besides the imposition of hands, was the moment of the Litany of the Saints. We lay there outstretched on the floor, praying that the Lord would show us the way, while surrounded by the increasingly urgent singing of the whole cathedral: "Pray for them."

It is a moment in which you profoundly experience your own helplessness—prostrate, not seeing and not touching the Other—the disproportion between one's own resources and the immensity of the task, one's own inability and the uncertainty of a far-reaching future, about which no one can say how it will continue, how this task will be accepted, rejected, or trampled in it. In all the wretchedness of an experience of inadequacy, we nevertheless heard the prayer of the whole cathedral, the invocation of all the saints. It told us ever more insistently and at the same time ever more consolingly and forcefully: You are not alone! You are walking in a great fellowship that will not abandon you! It is the great communion of the saints of all centuries. As people they were just as wretched, and yet the Lord granted them this path. He alone could do it. But we not only sensed the fellowship

of a past Church but were introduced into the communion of the Church of today, which supports and offers
companionship on the journey and does not abandon you,
introduced into the communion of the Church of tomorrow, for the ship of the Church is built to last forever.
Even though the Lord sometimes hides himself and seems
to be sleeping, he is there on board with us during all the
storms. The ship does not sink. It has the promise of eternity. This awareness entered into us, caused us to stand up
again and to say our Yes.

In the forty years of the path that we have now traveled,
the truth of this has been demonstrated: We are not alone!
Holy Church, the Church of the simple and of the great,
the Church of yesterday, today, and tomorrow, travels
with us. Beyond thanks to the Lord, this is above all an
hour of thanks also to the people who went before us and
led us, to the people who walked with us and who now
follow us and take over our task. We have received something from all of them, precisely from those who have
no name in history and do not appear in the newspapers.
From those humble people who are believers in the midst
of the burden of this time, we ourselves have received
again and again the grace of faith, the experience of the
Church's permanence and of the reliability of her promise.
We have learned firsthand that one can entrust oneself to
the ship of the Church. For the Church does not belong
to yesterday or today, she is situated neither in the Council
of Trent nor in Vatican I and II; rather, she was founded by
Christ, and all those other things are stages of her renewal,
in which again and again she finds him anew and finds
herself, too, and thus can keep going. This is the joyful
certainty in which we stand and in which we keep going.

Finally we had the privilege of celebrating Holy Mass
for the first time with the bishop, of saying for the first time

in the person of Jesus Christ: This is my Body. After this turn to the Lord with great devotion, there was another very memorable moment: the first time we turned to the believing community and had the privilege of extending our hands and blessing it. Blessing means handing on the force of a goodness that is stronger than what I personally could do or give. It was the promise to Abraham that he would become a blessing. We knew that we were now included in a special way in this Abrahamic promise and could be men who bless with Christ.

At the end of his Gospel, Saint Luke relates that the Lord, before he ascended, blessed the disciples and the world (Lk 24:51). He disappears with hands extended in blessing. He remains as one who blesses. The evangelist means to tell us: Precisely by stretching out his hands and blessing, he did not go away; rather, he remained, and the world always remained under the protection of his blessing hands, which cover it and at the same time lead it upward over and over again. This told us that we represent and, so to speak, are the blessing hands of the one who was taken up and is present and that we have the privilege of giving him our hands for the purpose of blessing. That explains at the same time what we hear today in the reading from the Letter to the Ephesians: Only someone who is blessed can bless. One can never bless oneself. One can only receive a blessing or give it to others. Only by giving it to others do we ourselves become blessed. In this cycle—as blessed, blessing, and receiving blessing—we walk full of confidence, knowing that the world always needs this, that the Lord who holds his hands over the world in blessing will also make sure that his blessing remains visible and is passed on.

It was a custom of our diocese that at the end of the ordination ceremony the newly ordained formed a procession and each carried a burning candle in his hand, which we then individually gave to the bishop. As we went forward holding in our hands the burning candles, it seemed to me that this was an image of our life. We had to carry this light and to keep it lit in the winds and storms of this age. We were supposed to bring a spark of this light, of its brightness and warmth, of God's light, to the people who toil in many sorts of darkness. We knew that the light would remain precisely by being handed on and that it would grow as we passed it on. Somehow the candle seemed to be an image of ourselves, also: we were supposed to make available the material of our own life, so to speak, so that the light of the Gospel might burn and shine and warm.

Now we have traveled through time for forty years with the light of the Gospel, the light of word and sacrament. Sometimes it was in danger of slipping from our hands; sometimes it was in danger of going out in the confusion of the times. But there was always a goodness there that covered us. Precisely because the light had been passed on, it always came back to us. That is why we are grateful and are, not fixated on the past, but full of confidence in what is to come:

> We thank you, Lord,
> for giving us a light,
> for sending us again and again someone
> to help us carry it.
> We ask you
> to give us again and again hands that will take
>   it up and pass it on.
> We ask you
> to make sure that we arrive with our lamp
>   burning and to welcome us someday to the
>   feast of your eternal love.

The Interior Center of Priestly Life

Twenty-Fifth Priestly Jubilee
of Father Martin Bialas

Schwarzenfeld, 1993

Gospel: Matthew 16:13–20

Dear Father Martin,
dear confreres in the priestly ministry,
dear sisters and brothers!

Twenty-five years ago, in the turbulent year 1968, before
he was ordained a priest, Father Martin answered when
his name was called: *Adsum!*—Here I am, I am ready. And
this was more than a sort of verification of his presence.
It was the gesture of his life making itself available to the
Lord as it set out on his way. With this word, he entered
the extensive ranks of those who have given themselves
over to the Lord's service. We find this word for the
first time in the account of Abraham, in the hour when
God called him to the mysterious sacrificial journey to
Mount Moriah. "Here am I", he says (Gen 22:1). And

"Die innere Mitte des priesterlichen Lebens", for the silver priestly jubilee
of Fr. Dr. Martin Bialas in the church of the Passionists' Miesberg monastery
in Schwarzenfeld, Oberpfalz, on August 22, 1993. Previously unpublished.
[B 965]

297

then we encounter it again with Samuel, whom the Lord calls at night. And the youth, who still has no idea what it is actually supposed to mean, nevertheless answers with the words that the priest Eli has given him: "Lord, here I am—I am ready" (cf. 1 Sam 3:1–21). And I would like to mention another great scene: Isaiah has beheld the glory of God in the Temple, and while he is still frightened by the power of him who fills heaven and earth with his glory, he hears God say, as though begging: "Who will go for us? Whom shall I send?" And he bursts out with: "Here am I! Send me" (Is 6:8). And this first word of the sacred rite is continually the interior origin of priestly ministry, the interior center of priestly life; it continually means being at His disposal and putting this initial word into practice day by day.

But to what is the Lord actually calling men thereby? Let us try to find an answer by looking into today's Gospel. First of all, as we just heard, it speaks about the origin of the Church. The Church begins with Jesus being known and acknowledged, with the recognition and acknowledgment of Jesus. In the moment, and only in the moment, when he himself has arrived in the heart, the understanding, and the will of men, the Church is there, for she is Jesus' coexistence with us and our coexistence with him. Thus Christ's being known, his being acknowledged is the point of departure. Next comes Jesus' answer. Now he can give Peter the power of the keys over this living house, which is thereby in the process of coming into being.

But the rise of the Church is not the only thing being depicted for us in this way. In the service of Peter and of the other eleven apostles, the priesthood in general begins, also. It is the origin of priestly ministry. Priesthood, too, begins decisively with the fact that we recognize and acknowledge Christ. Becoming a priest means first entering into an acquaintance with Jesus Christ, knowing him not only second-hand but firsthand, based on one's own coexistence with him. Knowing him correctly always means also loving him, becoming his friend. Finally, priestly ministry consists of living in this friendship and leading others to friendship with him, into the fellowship of Jesus' friends that we call Church and, thus, into the true, supportive friendship that extends into eternity. Then there is this other point, too, that Jesus says to Simon: You could not say this on your own but, rather, because God opened your eyes and your heart. This means that one cannot simply *make* himself a priest. It is not a rung on a career ladder that one builds for himself. A man can only *become* a priest; this means that there is always something passive about it, receptive, allowing oneself to be called and gifted. One cannot seek it out for oneself as a job worth striving for, but only allow oneself to be called, accepted, and accompanied. Recognizing Christ happens only when the recognition about which we have just heard takes place: when he is recognized as the "Son of the living God". Not some ideal man, not some great personality, not a moral ideal that we want to emulate, but rather God's being with us, God as man. Therefore, following Christ—whether as a Christian in the midst of the world or as a priest—always means more than imitating a human ideal. It means that we walk after him along his whole way; this means going after him in his Being-God, in his sitting at the right hand of the Father; this means following him to his Cross and Resurrection. Of course we cannot do that by ourselves. We can walk along this great way that he opens up for us, that surpasses all our potentialities and is the only true fulfillment of human existence, only if he himself grants us the wings of faith that reach farther than our own footsteps; if he gives us, as it were, the vehicle of the sacraments, in which he himself takes us up and guides us and drives us to communion with the living God—a destination we could not reach by our own powers. Recognizing the Son of the living God, the whole Christ, and, consequently, for the first time the whole greatness of our human calling as well—that truly is knowledge, and that is the task of acknowledgment.

Saint Paul of the Cross, the founder of our dear Father Martin's religious community, particularly emphasized in this connection another perspective that we would hear in Matthew, too, if we could continue the Gospel reading and that then the apostle Paul emphatically brought into the world when he said: We do not proclaim ourselves, "we preach Christ crucified" (1 Cor 1:23). This seems to be a contradiction: God's glory and the Crucified. Yet the two go together, and we have known God's glory only if we have recognized Christ as the Crucified. The true God does not rule like the rulers of this world by smashing and destroying; he does not rule with bombs and violence or through technological prowess; he rules in a completely different way. He rules by coming among us, loving us, and suffering with us and for us. This weakness is the real strength of God, the strength by which he renews the world again and again, the only power that survives all the downfalls of worldly powers and always opens new doors of life. That contradicts our current mind-set to a great extent. Suffering ought to be eliminated and banished; it should not be. We want pleasures, we want success, we want to exhaust the fullness of life. But this same inability to renounce makes us unable to put up with each other anymore, to keep loving each other, and we lose the joy that we are pursuing. Pope Saint Pius X, as a simple rural pastor, personally compiled a catechism for his school, and in it he noted also the question: "Why did Christ come to earth?" The amazing answer, which reflects all the hardship of life in poverty-stricken Veneto of that time, was: "He came to help us to suffer." Precisely by suffering with us and teaching us to find meaning in it and to become better in the midst of it, to allow ourselves to be purified, he opens for us the door of humanity and joy: this is precisely how he demonstrates that he is the Son of the living God. Only when we mention this, too, do we learn to live and to love, because only then are we in harmony with God, too. So I think that it is nice that during this priestly jubilee we have before us also the figure of Saint Paul of the Cross, about whom the jubilarian has written so much, a figure who helps us to understand in its entirety the acknowledgment that is perpetually the content of priestly ministry and life.

The Lord responds to Simon's acknowledgment by handing over to him the power of the keys. In the First Reading, we saw what this means in the broader sense: he is appointed God's steward. And we could look at priestly ministry in this way, too: being the administrator in God's household. The Lord described this in many parables. The essential element is: the priest does not manage business for his own sake. He does not start a fan club but, rather, is a trustee, a house steward, so that God's goods are among us—goods that belong to all of us and lead us all to one another. He is a trustee. This is the first thing: fidelity, which does not claim for itself what belongs to someone else; the faithful steward does not make himself the center of attention but, rather, sees to it that the Lord's property lasts. Part of this is vigilance, which watches out to make sure that this property is not squandered or ruined or spoiled, that it does not sink into indifference. Part of it is justice and kindness, which hold God's house together and give to each his own at the proper time. Then, too, another part is prudence, which is able to care in the right way for these goods of God. Another part of fidelity is creative courage. There is the parable of the talents (Mt 25:14–30): the servant who managed best was not the one who buried his talent so that nothing would happen to it but, rather, the one who invested it in the world's "business" so that it could grow and increase. Thus being God's steward, God's trustee, always means this, too: putting God's goods, the living word of faith, the grace of life with Christ, and the sacraments, right in the middle of the living struggle of an era, so that God's property might grow in it, so that the mystery of the word may be spread, so that we become more and more aware of it, so that it permeates the life of this world more and more. Being God's steward means striving to make God's treasure grow in this world, so that it is a living presence in it, so that the salt saturates the earth, and the yeast leavens the whole lump of dough, mankind.

Priestly ministry, therefore, I will say it again, does not mean positioning oneself. Unfortunately, many people today see the priesthood in this way: as a chance to "have a place at the table" and "to have something to say" about the Church. But that is not what it is about. If we look at the great priests, starting with the apostle Paul, down through the ages to Charles Borromeo, the Curé of Ars, and Saint Paul of the Cross, then we see that it is always about something quite different, namely, about just what Christ did, who once told us: "The last will be first" (Mt 20:16), and who truly being the First, the living God, personally became the last among men so as to come to us all. Being a priest means again and again entering into this gesture of Jesus Christ, being for all and with all, even desiring to be one of the last, so that the light of the living

God might shine everywhere. And of course this is then very promising.

The Lord once said that whoever "has left house or brothers or sisters or mother or father or children or lands, for my sake" (Mk 10:29) will receive all this again a hundredfold on earth, although amid hardships, and in eternity as well. And this is demonstrated over and over again in priestly ministry, and I think we see it in this living congregation, too: that through this existence for Jesus Christ a family grows, in which we notice how all this bears fruit, how it renews us and brings us to one another, how we are gifted in this way by the Lord, not only in the next life, but with a new love, with a new friendship, with a new breadth even in the middle of this world.

And finally, in conclusion, we return once again to today's Gospel: The power of the keys is conferred on Peter. This has a twofold meaning: first, the authority of the discipline to shut out or to let in; and as the core of this authority, the authority to forgive, to say in the Lord's name: I forgive you your sins, they are taken away from you, you are made new. And this then implies the authority to teach, to determine what belongs to the faith and what contradicts it. This power of the keys was first given to Saint Peter, but the others have it, too, each in his own way: the bishops, the priests, indeed, the whole Church, for we are all responsible for the faith, for the presence of the truth. For we could also summarize this power of the keys as service to the truth, service to love, and service to unity. We are all commissioned to serve the truth: to fight to keep the faith alive and unadulterated; and we are all commissioned to love, we are all commissioned to forgive again and again so that we might be forgiven. And we are all commissioned to seek unity, to love unity, and to live it. The priest is commissioned in his special way to do these things. He, too, must repeatedly perform the service of the truth, undergo the suffering of the truth, and have the courage to reject conjuror's tricks and to make sure that the Lord's property remains pure. He is, as the Gospel says in another passage, the doorkeeper who must know when to lock up and when to open; who must take care of God's house in all its breadth, but must also prevent the introduction, by God knows what tricks, of falsifications by which men serve only themselves. In this era, in which so much manipulation of our souls occurs through advertising and by all sorts of other means, it is all the more important to perform the humble service of truth, in which the essential thing, the word of God, remains alive among us. Then there is the service of reconciliation. Here the priest must begin personally with himself. This means that he acknowledges again and again that he himself, too, is guilty and a sinner. That he has the humility to see that he, too, has done things wrong in the sight of men and in the sight of God; the humility to acknowledge it and then to be transformed in forgiveness. By doing it in his own case, he can teach it to others. This ability to acknowledge guilt and consequently the ability to accept the grace of forgiveness is one of the fundamental conditions for love, one of the fundamental conditions for human life together, and, thus, also a fundamental condition for the unity of the Church.

And finally: the power of the keys of which we are speaking is given to Peter and, as we said, to the bishops, the priests, and all the faithful, each in his own way, which means that it is always a service to the truth, also. The priest never works only for himself or only for his congregation; the service is always directed to the whole. It is always the commission of Jesus Christ to put down the barriers in the world and to lead us to unity, to communion with one another. It is always in the true sense of the word a catholic service, that is, a service that leads into the worldwide communion of the Church of all places and all times and, in this broad sense, a service of reconciliation. That is why part of the priesthood is being with the other priests, being with the bishops, being with the successor of Saint Peter, so that unity might grow. And, ultimately, unity is with the one God himself. We can come to the one God only if we ourselves are and become unity. Striving for the unity of the Church is intrinsically part of acknowledging Jesus Christ, the Son of the living God.

"We give you thanks that you have held us worthy to be in your presence and minister to you." So priests pray in Eucharistic Prayer II, which goes back to the early third century. We thank you for letting us be in your presence. These are the thanks of us all, and it is our thanks for the priesthood that Christ gave to his Church as a gift. For what could be more beautiful than to stand in the presence of the living God, to serve him, and thus to serve the world! Now this prayer of thanksgiving also expresses mysteriously and humbly the most profound core of the priesthood: Thanks for the privilege of celebrating the Eucharist, of saying in Christ's own person: "This is my Body, this is my Blood." Thanks that through the priestly ministry he himself comes among us, distributes himself to us, and lifts us up again and again. In this hour, we thank the living God for the twenty-five years of priesthood that he has granted Father Martin, for the fact that in an era that has not always been easy he has had the privilege of standing at the Lord's service with a cheerful heart, generously, and even globally. We thank you yourself, Father Martin, for all that you have given us in these twenty-five years, and we pray to the living God that he may grant you to keep walking along the priestly path with a cheerful heart and the courage to serve.

Preparing People to Receive Jesus

Eightieth Birthday and Golden Jubilee of Father Ignatius Glasmacher

Maria Eck, 1994

Reading: Isaiah 58:9b–14; Gospel: Luke 5:27–32

Dear Father Ignatius,
dear confreres in the episcopal and priestly ministry,
dear sisters and brothers in the Lord!

On this Saturday after Ash Wednesday, the Church presents to us in the Gospel the story of a vocation, which plays out like a drama in three acts: there is the background, the actual occurrence of the encounter with Jesus, and then the response to the call.

The background: this man's name is Levi, which means that he comes from the priestly tribe of the Old Covenant and, thus, by his heritage is destined for the priesthood according to the laws of the Old Testament. Of course his life has driven him far away from that, for according to the oriental custom, tax collectors raised money not only for the state but above all for themselves—often cruelly and

"Die Menschen für den Empfang Jesu bereiten", for the eightieth birthday and golden priestly jubilee of Father Ignatius Glasmacher, O.F.M. Conv., in Maria Eck on February 19, 1994. Previously unpublished. [B 976]

almost always unscrupulously. But some sort of interior uneasiness must have remained in this man, an awareness of the fact that he was not living his authentic life and his real destiny. And now Jesus appears before him and says: Follow me.

It is the moment when he finds his way back to himself and, at the same time, finds his way out of himself. The Lord calls him to authentic service, to the real priestly ministry, to the ministry of the Twelve who are appointed to go out and gather men, sinful men, from all the ends of the earth for the communion of God's new people.

Then comes the third act: the actualization of the call. Levi holds a reception for Jesus and calls his friends to attend it. All of them are people publicly marked out as sinners; he himself knows that something in them yearns for what is greater and purer but that their life is going right past this authenticity. He calls them so that the same thing can happen to them, this same transformative renewal leading into real life that he himself has just experienced. And so what he does is the content of all priestly ministry: holding a reception for Jesus. This is the genuine thing: bringing people to the reception for Jesus so that he finds a response and the world becomes his living house.

We celebrate also today a vocation story—fifty years of priestly ministry. You, dear Father Ignatius, were certainly not sitting at a tax collector's booth like Levi when the call to the priesthood hit you. As you have often told me, you come from the blessed poverty of a large Catholic family in which Christian joy was at home. Nevertheless, the priesthood is never simply the result of disposition and upbringing. No one can simply give it to himself or take it; the Lord must call. And the call must be accepted anew again and again throughout a lifetime. Another part of the priestly path, again and again, is that we lift the barrier and clear away the barricade that we have set up in our life, with which we have become set in our own plans and ideas. Again and again the call must be heard and accepted: Follow me! Break out! Get away from that barricade! Set out on the way so that world history may become a reception for Jesus!

One could probably depict this life in terms of the major stops at which it played out: Cologne, the Palatinate, Rome, and now Adelholzen and Maria Eck. But something else seemed more appropriate to me. Everyone becomes himself—authentically and most often—in his encounter with others. What we are and what we become depends to a great extent on whom we meet and how we are able to encounter him. And so this life is perhaps best depicted in the major figures, in the figures of the saints who stood at the various turning points along the way and pointed the way: Francis of Assisi, Peter the fisherman from Bethsaida who became the prince of the apostles, Mary, the Mother of the Lord.

With Francis of Assisi—we just heard—and in fellowship with him you found the path to the priesthood. You wear his garment. You have his joyful, unaffected faith. You have in common with him also the cheerful simplicity with which you are able to beg—and the generosity with which you can then give. For you do not beg for yourself, after all, you beg in order to spread joy. And both things: the humility of begging and the magnanimity of giving, are part of man. When one or the other is lacking, we become hardened. If we are no longer able to beg, arrogance comes over us. And if we no longer give, we become self-willed and reserved and by that very fact empty.

But let us return again to Saint Francis. It occurs to me that we cannot understand this figure without first of all thinking about his Levi hour, his experience of being called. He most certainly had something in common with the Levi of this Gospel. He was a rich merchant's son who tossed money around by the handfuls and thus enjoyed life and enjoyed being a ringleader of those who lived as he did. After his imprisonment in Perugia, he noticed that this seemingly so full, adventuresome life had been futile. He was sick of loafing around as a wealthy playboy and now sought something truly great, but he did not yet know of what it would consist or how he could find it. Then, in the little, half-ruined church in San Damiano the Lord spoke to him from the Cross: "Francis, rebuild my house, which is in danger of falling down." And now he had to emerge from his dreams. He, the spoiled youth, had to tackle hard construction work, the difficult and often dirty job of gathering stones, making mortar, finding friends who would pitch in, and doing hard physical labor. He became at first in a literal sense what we just heard about in the reading from the prophet: a stonemason who repairs the breaches. And as he did so, he learned about the more profound sort of construction. He learned: not only are there fissures in this chapel, and not only is it necessary to apply mortar with his hands, but also the living Church of God is in danger of falling down, and it needs a stonemason who will restore her again.

By learning to work, he now learned to serve in this deeper sense. The Church is never entirely done. And again and again she looks as if she is about to fall down. There are fissures in the walls, and the Lord needs men, stonemasons, to repair the breaches and to restore his house. Francis did this by giving his whole life for the cause; not only by proclaiming the Word with his lips but by living it in its entirety; by becoming a lover, a beggar, and a giver. And then there is the fulfillment of what we just heard in the reading also: where this happens, a light goes on even in the gloomy night and living water springs up in the desert.

You, dear Father Ignatius, worked as a stonemason, erected buildings in Cologne, and from these difficult external demands, which at first seemingly lead so far away from genuine pastoral service, you learned to obey the Lord's will simply; you learned to build up the Church from within with all that he demands. And so for fifty years now you have been preparing the reception for Christ by calling people to leave their lives, which they have often been living badly, so as to become persons who are received and receiving, so that as receivers they might give and thus a light might go on in a dark world.

And then, with the path to Rome, the figure of Saint Peter left his mark on your life. The two keys became his symbol, as a result of Jesus' words: "I will give you the keys of the kingdom of heaven." What does that actually mean, the keys of the kingdom of heaven? Certainly the popular image is not correct: a bearded old man who stands at a gate somewhere beyond the clouds and somewhat peevishly and irritably opens up the register to see whether or not he should unlock the gate. The keys to the kingdom of heaven are something very much present. They are simply the keys to happiness—for that is what the kingdom of heaven is—the keys to right living. But are they to be found? Of what do they consist? What do they actually lock up? Jesus' words about these keys mean the authority to forgive. Indeed, the core of all misery in the world is uncleansed guilt, the darkness of the human heart, and the silencing of conscience. Today we are acquainted with an immense amount of misery in the world, whether we look at Bosnia, at Somalia, at Angola, or even at the drug scene, at the whole set of problems in our own country and in the Western world. We can recite a whole litany of evils that are devastating the world. But all this cannot be cleansed unless we get at the real root, the fact that man turns away from God, which leads to a loss of standards in which man now wants only himself and whatever he wants to have and therefore becomes violent, wicked, and disorderly. Only when guilt is overcome from within can there be healing, too. Today, in this world of ours, the word "sin" has become a foreign word. Around fifty years ago a French author said that now it belongs only in an operetta. And, therefore, the word "redemption" is meaningless, too. Yet "being unredeemed" is something with which we are all familiar, of course. Discontent or, as we say nowadays, frustration with life in this world. The only possible key by which to escape this and become new is overcoming sin, the grace of forgiveness.

You, dear Father Ignatius, devoted the best years, actually all the years of your priestly life to precisely this task of forgiving sins. You called people who recognized that something was not right in their lives to Christ's reception and had the privilege of speaking to them the words: "You are forgiven. Now follow me." Consequently, you have been able to open the door to new life, repair the breaches in the walls, rebuild the crumbling house, and thus caused light to shine.

And finally there is Mary, the Mother of God, who is so close to us in a special way here in this little homey, familiar shrine. Adelholzen, Maria Eck—*Holz und Eck*, "wood and corner". One might think, after the work that you have done in major metropolises, that now at the end of your career you had been "pushed into a corner". But someone who goes to Mary is never on the wrong track, and the corner in which we find her is always the right spot, where we are at home. The mystery of the Incarnation is the center of our redemption and of our faith;

what I find particularly beautiful about it is this: from that moment on, God wanted to have a mother. And now she is our Mother, so that the People of God has thereby become the family of God, in which we are so thoroughly at home. And full of simple trust, we can go again and again to our Mother.

Once again Francis of Assisi. His path, his spiritual path, started in San Damiano, but the Portiuncula became the real home of his heart—the "little lot and portion", the "corner" where the Mother of God resides—Maria Eck. There he started the Order, there he gave his life back to the Creator. So you have arrived at a truly Franciscan place. Mary is always there for us. In fellowship with her, we know that we are safe. Someone who is with Mary can also look forward, even in the latter days of life. He does not need to look back nostalgically because the way forward might be short. No! She, who went through death without being harmed by it, shows us the totality of life, which is still and forever the future. Whether we are here or there, says Paul, in other words, this side of death or beyond it, is not the decisive thing, but, rather, the fact that we are with Jesus. Then we live. This life is always the future, because it becomes ever richer, greater, and deeper. At the end of the Salve Regina we pray to Mary: Turn your eyes of mercy toward us. And after this our exile, show us the blessed fruit of your womb, Jesus. We do not like to hear the word "exile" because we find the world beautiful—and it is beautiful. But, nevertheless, we all know, too, when we think about all the shadows that exist, that we are not entirely at home, that we remain on the way, and that a situation is best, that we are most at home in a place, when it contains the prospect of a lasting city, when Christ is with us. That is home, and there we are at home; there the saying is fulfilled: "For here we have no lasting city, but we seek the city which is to come" (Heb 13:14). So we pray for you and for all of us to Mary, that she might turn her eyes of mercy toward us and show us Jesus.

We thank you, dear Father Ignatius, for showing Jesus to so many people in their lives and for still continually showing him. And we pray all the more for you on this day, that you yourself might continually see him, might see him forever and, thus, truly live.

Teaching and Learning the Love of God

Fortieth Priestly Jubilee of
Monsignor Franz Niegel

Unterwössen, 1994

Gospel: Mark 12:28b–34

Dear Franz!
Dear sisters and brothers
  of the parish in Unterwössen!

As I was thinking ahead to this Sunday in Unterwössen to give thanks again for the forty years of our Monsignor's priesthood, an old story from my days as a recruit occurred to me again. We had just received our uniforms, and the lieutenant then asked each one what he thought his profession would be. I answered that I wanted to become a Catholic priest, whereupon, as a staunch representative of the regime, he shouted at me: "Then you will have to find something else to do! In the future priests will no longer be needed." Just a few months later, that Reich collapsed into rubble and ashes and left a trail of blood and tears behind that still plagues us today. In the resulting void, we felt

"Die Liebe Gottes lehren und lernen", for the fortieth priestly jubilee of Msgr. Franz Niegel, in Unterwössen on October 30, 1994. Previously unpublished. [B 987]

again in a way that was very real and new that we still needed priests and would continually need them. By then the regimes in the East had also disappeared; they had said that after they had ruled for one generation, religion would dissolve by itself as something superfluous. But they were gone, and in the interior and exterior destruction that they left behind, a new thirst for God had appeared and for men who could proclaim God. What do we need priests for? We need them, quite simply, because we need God. And with that we have arrived at today's Gospel.

In it a man asks the Lord: "What is the most important commandment?" We would not ask him that, because commandments per se do not suit us that well. But we, too, ask him what he meant, namely: What is the most important thing that will make life right? What can I not omit under any circumstances? What is necessary in order to make this life rewarding, so that I can at last be happy and content and grateful? What is indispensable? The Lord's answer is: The most important thing of all is God! If he is not there in your life, none of the rest is right. It is as though someone had put the first button in the second buttonhole: then all the rest are wrong, too, and he has to start all over again. If the fundamental relationship to God is not right, then none of the other relationships of which our life consists and on which it is built can be set right. For then our life has no meaningful source: then it developed, not out of a thought and a heart, but, rather, as an accident of evolution, which attempted this play and may have played the card wrong. Then all of this has no reason and is empty, and it is also without purpose. When God no longer exists, everything else becomes gloomy and empty. People do not notice it right away. For a generation, maybe two, the afterglow of his presence still remains, but when this gleam has finally disappeared, then all that is left is a great darkness, and then all that is left is doubt about everything, flight into intoxication, stupor. A Yes no longer makes sense. That is how we understand the Lord. If we reflect a little, if we investigate the history of the present day a little, although it is not immediately evident and other things seem more urgent: if God is not there in our lives, if I have not found him and am not right with him, then nothing else can be set right, either. Therefore, there is a need for men who are "men of God", as the Bible calls them, who speak to us about God and, even more, who bring God into our lives.

But if we look even more closely at the Lord's answer, another very important key word appears. He does not simply say: The first thing is for you to know God and to know about him, although that is very emphatically stated at the beginning: "Hear, O Israel, the Lord our God is one Lord." First you have to know about him, to have opened your ears and eyes for him, so that he comes into your life's field of vision. But then it goes farther: Because of that you must love him with your whole heart, and there is something moving about the way in which the Israelites in the Old Testament reading are taught as though by a good teacher: You must keep this continually in mind, because it is so easy to forget it; before you go to sleep, I will remind you about it once again; when you get up, when you are on your way, think of this, keep God's presence in your life close to your soul, so that it really penetrates it and becomes something within you. But then, when this happens, you will also notice that you must love this God and that this love alone sets all other love free, that when you learn to love God, you also see in people a reflection of God, and the people who are either distant or annoying or indifferent to you are neighbors, because they all belong to the same family of God and therefore are all your siblings, and all of them, in whom God's image shines, can be loved. And so we could say now that the Lord gives two answers, which, however, are only one, about the most important thing in life. The most important thing is that God is there. But, conversely, he also says: The most important thing in life is love. And if you do not find love, then you have lived in vain. And these two things are the same. For if God walks away from our life, then ultimately we cannot really love anymore. Then the Other becomes dangerous, weird, strange. We cannot like our own life anymore because it so often plays dirty tricks on us. Then love disappears, too. Knowing God and learning to love are one and the same thing; love is the most important thing, and if that is true, then God is the most important.

A similar line from the Holy Father's new book occurs to me, in which he tells about his years as a young priest and then describes what an experience it was for him to discover the love of young people and to recognize the beauty of their love. And how he recognized that the priest's task is to teach people to love. To love love and to teach them to love. For, indeed, we must learn it. After all, love does not consist only in the first great moment of being swept away. Love consists precisely in the patience of accepting one another, of becoming ever closer to one another from within. It consists in the fidelity of putting up with one another; it consists in walking together. Love, like the Gospel, is not sugar water, not comfortable, but, rather, a great challenge and, for this very reason, the purification and transformation and healing of our life, which leads us into the big picture.

Teaching and learning love. That is the real task of someone who speaks about God. And this is what we need most, for if we do not become loving in the right way, we separate ourselves from God and from ourselves, and life becomes dark and pointless.

Allow me in this connection to say something very concrete about the present situation: Very recently a document was issued by Rome (*Ordinatio sacerdotalis*, dated May 22, 1994), which surprised and hurt many of you because it seems to speak so harshly about man and seems to be so unloving. Indeed, in Jesus' life we always find both of these factors. On the one hand, the great, infinite understanding for each individual and, on the other hand, the message that challenges us all again and again, purifies us, and shows us the high road to being human in communion with God. Therefore we find in the Church, too, that both factors are always present: That the Lord's great challenge is continually present among us undistorted and with its demands undiminished, that he continually challenges us and leads and purifies and even defends us against ourselves and defends mankind against the tendency increasingly to let itself go and get lost. That the Church continually upholds the greatness of fidelity and perseverance and willingness to walk with Christ. But that at the same time, all of his personal kindness is still present. This is why both factors have to be in the Church: the word that continually imposes its challenge anew on our life and calls us and makes demands on us, and maybe even hurts, and the priest who personally does this, who brings it into the life of each individual and brings about the reconciliation between the big picture and the individual. Who enters into the agreement of the conscience with God and walks with it along the way. It is not a matter of driving people away or dismissing conscience but, rather, of not losing this joint effort. So that the Lord's challenge does not lose its greatness and so that at the same time through the ministry of the priest the Lord's personal kindness applies this word to us and brings it along with his kindness into our life in a way that is purifying and healing and helpful.

And this brings a third consideration into view. We need priests because we need God, and because we need him to be near, because the great word of his message has to become personal. This means that we need people who not only speak about God but also make him present. And, of course, that is too much to demand of anyone, because none of us can, so to speak, reach up to heaven and pull God down. No one is so great that he personally would be capable of putting him into our life. So He came to meet us. He himself became man and our priest, present among us. If we look to him, to Jesus Christ, then we see God. In the Lord, who stands before us fully displayed in the Gospel, the face of God, indeed, the Heart of God is right there in front of us. We must look to him, and then God is present. And by looking to him, who allowed himself to be crucified for us, we see love at the same time, we see that they are one: God and love. The most sublime thing about the life of the priest is that he has the privilege of being quite simply the servant of Jesus Christ, who in the mystery of the sacraments not only speaks about him but can give us his presence: "This is my Body", "this is my Blood", "I absolve you." We not only speak about him; in the sacrament he gives himself to us and is present and transforms our life, leads us anew again and again out of ourselves and beyond ourselves to him in his forgiveness and in the purification of his message.

Dear Franz, you have been allowed to carry out this ministry for forty years now. We are indeed traveling companions; we remember starting out in the early years, when the world was wide open and we thought that we could, as it were, build up the kingdom of God in it and transform it. Then come the years of battles and hardships, transformations, the complications of history, and now, too, this beautiful autumnal time with its colors, with the fruit that it bears, with its silent pause. We are grateful for all this. Of course we could now list a whole lot of things that you have done, but the essential thing, I think, is this: that with the grace of the priestly sacrament, you were able to give people again and again light from God. And that is indeed the most important thing in life. Not what we own or what we can do matters in the end, but the light that we have lowered down into others and that remains in them. It occurs to me that all of us have to do that, naturally. The nice thing about the priest is that he has the privilege of doing as his main job what we all actually have to try to do: to give each other light, to let each other sense God's closeness.

And so today we thank you, and we thank God who gave you this path as a gift. We ask him to lead us all, that we might continually recognize his goodness, even in things that seem dark to us, so that in this way, as we said today in the Church's prayer, freed again and again from the obstacles we meet along the way, we might "walk with great strides toward the joy that is promised us".

... Enlisted in Service so that Jesus' Mission Remains Effective

Twenty-Fifth Episcopal Jubilee of Doctor Hubert Luthe

Essen, 1994

First Reading: Isaiah 61:1–2, 10–11
Second Reading: 1 Thessalonians 5:16–24
Gospel: John 1:6–8, 19–28

Dear confreres in the episcopal and priestly ministry,
dear sisters and brothers in the Lord,
dear Bishop Luthe!

Twenty-five years ago, in the Cologne Cathedral on Gaudete Sunday, the Advent day of joy, you were consecrated a bishop. We encountered then the same readings that we heard again today in this hour, as an explanation of the day and as an explanation of your task. A quarter of a century later, with all its experiences, its sufferings, and its greatness, you hear them, we hear them anew and wonder:

"... in den Dienstgenommen, damit die Sendung Jesu wirksam bleibt", for the twenty-fifth episcopal jubilee of Bishop Dr. Hubert Luthe in the Essen cathedral on December 14, 1994, *Ruhrwort*, no. 50 (December 17, 1994). [B 990]

What do they tell us in this hour of remembrance, meditation, and new beginning?

"The Spirit of the Lord God is upon me, because the LORD has anointed me" (Is 61:1). In the synagogue in Nazareth, Jesus presented this verse from the prophet Isaiah to his fellow countrymen and to all generations as an explanation of his mission. And because episcopal ordination means being grafted onto Christ's mission so that it might continue and remain present down through the ages, we can see in this verse also an interpretation of episcopal consecration. "The Spirit of the Lord God is upon me, because the LORD has anointed me." In the ancient signs of anointing, the liturgy represents the gift of the Spirit. But at this point we start to ask: Is that really true? Does he rest upon me? Is he there? Do I have him? Can I simply call on him? And in doing so, we need not be thinking at all of the slogans popular in circles that are critical of the Church, who are of the opinion that nobody is so godforsaken as the hierarchy and, to express that view, have coined the disparaging term *Amtskirche* ["official Church"], as though bishops and priests lived in a Church different from that of other believers. We have only to think of our own experiences of how dark, how oppressive, how difficult it can be when a word of instruction is expected of us or when a decision is required. How grateful we are then that we can go to our brothers and sisters and confer with them and together with them pray for the Spirit. Does this then belie the word of the Lord, the word of the liturgy, or have we just interpreted it incorrectly? If we go back to the original texts of the Old and New Testaments, we can ascertain that the verb "rests", the idea that the Spirit of the Lord "rests" on me, is not in them. This was only interpolated into some modern translations. And in fact, resting, simple existence, is not the way the

Spirit works. He is not something that I have, in the way that I own a coin, for instance, or have furniture or pictures. He is not something that is had at all, that I could regard as my property, and that might be added to other qualities of mine as an additional one. The Spirit is not *property* that rests; rather, the Spirit is the power of transformation. He tears us away from our habits in life, from our contentment with ourselves; he burns and consumes, he purifies and renews. We do not have the Spirit; he takes us. He summons us and sets us on our way. Receiving the Spirit means being given over to him, so that we become servants of Jesus Christ; it means being taken away from ourselves so that we might be there for him, the Other. And so in fact we then read also in the next sentence: "He has sent me" (Is 61:1). Receiving the Spirit in the holy sacrament means being sent, being there so that Christ might send me wherever he wants, even though I may have had quite different plans.

But with that, something further has already become clear. The Spirit is storm and fire. But not just any storm, not just general excitement that tries to destroy in order to make something different, not just any vague theory for improving the world. The Spirit has a name: he is the Spirit of Jesus Christ. He comes from him and leads to him. Saint Paul the apostle said this unambiguously in the First Letter to the Corinthians: No one can say the words, "Christ is Lord" except in the Holy Spirit (1 Cor 12:3). By that he means that the proof of the Spirit is the Church's profession of faith in her Lord. The Spirit does not lead somewhere; he leads to Christ. And Christ leads us to each other, so that with each other we become his Body, the Holy Church. Saint Luke elaborated on this even more in the Acts of the Apostles with the picture of the early Church, and in terms of it he gave four standards that show the nature of the abiding Pentecost event and of the Spirit who comes again and again and transforms and builds. He depicts the early Church in these words: "They held steadfastly to the apostles' teaching and fellowship, to the breaking of the bread and to the prayers" (Acts 2:42). These are the standards by which we recognize the Spirit even today. And perhaps we should reverse the sequence in order to understand it better: they held, they hold steadfastly to the prayers. The first thing is God. Church comes about, and true communion or fellowship comes about, only when we turn to him in prayer and let him guide us. And only when this happens, when people begin to look away from themselves and become people who pray together, call on God, and begin to listen to God, can the breaking of the bread occur. Then he gives himself, gives us his Body, and leads us to one another, so that in the one bread we become one with him and with one another. And this is how fellowship is formed. And in all this our eyes and our hearts are opened, so that we recognize that the simple teaching of the apostles that they received from the Lord is the true light of this world. Not just some exciting new theories, but this word that they gave us for all times to take on our way, this message that remains truly ever-new and inexhaustible. Dear Hubert, in this hour you could give a commentary on these words based on twenty-five years filled with life and sorrows and joys. Here we simply want to thank you for accepting your ministry on these terms, for carrying out this humble service of the Spirit of God in our time. That you do not seek noisy displays or headlines but the essential, the center: leading us to one another in prayer and thus coming to one another in the breaking of the bread and the new life in the light of the apostles' teaching. We are grateful that you lead to the center, that you seek, not what is interesting, but what is essential. For that is the only possible source of what is saving.

But let us return again to the Old Testament reading. It speaks—as we just heard—about the gift of the Spirit, about mission. And this mission is described with various verbs: bind up, proclaim, comfort. But the first verb, which at the same time sums up everything, is *evaggelizesthai*, to be an evangelist, to tell good news, to bring good tidings. This word of the prophet, *evaggelizesthai*, waited for Jesus, so to speak. Only in him did it acquire its full meaning and all its greatness. He is the good news. And being a bishop is nothing other than being an evangelist of Jesus Christ, bringing this news into the world, which is full of grief and full of darkness and full of questions. And we just heard the echo to this summons in the First Letter to the Thessalonians, where Paul says to the Thessalonians what he says to the Philippians, what he says to us all: "Rejoice always" (1 Thess 5:16). And again we hesitate. Is that possible? Is that not just silly romanticism? Paul was a great man of suffering, and everything difficult that life can offer happened to him. When he says this, it is not the result of a superficial daydream; this is about something deeper. Today there is polling about happiness, research into contentment, perhaps because both have become so rare. They want to make clear what it actually is to be happy and how to go about it. And the researchers tell us quite frankly that they do not know. That they have not identified the key, that at any rate they know one thing: where happiness does not come from. That happiness is not based on possessions or career or success, that it does not appear when I learn that I have won the lottery or have become something. That it is something quite different that enters into my life mysteriously, as

though unbidden. The bishop, a successor of the apostles, is therefore in fact not a messenger of happiness who
brings money, offers possessions, or has prescriptions for
transforming the world into an earthly paradise. He has
none of those things. And Peter already said this to the
crippled man at the Temple gate: "I have no silver and
gold" (Acts 3:6). And by that he means all property in
general. But what does he have, then; what can he bring?
Joy. And now we ask once again: What is that, actually?
And someone could say: Joy is when love happens to me
and reaches deep down into my life. It lets me know that
I am not alone, that I am accepted, reliably and forever.
Then someone else might say: But how fragile is that?
After all, the person who gives me this experience can die
or be taken away from me. And he may say: No, joy is
hope. For we men live toward the future, and this life
is good only if a light goes ahead of me, if I know that
the future is good; for that means being able to hope. And
yet another might say: But if that is deception, what then?
And he would answer: No, only truth is joy. Only that
can be a reliable foundation. And then we will ask again:
Is truth, then, joy? Or is it not rather sad? Is it good to be a
man? Is the world really good? The ancients said: Knowledge makes you sad. The more a man learns, the more
sadness he knows and the less he can be happy.

And today if we look this world in the face, how many
terrible things we learn day after day that depress us, discourage us, and very seriously raise the question: Can
truth be good? Is the world good, then? And if it is not
good, if the truth is not good, is not all our joy just a passing will-o'-the-wisp that quickly dissolves? As this point
Jesus Christ meets us. For if we see him, then we see right
through all the affliction and all the terrible things in the
world to the Sacred Head surrounded with a crown of

thorns and the unveiled face of the truth, and we see that it is good. That he who is the Truth because he is God is a lover—so much so that he became a man of suffering with us. And if this really dawns on us and shines into our souls, if I really recognize from his face that, yes, despite all the terrible things, the Truth is good, then I also know that it is good to be a man, that life is beautiful. Then I have hope. For even if I am still far away from the complete encounter with him, the light reliably shines ahead of me, and love ultimately does not deceive. And I think that precisely in our time we need to hear this message anew, for the doubts about whether we can be happy, whether truth is good, whether it is right to be a man, are becoming almost insoluble. We can begin over again only if he encounters us and it becomes evident again in light of him that truth is liberating, great, and good. He is redemption because he gives the answer to the affliction of our doubts. A message that of course is ever new, for men will repeatedly dip into the abyss of their doubts and their sorrowful experiences. And only by getting through them can we repeatedly recognize the greatness of what it means that he, the Son of God, is a lover and a suffering man with us. He is the torch of hope that goes ahead of us, and with him we can walk confidently.

Being an evangelist. This is the task of the successors to the apostles, to proclaim true joy, redemptive joy. And a bishop will be more able to do this, the more the light of Christ has penetrated into his own heart, the more profoundly he is filled with it. All of us, even and especially we bishops, experience dark hours. But the hand of the Lord that was laid upon us does not let us go. And therefore the narrow, perhaps sometimes faint beam of light does not disappear. It remains, and it will shine all the brighter for us, the more we also show it to others.

Dear Hubert, on this day our wish for you is that the light of Jesus Christ may shine ever more deeply in you. That it will fill you and that, from this fullness, you can bring to men the word that they need, that we all need. Our wish for you is that you will be able to say more and more, out of an ever deeper assurance: Rejoice always.

On the Ministry of the Bishop

Thirtieth Episcopal Jubilee of
Friedrich Cardinal Wetter

Munich, 1998

Gospel: John 21:15–19

"We give you thanks that you have held us worthy to be in your presence and minister to you." So we pray in the Second Canon of the Mass with the Christians from the first centuries who created this Eucharistic Prayer; so we pray with the people of the Old Covenant, for the text goes back to the Book of Deuteronomy, which describes the vocation of the tribe of Levi as standing in the Lord's presence and serving him. When the early Church included this verse in the Eucharistic Prayer, she meant to announce the unity of God's history, the intrinsic unity of the Old and the New Covenant, but at the same time the newness of the priesthood that now comes from communion with Christ, from his standing in the presence of the Father, and from his submission, from the liturgy of his life, suffering, and Resurrection. In terms of today's reading, we

"Vom Dienst des Bischofs", for the thirtieth episcopal jubilee of Friedrich Cardinal Wetter, Archbishop of Munich and Freising, in the Liebfrauendom, Munich, on June 28, 1998, in *Priester aus innerstem Herzen* (Munich, 2007), 304–8; previously in *KlBl* 78 (1998): 152–53. [B 1079]

will think, too, about how Christ restored to us through
faith the ability to stand upright and takes away from us
the crippling effect of sin, which cuts off our path to God;
how Christ frees us from the distortion that keeps us from
seeing beyond material things, from seeking and finding
the face of God.

"We give you thanks that you have held us worthy to
be in your presence and minister to you." Today this sentence has a special resonance. We thank God for the thirty
years of episcopal ministry that he has granted to you, dear
Cardinal Friedrich, and so to us. We thank the Lord for
this vocation and for accompanying you on the way, for no
one can make himself a bishop and no one can perform
this ministry in Christ's place without his constant accompaniment, which is always an accompaniment of forgiveness, too. But we also thank you yourself for saying Yes
again and again to this task, for carrying out the bishop's
ministry cheerfully and kindly, but also decisively and
firmly, for walking ahead of Christ's flock that has been
entrusted to you.

A bishop—what actually is that? The word is an Anglo-
Saxon form of the Greek word *episkopos*, which first simply means overseer and in the pre-Christian world was
used for various functions. The early Church gave it a new
meaning, connected it with the word *shepherd*, and thus
placed it in the great line of biblical tradition, in which
God himself appears as the Shepherd of Israel. He becomes
quite close and quite practical in Jesus, who does not live
on the sheep but for them. The true shepherd is the one
who gives his life for his own. The Shepherd God himself became the lamb in Christ, the sacrificial Lamb. In
the Incarnation, he pursued the lost sheep even into the
thornbush of the Cross, so as to take this sheep—us, mankind, human nature—onto his shoulders and to carry it

home. Thus the initially rather unsympathetic word *episko-pos*, overseer, was transformed in the direction of respon-sibility, love, service, and self-giving. Being an *episkopos*, a bishop, means to place oneself into this responsibility and this mind of Christ. The sheep remain Christ's sheep. Thus, the Lord says quite clearly to Peter in today's Gos-pel: Feed my sheep. Not yours—they do not become Peter's sheep; they remain Christ's sheep. The Church is not our Church, but Christ's Church. Being a shepherd means being a trustee. Safeguarding God's property, caring for it, fighting for it, so that others do not seize the Church and the people in her. So that our ideas and wishes do not rule, but, rather, so that his light stays in it and his way opens up again and again.

Today's Gospel gives us a few additional aids to under-standing the meaning of episcopal ministry. The com-mission given to Peter, every pastoral commission in the Church, is connected with the question: Do you love me? Not: Are you a skilled administrator? Are you a great speaker? Do you enjoy power? Rather: Do you love me? It is a service that is performed for Him, and only if He really matters to us more than our own life can we also place our lives at His disposal for it. A man who is just looking for an interesting profession, who seeks power, financial support, or himself, cannot do it right. Do you love me: in this question the Lord uses two different words for "love": ἀγαπᾶν and φιλεῖν. The first is the new love that comes from God and goes to God. The second is in a certain respect something very human: the love of friendship. In the Gospel of John, Jesus describes his dis-ciples several times as his friends. A disciple is someone who is a friend. And only someone who is a friend can be a shepherd. Only with the third question does Jesus ask about the love of friendship, this very special and also

human association with him, and only with it do the question and the commission arrive at their goal. Above and
beyond the love of God that binds us to Jesus, the bishop
must in a very human way also have become Jesus' friend
and have grown fond of him. He must be a friend, which
means to want the same things he wants and not to want
the same things. He must, so to speak, share his preferences, his choice, his taste in life with him. Confronted
with this question, again and again we will be abashed.
And we will sense the inadequacy of all our love, but also
the magnanimity of Jesus, who embraces our weakness,
accepts it, and in spite of everything makes us his friends.
Precisely from the gift of this magnanimity grows the
friendship that helps to lead others to Christ, too, and to
teach them to love him.

Then there is the commission to feed the sheep. Again
the Lord uses two different words: βόσκειν and ποιμαίνειν.
The one means providing, giving the flock what it needs,
leading them to pastures, to "the living waters", giving life.
The other means protecting and leading, going ahead
and guiding, deciding and also reprimanding. This will
remind us of the Acts of the Apostles, in which the apostles, while instituting the new ministry of the seven, very
precisely formulate their own task: prayer and the ministry of the word (Acts 6:4). Prayer—this means first and
foremost the celebration of the Eucharist and then, of
course, praying in general and leading others to pray.
God must be continually brought into the world, and
the world must be placed before God, otherwise it not
only loses its sense of direction, it loses the source of life
and staggers into the darkness. Therefore the ministry of
the Eucharist and of prayer in general is not at all a special activity of a few pious souls; rather, it concerns the
world and its life and its survival. Ministry of the word:

the message that gives direction and meaning to life has to be spoken. Often it goes against the stream, against the things that seem plausible and flatter the ear—in the days of the prophets, in the time of Christ, and in every era. We thank you, dear Bishop Friedrich, for performing this ministry courageously and decisively, with heart and understanding, and consistently leading the fight for life, the fight for biological life and the fight for the deeper sources of life. Ministry of the word—this involves not just speaking; it means deciding, leading, protecting, reprimanding. Unpleasant things are part of it, too. When it is a matter of defending goods—like protecting the environment, protecting the consumer, protecting our rights—then we understand this necessity without further explanation. But because today we often do not regard the faith as a good at all, speaking up for it can easily appear to us to be a restriction of our freedom, as an inappropriate curtailment of our rights. And yet our rights deteriorate if the source of justice, the word of God, runs dry.

Finally, there is a third instruction that the Gospel gives us. It is the prophecy about martyrdom. "When you are old, you will stretch out your hands, and another will fasten your belt for you and carry you where you do not wish to go" (Jn 21:18).

This saying about stretching out his hands reminds us once again of the Second Eucharistic Prayer: "He stretched out his hands as he endured his Passion." Stretching out hands is a reference to arms spread on the Cross—a prophecy that Peter will die on the cross like his Master and that in precisely this way he will have the distinction of being conformed to the supreme Shepherd, who lays down his life for his sheep. The early Church, however, which included this saying in the Canon, sees in it also a profound interpretation of the mystery of the Cross. The outstretched hands are, first, signs of suffering, of loss of freedom, of being bound by others. But at the same time they are the posture of prayer, the posture of adoration—of "standing in your presence" and of serving you and yours. And finally they are the great gesture of embracing: "I, when I am lifted up from the earth, will draw all men to myself" (Jn 12:32). They are the expansive gesture of love with which Jesus brings us into communion with his life. Divine worship becomes love, divine love becomes human love. Peter with his outstretched arms is taken into the communion of the Cross, taken into the gesture of Jesus' open arms. From this perspective, being a bishop means: allowing yourself to be bound and led where you yourself do not want to go, allowing yourself to be taken and stretching out your hands in the presence of God and for mankind. Episcopal ministry must continually come from adoration and lead into love. It can never be lived out without a willingness to let oneself be controlled and led into unwanted suffering—into the communion of the Cross. Only in this way is the ministry of feeding the flock accomplished.

After the destruction of World War II, Cardinal Wetter continued the previous stages of the rebuilding of our cathedral in Munich by restoring to it the fullness of its history in the side chapels. In the center, our gaze is focused entirely on the Lord: it falls on the cross that Catholic young people promised to Cardinal Faulhaber and then delivered to Cardinal Wendel; then it goes down from the cross to the altar—from the image to the reality. For here it is perpetually Good Friday and at the same time Easter: the Lord steps through the veil to the Holy of Holies and stands before the Father interceding for us, stretches out his hands to him and to us, draws us all in the mystery of the Eucharist into his arms and thus to one another. But this center, which stands there in grandeur and purity, is rightly surrounded in turn by a wreath of chapels, in which the whole history of the faith and prayer of our home is present—the procession of history toward the Lord. Our ancestors pray with us, and we with them: what has returned here to the Munich Cathedral is not just a magnificent collection of art history; here there is more than history; here there is the presence of the communion of saints, of our common faith and common prayer in every age. As part of this return of the praying art of the Munich Cathedral, Peter's altar and Paul's have also returned, which Duke Wilhelm V had erected at the Benno Arch, so as to confirm the profession of faith implicit in the relics of Saint Benno and to explain why they were brought into the cathedral. It is supposed to be an acknowledgment of the two princes of the apostles, an acknowledgment of communion with Rome and a conscious acknowledgment of the Catholic faith. Today the two altars are found in more modest locations in the side chapels, as part of the whole great procession of saints that leads to the Lord. Yet their message has remained the same. We profess our faith in the communion of saints and thus know that we are in communion with Christ; we acknowledge Peter and his successor and thus know that we are in the living unity of the Church of all places and all times. We thank you, dear confrere, for helping us to practice this faith as part of the one flock of Christ that is entrusted to Peter, and we ask the Lord to continue to bless your ministry.

The Church Lives by Abiding with Christ and Standing by Him

Silver Episcopal Jubilee of Cardinal Meisner, Auxiliary Bishop Dick, and Auxiliary Bishop Plöger

Cologne, 2000

Gospel: John 15:1–8

Dear Cardinal Meisner!
Dear Auxiliary Bishops Dick and Plöger!
Dear brothers and sisters in the Lord!

The liturgy of this Easter Sunday, on which we observe with grateful joy the silver episcopal jubilee of Cardinal Meisner, Auxiliary Bishop Dick, and Auxiliary Bishop Plöger, places before us one of the great images for the mystery of Christ that the Gospel of John gives us, bread—light—wellspring—grapevine. The grapevine is an image

---

"Die Kirche lebt vom Bleiben bei Christus, vom Stehen zu ihm ...", homily for the silver episcopal jubilee of Joachim Cardinal Meisner, Auxiliary Bishop Dick, and Auxiliary Bishop Plöger in the Cologne cathedral on May 21, 2000, in *Priester aus innerstem Herzen* (Munich, 2007), 309–12; previously in *KlBl* 80 (2000): 147–48; under the title "Bleiben und Reifen—Formen christlicher Existenz", *L'Osservatore romano* (German ed.), no. 22 (June 2, 2000): 12. [B 1149]

for the exquisite character of creation, for the festivity and the joy that it provides. It immediately became an image of election, of the story of the love that God seeks with mankind, and thus an image of the People of God.

The grapevine is smaller than the other trees, the teachers in Israel used to say; but by its fruit it surpasses them all. Thus the grapevine became an image for Christ, an image for the unity between Christ and the Church, an image for the unity of Creator and creation, an image of the promise: God is everything to everyone [1 Cor 15:28]. And of course in this the Eucharistic mystery shines through, in which the Lord gives us himself as the fruit of the vine, gives us the sacred wine of his love, of his life.

Standing by Christ

All the great themes of the faith—creation, Christ, Church, sacrament—are intertwined in this image, which thus becomes also a parable for the priestly ministry in being with Christ and for Christ, in standing up in the Church and for the Church, in going toward his kingdom. Therefore, on this day it is addressed in a particular way to you, dear confreres, who today are looking back on twenty-five years of episcopal activity in the Church of God.

If you read the Gospel (Jn 15:1–8) carefully, you can tell that it is constructed like a fugue with three themes that intertwine more and more and thus interpret the message of the grapevine: abiding—pruning—fruit—these are the three basic terms of this parable; just in the eight verses of the Gospel reading the word "abide" occurs six times, and so in it we heard the basic theme that Jesus intended to present to us with this image—the basic theme that is developed and deepened in the two other accompanying themes.

"Abiding" therefore is the first basic term that stands in front of us like a signpost for us and also for the priestly ministry: only the one who abides lives with the grapevine and stays alive. "Abiding"—that is certainly not one of the favorite words of our time. Quite the contrary— what counts is change, things that are new and different, mobility that does not let itself be pinned down but is able to detach itself quickly from former things and to turn to changed circumstances.

And yet: without abiding, there is no growth; without connection, there is no progress. Where there is no connection, there are only torn-off branches that are doomed to wither and belong to the world of the dead, even though they still appear ever so strong and alive. The Church lives by abiding with Christ, standing by him, even if that does not seem modern. "Do you too want to leave me?" the Lord asks us. And you, dear brothers, answered along with Peter: Lord, to whom should we go? You alone have the words of eternal life (Jn 6:67–68). We stand by you; we do not let the winds of the moment bend us and drive us away. You are the root that supports and gives life. You, O Lord, said: No one will snatch from my hand those whom my Father has given to me (Jn 10:28–29). Therefore, we ask you, Lord, let us not be snatched from your hand. Let not the faithful whom you have entrusted to us be snatched from your hands. Let not the wolves tear to pieces your sheep, who after all are your flock.... "Abiding"—dear Cardinal Joachim, in difficult times in the German Democratic Republic you experienced what that means: abiding. You did not bow to the dictatorship. You made no false compromises, for you knew: only Christ abides. And if we abide with him, even in adverse winds, then we stand aright. And in doing so, you also had in view the other, the ecclesial dimension of this abiding.

Peter spoke the word about abiding, and we pronounce it with him. Another part of abiding in the grapevine is precisely abiding in the great communion of saints, for whose cohesiveness Peter stands.

Ministry of Pruning

When we read the acts of the martyrs of the century that has just passed, we repeatedly encounter this: knowledge about the great communion of the Church, knowledge about Peter as the seal of unity supported people in the confusion: it was for them a signpost pointing to where the whole grapevine is and a sign that all the parts of the grapevine belong to one another. Only in the whole, in the one grapevine, do we also abide with Christ.

Since you came to the West, your witness of standing firm and abiding assumed other forms that demanded no less of the courage of humility. A saying of Saint Ambrose comes to mind; he had to fight quite similar battles: "Since the Church has been living under Christian emperors, she has no doubt grown in power and wealth, but has become weaker in moral strength" (*In Luc* IX, 32). How true that is today, too! "Abiding" is not something static and comfortable. Part of abiding is the ongoing service of pruning. Today in this connection, we find it very easy to mouth the remark about the "Ecclesia semper reformanda" [The Church must always be reformed] because we are always thinking about others and about the structures that are to be changed, especially far away in Rome. But pruning means in reality something very personal and, if we understand it correctly, shifts us directly to the body.

Here a remark that Saint Augustine made in his sermons on the psalms comes to mind; in it we can hear the autobiographical element, the retrospective view of his own life: "Before such people enlist in God's service, they enjoy delightful freedom in the world, like grapes or olives hanging there.... Any who approach God's service must know that they have come to the winepresses. They will be bruised, trampled, and squeezed, not so that they may perish in this world, but to ensure that they trickle down into God's storage vats" (*Exposition of Psalm 83*, 1).

You too, dear brothers, in the twenty-five years of your episcopal ministry, have certainly had in abundance this experience of being bruised and trampled. Otherwise, we cannot become mature wine. This applies to all of us, priests, bishops, and laity, each in his own way. In order for ripe fruit to develop, rain, storms, and sunshine are necessary. And in order for the fruit to serve its purpose, we have to go through the winepress of suffering, whether we like it or not.

Christ himself went ahead of us: on the Cross, as God's sacred cluster, he allowed himself to be pressed, and so he offers himself to us down through the ages in the Eucharistic chalice as the wine of God's love. And again and again Eucharist comes about only by gathering and pressing the grapes, through their fermentation and maturation, in which the whole Church must become good wine and thus one with Christ, the grapevine that supports and enlivens us all.

With the saying about pruning, the third leitmotif of this Gospel has now been introduced: the theme of the fruit for which the grapevine is intended. The parable silently contrasts the grapevine that puts forth leaves only and the grapevine that is pruned and thus bears fruit. A Church that produces many papers but no vocations of persons who give themselves entirely to the Lord is a grapevine that puts forth leaves but no grapes. Papers pass away; words resound.

Faith Becomes Love

Structures become outdated—but the Lord looks for fruit that lasts. God does not want dead, artificial things that ultimately are thrown away: he wants living things, life. The grapevine is Christ; along with him the grapevine is his Church, the People of God, which grows on its pilgrimage through the ages. But the remark once made by the Jewish philosopher of religion Philo of Alexandria—a contemporary of Jesus—still applies also: "The soul is the most sacred vineyard" (*Somn* II, 172f.). The Lord waits for the grapevine to set down roots in the soul and, through all the prunings, to bring forth the fruit of faith, hope, and love.

He waits for men who make themselves available, not just for a more or less long-term experiment, but entirely and unconditionally with their life, full-time, who also allow him to lead them where they actually did not want to go. He waits for our Yes—that is the real fruit for which he created us.

When faith becomes the force that supports a person and the person relies entirely on God, then faith automatically becomes love. The great figures of faith—from Paul via Francis of Assisi down to Maximilian Kolbe and Mother Teresa—show us this. Where faith deteriorates, love also grows cold and selfishness increases. However, when Christ dwells in our souls, his love is enkindled there, too, and the face of the earth is renewed through the love in which God himself enters into this world.

"You crown the year with your bounty", it says in Psalm 65:11. Dear brothers, twenty-five years of episcopal ministry are a sort of harvest festival of thanksgiving. In looking back on these twenty-five years, with all their toils and their blessings, we sense it: Yes, you crown the

years of ministry with your goodness. On this retrospective day, the Church of Cologne thanks you, the Church
of God thanks you, and the Lord himself thanks you for
your fidelity in abiding, for your patience in the maturing
processes, and for the fruit that you bring him.

With you, we all thank God for the gift of fidelity, for
perseverance with the Lord and for the joy of faith that
you pass on in the midst of all tribulation. And we pray to
the good Lord that he will grant you again and again the
crown of his goodness. We ask him to help you to keep
going, so that your ministry, too, might continue to be
blessed and to produce abundant fruit unto eternal life.

Bringing Christ to the People and the People to Christ

Golden Priestly Jubilee of Monsignor
Georg Schuster, Pastor Emeritus Alfons Karpf,
Pastor Emeritus Ludwig Radlmaier,
Georg Warmedinger, S.T.D., and
Pastor Emeritus Johann Warmedinger

Munich-Pasing, 2000

Gospel: Matthew 16:13–19

A half century has passed since your names were called in the cathedral in Freising at the hour of your priestly ordination and you responded: *Adsum*—I am ready! This is the word with which Abraham placed himself at the service of God's call, as Samuel, the prophets of the Old Covenant, and finally the witnesses to Christ did after him down through the centuries. *Adsum*—I am ready, Lord, do with me what you will. Send me. I want to be your

"Christus zu den Menschen, die Menschen zu Christus bringen", for the golden priestly jubilee of Msgr. Georg Schuster, Pastor Emeritus Alfons Karpf, Pastor Emeritus Ludwig Radlmaier, Georg Warmedinger, S.T.D., and Pastor Emeritus Johann Warmedinger, in the parish church of Maria Schutz in Munich-Pasing on July 2, 2000, in *Priester aus innerstem Herzen* (Munich, 2007), 313–18; previously in *KlBl* 80 (2000): 175–77. [B 1153]

instrument. It was a Holy Year then, too, and it really was true that the Lord opened the door for us. Behind us lay the dark years of the war that had devastated Europe and in particular our land. Germany was excluded from the community of nations; hunger and privation of all sorts kept it down. During the Holy Year, the doors opened to a pilgrimage to Rome. We encountered the great family of the Catholic Church, in which there are no boundaries, and the Church welcomed us all with the power of reconciliation that comes from God. The isolation had burst open, and we could see that ultimately Christ was the one who was leading the nations beyond all those terrible events and thereby was also bringing our people back together again.

Behind us lay the dictatorship of the Third Reich; ahead of us and beside us, on our borders in the middle of Germany, stood the power of the Soviet Union, bristling with weapons and ready to pounce. We scarcely dared to hope that it would halt at those borders. But in our midst stood Jesus Christ, and we knew that from him—and only from him—salvation could come for all: the empires of men, which were built contrary to God's will, proved to be empires of inhumanity. The true kingdom of men and of humanity could come about only in the kingdom of God, from Christ, who is the kingdom of God in person. To him you said your *Adsum* with the passion and determination of your hearts after all that you had experienced: Here I am, Lord—take me into your service for the coming of your kingdom. You, dear friends, held high the flame of this Yes in the dark and bright hours of these fifty years, in storms as well as in good times, and we thank you for that at this time.

The Gospel that we just heard (Mt 16:13–19) shows us that there are two ways of knowing Christ and encountering him. On the one hand, there are "men", the people who encountered Christ once, heard him preach, experienced a miracle, maybe even accompanied him for a stretch, and for a moment were enthusiastic about him, but then went their way. And on the other hand, there are the Twelve whom the Lord addresses as "you": "But what do you say about me?" "Men" perceived something about him; for them this Jesus is a great figure like the prophets and John the Baptist. You admire such figures, maybe you learn a thing or two from them also, but they do not change your way of living and dying after all. Christ is great, but, for those "men", just one of the many greats. The disciples know him in a different, deeper way. They share his life. They begin to become acquainted with him from within. They touch him, not only with their hands, but with their hearts. By way of comparison, you might think of the story of the woman with the hemorrhage who pushes her way through the crowd to him and touches him in order to be healed. "Who touched me?" Jesus asks. To the disciples, the question seems senseless, since people are pressing on him from all sides. But here another touch has taken place—the woman's faith touched Jesus' heart and from it received healing. It is different and yet quite similar with the disciples: by sharing Jesus' life, they begin to come to an interior encounter with him. They experience the hidden center of the figure of Jesus—the fact that he lives entirely with the Father. In his prayer, they sense this inmost center of his being, from which all the rest comes. And so they really know him: "You are Christ, the Son of the living God."

You too, dear friends, have touched Christ from within. Early on, you joined your path with his and sought a deeper closeness to him. As Jesus turned around to the healed woman, so he turned around to you, placed his hand on you, and imparted to you something of his power, so that in his name you might administer the sacraments, forgive sins, and call down his presence. He sent you, not only to hand on his words, but also to make him known personally, just as you had the privilege of becoming acquainted with him. For fifty long years, you strove to communicate to people more of Christ than what "men" say; you strove to communicate Christ himself. You pointed him out so that people could see the face of God in his face (Jn 14:9) and thus learn to live. You did not let yourselves be dissuaded when the waters of unbelief rose again and increasingly became a dangerous flood. You put up with it when you were dismissed as old-fashioned and not with the times. You knew who really holds time in his hands. You were able to say: I know whom I have believed. And thank God, you also had the privilege of witnessing again and again the fact that from this Jesus whom you proclaimed healing power came to the people, who experienced that Jesus really is more than a prophet, namely, life itself (Jn 14:6).

You brought Christ to the people and the people to Christ and thus gave them the friendship that is decisive in every human life. But you knew also that no one can have Christ merely for himself alone. The Gospel is not written in the first person singular but in the first person plural: We do not pray "my Father" but, rather, "our Father"; not "give me my daily bread" but, rather, "our daily bread"; not "deliver me from the evil one and from all evils," but, rather, "deliver us". Christ lives in the Us of his Church, and only in this great Us of the children of God can we be with him. You knew, furthermore, that the Church is always recognizable by the sign in which she appeared at her birth on Pentecost: then, right in her first moment, the new People of God could be recognized by the fact that it speaks in all languages. It overcomes the divisions that tear human society apart. It is the unity that reconciles the diversity and leads them together in terms of Christ through the power of the Holy Spirit. The profession of faith expresses this connection by saying: The Church is catholic—she is the Church of all nations and cultures, she spans all times and places, embraces both the living and the dead.

Allow me to weave in a personal note: in this Holy Year, we have the privilege of experiencing in Rome in a thoroughly realistic way the reality of this catholicity. When I cross Saint Peter's Square, indeed, when I simply step out of the house, I encounter people from all countries, of all ages, from all walks of life. They recognize me as a bishop and are glad because a bishop is for them a successor of the apostles, a bearer of the mystery of the Church, a messenger of Jesus Christ. Again and again it is as though we are all old friends. No one is a stranger to the other. Through the faith, we are all acquainted. Through the Church, we all belong to each other. And what is most moving for me is the joy that is alive in all these encounters. What it says in the Acts of the Apostles (4:32): "They were of one heart and soul", is for the moment a reality that can be experienced. Faith produces joy, and the faith unites us over and above all boundaries: that is the experience of catholicity, the experience of the living Church, even today, especially today. And when I see the many young people who share in this feast of faith, then I know: the faith, the Church, has a future; indeed, she is the future. In the everyday routine of your fifty years as priests, all this very often looked much more troublesome. And yet you, too, continually experienced how you, with Christ and in the Church, had the privilege of giving people the essential gifts that we need in order to live. The Church gives us the faith and consequently friendship with God and knowledge about where we come from, where we are going, what we live for, and how we should live. She teaches us to pray. Alone, we do not know how we ought to speak with God (Rom 8:26), but we can pray along with the people who have prayed before us and for us and, thus, find the relationship with God that simultaneously makes possible the relationship with those who have gone before us and still remain close to us in the Lord. From faith we receive the liturgical feast as a gift—we are experiencing this today. Feasts at which God does not appear may be splendid, but something or other is lacking in the end. Only the feast in which heaven and earth harmonize, in which God's Yes to us is palpable—only this is a complete feast in which we become certain that God was right when he said at the end of his work of creation: It is good, it is very good. If we experience the true feast, then above and beyond all the troubles and difficulties we can say: Yes, it is good that the world exists, that I exist, that we exist— and this is the joy that we men are constantly on the move pursuing. In the sacraments, the Church accompanies us from birth to death. There is Baptism as affiliation in God's family; there is the Eucharist, in which he personally gives us himself; there is the sacrament of Reconciliation, which renews us again and again; there is the sacrament that assists us in the hour of sickness; there are the two sacraments that are the foundation of the Church's essential states of life: Matrimony and Holy Orders. As pastors, you have accompanied people in all the seasons of life, in their hours of joy and in their hours of grief and suffering. You have helped people to live and to die. So you have many friends, on this side of the threshold of death and beyond it. When someday you knock at the door of heaven, you do not need to be afraid. There are so many people there who are waiting for you, who thank you: people to whom you showed the way. Yes, you will not be alone when you arrive. At this moment, I would like to thank you in the name of the Church, in the name of so many people, for the service of faith and life that you have given to countless people during this half century.

We find Christ in the Church, and by her nature she is a Pentecostal-Catholic Church. But you gave the people two more additional, very practical signs for the Church: where Peter is, there is Church, and where Mary is, there is Church. In the Gospel, we heard it from the mouth of Jesus: On this rock I will build my Church (Mt 16:18). In John's Gospel, we hear it again: Feed my lambs, feed my sheep (21:15–17). Christ gave us the successors of Peter as guarantees of unity, as reliable signs for the location of his Church. Of course the competencies of men, of popes, are not what sustain the Church. That was already the case with Peter, and in various ways it is always the case: God's power works precisely in the weakness of men; precisely because men could not do it by themselves, we see that Christ is at work in the successors to Peter, holding up his Church. That is why in the confusion of the ages we remain faithful to the Holy Father and thank him for the ministry of unity that he humbly and faithfully performs for all of us amid the contradictions of the world.

And there is Mary: as at Cana, through the ages she leads people to Christ. When the Christian faith was proclaimed to the native peoples of America, the message of the conquerors must have seemed dubious. But in the image of the Mother they were then able to recognize the Lord, too. The Mother—that was not the conquerors' religion; that was the kindly face of the true God that unveiled itself through her—in a unique way in Guadalupe. Mary became the icon of Christ for them; led by her, they could find him. And so it is down through all the ages. Anyone who says that Mary conceals Christ or leads away from him is speaking nonsense. In all centuries she brings forth Christ; through her maternal goodness, we learn to know and love him. That is why our ancestors were right to entrust our land [Bavaria] to her. That is why it was a good thing that here in Pasing—not least importantly through the initiative of Monsignor Schuster—the image of the Mother of God recovered its hereditary place at the heart of the locality, so that she encounters us right there in the middle of our daily routine and leads us to that heartfelt, uniquely saving contact with Christ.

As chance, or rather Providence, would have it, two dissimilar news items dominated the media on the same day. On the one hand, there was the decoding of the human genome, the mathematics of our body, so to speak; on the other hand, there was the publication of the secret of Fatima, in which the genetic structure of our souls becomes apparent in a certain way: Repent and believe in the Gospel (Mk 1:15); do whatever he tells you (Jn 2:5). Scientific knowledge about the blueprint of our physical life, however many questions it may still leave unanswered, is a wonderful gift. We may hope that as research continues it may also be of help in the fight against sickness and death.

But, of course, it cannot do away with pain and death. Unless we receive something deeper in addition to it, we always ultimately remain the losers in this battle; for in the end, despite everything, it will be for us as it was for the woman with the hemorrhage about whom we spoke at the beginning: after long years of suffering, she had to admit that she had spent all that she had to live on and yet had not been healed (Lk 8:43). Medicine does great things and is an important help in life, but above and beyond it, we still need a more profound healing in order to be able to undergo the mystery of suffering and death. This healing can come only from the touch of Jesus Christ. Him we seek, to him we go. Mary, the Mother, leads us to him. We ask her to commend us, in our final hour and continually, even now in the middle of our life, to him whom we have the privilege of calling the blessed fruit of her womb: Jesus Christ, our Lord.

APPENDIX

Letter of Pope Benedict XVI Proclaiming a Year for Priests on the 150th Anniversary of the *Dies Natalis* of the Curé of Ars

Dear Brother Priests,

On the forthcoming Solemnity of the Most Sacred Heart of Jesus, Friday, 19 June 2009—a day traditionally devoted to prayer for the sanctification of the clergy—I have decided to inaugurate a "Year for Priests" in celebration of the 150th anniversary of the *dies natalis* of John Mary Vianney, the patron saint of parish priests worldwide.[1] This Year, meant to deepen the commitment of all priests to interior renewal for the sake of a stronger and more incisive witness to the Gospel in today's world, will conclude on the same Solemnity in 2010. "*The priesthood is the love of the heart of Jesus*", the saintly Curé of Ars would often say.[2] This touching expression makes us reflect, first of all, with heartfelt gratitude on the immense gift which priests represent, not only for the Church, but also for humanity itself. I think of all those priests who quietly present Christ's words and actions each day to the faithful and to the whole world, striving to be one with the Lord in their

---

[1] He was proclaimed as such by Pope Pius XI in 1929.

[2] "*Le Sacerdoce, c'est l'amour du cœur de Jésus*" (in *Le curé d'Ars: Sa pensée—Son cœur*, presented by Fr. Bernard Nodet [Paris: Éditions Xavier Mappus, 1966], 98). The expression is also quoted in the *Catechism of the Catholic Church*, no. 1589.

thoughts and their will, their sentiments and their style of life. How can I not pay tribute to their apostolic labors, their tireless and hidden service, their universal charity? And how can I not praise the courageous fidelity of so many priests who, even amid difficulties and incomprehension, remain faithful to their vocation as "friends of Christ", whom he has called by name, chosen and sent?

I still treasure the memory of the first parish priest at whose side I exercised my ministry as a young priest: he left me an example of unreserved devotion to his pastoral duties, even to meeting his own death in the act of bringing viaticum to a gravely ill person. I also recall the countless confreres whom I have met and continue to meet, not least in my pastoral visits to different countries: men generously dedicated to the daily exercise of their priestly ministry. Yet the expression of Saint John Mary also makes us think of Christ's pierced Heart and the crown of thorns which surrounds it. I also think, therefore, of the countless situations of suffering endured by many priests, either because they themselves share in the manifold human experience of pain or because they encounter misunderstanding from the very persons to whom they minister. How can we not also think of all those priests who are offended in their dignity, obstructed in their mission and persecuted, even at times to offering the supreme testimony of their own blood?

There are also, sad to say, situations which can never be sufficiently deplored where the Church herself suffers as a consequence of infidelity on the part of some of her ministers. Then it is the world which finds grounds for scandal and rejection. What is most helpful to the Church in such cases is not only a frank and complete acknowledgment of the weaknesses of her ministers, but also a joyful and renewed realization of the greatness of God's gift, embodied in the splendid example of generous pastors, religious afire with love for God and for souls, and insightful, patient spiritual guides. Here the teaching and example of Saint John Mary Vianney can serve as a significant point of reference for us all. The Curé of Ars was very humble, yet as a priest he was conscious of being an immense gift to his people: "A good shepherd, a pastor after God's heart, is the greatest treasure which the good Lord can grant to a parish, and one of the most precious gifts of divine mercy."[3] He spoke of the priesthood as if incapable of fathoming the grandeur of the *gift* and *task* entrusted to a human creature: "O, how great is the priest!... If he realized what he is, he would die.... God obeys him: he utters a few words and the Lord descends from heaven at his voice, to be contained within a small host...."[4] Explaining to his parishioners the importance of the sacraments, he would say: "Without the sacrament of Holy Orders, we would not have the Lord. Who put him there in that tabernacle? The priest. Who welcomed your soul at the beginning of your life? The priest. Who feeds your soul and gives it strength for its journey? The priest. Who will prepare it to appear before God, bathing it one last time in the blood of Jesus Christ? The priest, always the priest. And if this soul should happen to die [as a result of sin], who will raise it up, who will restore its calm and peace? Again, the priest.... After God, the priest is everything!... Only in heaven will he fully realize what he is."[5] These words, welling up from the priestly heart of the holy pastor, might sound excessive. Yet they reveal the high esteem in which he held the sacrament

[3] Nodet, "Sacer doce", p. 101.
[4] Ibid., p. 97.
[5] Ibid., pp. 98–99.

of the priesthood. He seemed overwhelmed by a boundless sense of responsibility: "Were we to fully realize what a priest is on earth, we would die: not of fright, but of love.... Without the priest, the passion and death of our Lord would be of no avail. It is the priest who continues the work of redemption on earth.... What use would be a house filled with gold, were there no one to open its door? The priest holds the key to the treasures of heaven: it is he who opens the door: he is the steward of the good Lord; the administrator of his goods.... Leave a parish for twenty years without a priest, and they will end by worshiping the beasts there.... The priest is not a priest for himself, he is a priest for you."[6]

He arrived in Ars, a village of 230 souls, warned by his Bishop beforehand that there he would find religious practice in a sorry state: "There is little love of God in that parish; you will be the one to put it there." As a result, he was deeply aware that he needed to go there to embody Christ's presence and to bear witness to his saving mercy: "[Lord,] grant me the conversion of my parish; I am willing to suffer whatever you wish, for my entire life!" With this prayer he entered upon his mission.[7] The Curé devoted himself completely to his parish's conversion, setting before all else the Christian education of the people in his care. Dear brother priests, let us ask the Lord Jesus for the grace to learn for ourselves something of the pastoral plan of Saint John Mary Vianney! The first thing we need to learn is the complete identification of the man with his ministry. In Jesus, person and mission tend to coincide: all Christ's saving activity was, and is, an expression of his "filial consciousness" which from all eternity stands before

[6] Ibid., pp. 98–100.
[7] Ibid., p. 183.

the Father in an attitude of loving submission to his will. In a humble yet genuine way, every priest must aim for a similar identification. Certainly this is not to forget that the efficacy of the ministry is independent of the holiness of the minister; but neither can we overlook the extraordinary fruitfulness of the encounter between the ministry's objective holiness and the subjective holiness of the minister. The Curé of Ars immediately set about this patient and humble task of harmonizing his life as a minister with the holiness of the ministry he had received, by deciding to "*live*", physically, in his parish church: As his first biographer tells us: "Upon his arrival, he chose the church as his home. He entered the church before dawn and did not leave it until after the evening Angelus. There he was to be sought whenever needed."[8]

The pious excess of his devout biographer should not blind us to the fact that the Curé also knew how to "live" actively within the entire territory of his parish: he regularly visited the sick and families, organized popular missions and patronal feasts, collected and managed funds for charitable and missionary works, embellished and furnished his parish church, cared for the orphans and teachers of the "*Providence*" (an institute he founded); provided for the education of children; founded confraternities and enlisted lay persons to work at his side.

His example naturally leads me to point out that there are sectors of cooperation which need to be opened ever more fully to the lay faithful. Priests and laity together make up the one priestly people[9] and in virtue of their ministry priests live in the midst of the lay faithful, "that they may

---

[8] A. Monnin, *Il Curato d'Ars. Vita di Gian.Battista-Maria Vianney* (Turin: Marietti, 1870), 1:122.

[9] Cf. *Lumen Gentium*, 10.

lead everyone to the unity of charity, 'loving one another with mutual affection; and outdoing one another in sharing honor'" (Rom 12:10).[10] Here we ought to recall the Second Vatican Council's hearty encouragement to priests "to be sincere in their appreciation and promotion of the dignity of the laity and of the special role they have to play in the Church's mission.... They should be willing to listen to lay people, give brotherly consideration to their wishes, and acknowledge their experience and competence in the different fields of human activity. In this way they will be able together with them to discern the signs of the times."[11]

Saint John Mary Vianney taught his parishioners primarily by the witness of his life. It was from his example that they learned to pray, halting frequently before the tabernacle for a visit to Jesus in the Blessed Sacrament.[12] "One need not say much to pray well"—the Curé explained to them—"We know that Jesus is there in the tabernacle: let us open our hearts to him, let us rejoice in his sacred presence. That is the best prayer."[13] And he would urge them: "Come to communion, my brothers and sisters, come to Jesus. Come to live from him in order to live with him."[14] "Of course you are not worthy of him, but *you need him!*"[15] This way of educating the faithful *to the Eucharistic presence and to communion* proved most effective when they saw him celebrate the Holy Sacrifice of the

[10] *Presbyterorum Ordinis*, 9.

[11] Ibid.

[12] "Contemplation is a gaze of faith, fixed on Jesus. 'I look at him and he looks at me': this is what a certain peasant of Ars used to say to his holy Curé about his prayer before the tabernacle" (*Catechism of the Catholic Church*, no. 2715).

[13] Nodet, "Sacerdoce", p. 85.

[14] Ibid., p. 114.

[15] Ibid., p. 119.

Mass. Those present said that "it was not possible to find a finer example of worship.... He gazed upon the Host with immense love."[16] "All good works, taken together, do not equal the sacrifice of the Mass"—he would say— "since they are human works, while the Holy Mass is the work of God."[17] He was convinced that the fervor of a priest's life depended entirely upon the Mass: "The reason why a priest is lax is that he does not pay attention to the Mass! My God, how we ought to pity a priest who celebrates as if he were engaged in something routine!"[18] He was accustomed, when celebrating, also to offer his own life in sacrifice: "What a good thing it is for a priest each morning to offer himself to God in sacrifice!"[19]

This deep personal identification with the Sacrifice of the Cross led him—by a sole inward movement—from the altar to the confessional. Priests ought never to be resigned to empty confessionals or the apparent indifference of the faithful to this sacrament. In France, at the time of the Curé of Ars, confession was no more easy or frequent than in our own day, since the upheaval caused by the revolution had long inhibited the practice of religion. Yet he sought in every way, by his preaching and his powers of persuasion, to help his parishioners to rediscover the meaning and beauty of the sacrament of Penance, presenting it as an inherent demand of the Eucharistic presence. He thus created a *"virtuous"* circle. By spending long hours in church before the tabernacle, he inspired the faithful to imitate him by coming to visit Jesus with the knowledge that their parish priest would be there, ready to listen and offer forgiveness. Later, the growing numbers of penitents

---

[16] Monnin, *Il Curato*, 2:430ff.
[17] Nodet, "Sacerdoce", p. 105.
[18] Ibid.
[19] Ibid., p. 104.

from all over France would keep him in the confessional for up to sixteen hours a day. It was said that Ars had become "a great hospital of souls".[20] His first biographer relates that "the grace he obtained [for the conversion of sinners] was so powerful that it would pursue them, not leaving them a moment of peace!"[21] The saintly Curé reflected something of the same idea when he said: "It is not the sinner who returns to God to beg his forgiveness, but God himself who runs after the sinner and makes him return to him."[22] "This good Savior is so filled with love that he seeks us everywhere."[23]

We priests should feel that the following words, which he put on the lips of Christ, are meant for each of us personally: "I will charge my ministers to proclaim to sinners that I am ever ready to welcome them, that my mercy is infinite."[24] From Saint John Mary Vianney we can learn to put our unfailing trust in the sacrament of Penance, to set it once more at the center of our pastoral concerns, and to take up the "dialogue of salvation" which it entails. The Curé of Ars dealt with different penitents in different ways. Those who came to his confessional drawn by a deep and humble longing for God's forgiveness found in him the encouragement to plunge into the "flood of divine mercy" which sweeps everything away by its vehemence. If someone was troubled by the thought of his own frailty and inconstancy, and fearful of sinning again, the Curé would unveil the mystery of God's love in these beautiful and touching words: "The good Lord knows everything. Even before you confess, he already knows that you will sin

---

[20] Monnin, *Il Curato*, 2:293.
[21] Ibid., 2:10.
[22] Nodet, "Sacerdoce", p. 128.
[23] Ibid., p. 50.
[24] Ibid., p. 131.

again, yet he still forgives you. How great is the love of our God: he *even forces himself to forget the future*, so that he can grant us his forgiveness!"[25] But to those who made a lukewarm and rather indifferent confession of sin, he clearly demonstrated by his own tears of pain how "abominable" this attitude was: "I weep because you don't weep",[26] he would say. "If only the Lord were not so good! *But he is so good!* One would have to be a brute to treat so good a Father this way!"[27] He awakened repentance in the hearts of the lukewarm by forcing them to see God's own pain at their sins reflected in the face of the priest who was their confessor. To those who, on the other hand, came to him already desirous of and suited to a deeper spiritual life, he flung open the abyss of God's love, explaining the untold beauty of living in union with him and dwelling in his presence: "Everything in God's sight, everything with God, everything to please God.... How beautiful it is!"[28] And he taught them to pray: "My God, grant me the grace to love you as much as I possibly can."[29]

In his time the Curé of Ars was able to transform the hearts and the lives of so many people because he enabled them to experience the Lord's merciful love. Our own time urgently needs a similar proclamation and witness to the truth of Love: *Deus caritas est* (1 Jn: 4:8). Thanks to the word and the sacraments of Jesus, John Mary Vianney built up his flock, although he often trembled from a conviction of his personal inadequacy, and desired more than once to withdraw from the responsibilities of the parish ministry out of a sense of his unworthiness. Nonetheless, with

[25] Ibid., p. 130.
[26] Ibid., p. 27.
[27] Ibid., p. 139.
[28] Ibid., p. 28.
[29] Ibid., p. 77.

exemplary obedience he never abandoned his post, consumed as he was by apostolic zeal for the salvation of
souls. He sought to remain completely faithful to his own
vocation and mission through the practice of an austere
asceticism: "The great misfortune for us parish priests—he
lamented—is that our souls grow tepid"; meaning by this
that a pastor can grow dangerously inured to the state of
sin or of indifference in which so many of his flock are
living.[30] He himself kept a tight rein on his body, with
vigils and fasts, lest it rebel against his priestly soul. Nor
did he avoid self-mortification for the good of the souls in
his care and as a help to expiating the many sins he heard
in confession. To a priestly confrere he explained: "I will
tell you my recipe: I give sinners a small penance and the
rest I do in their place."[31] Aside from the actual penances
which the Curé of Ars practised, the core of his teaching
remains valid for each of us: souls have been won at the
price of Jesus' own blood, and a priest cannot devote himself to their salvation if he refuses to share personally in the
"precious cost" of redemption.

In today's world, as in the troubled times of the Curé
of Ars, the lives and activity of priests need to be distinguished by *a determined witness to the Gospel*. As Pope Paul
VI rightly noted, "modern man listens more willingly to
witnesses than to teachers, and if he does listen to teachers,
it is because they are witnesses."[32] Lest we experience existential emptiness and the effectiveness of our ministry be
compromised, we need to ask ourselves ever anew: "Are
we truly pervaded by the word of God? Is that word truly
the nourishment we live by, even more than bread and the
things of this world? Do we really know that word? Do we

[30] Ibid., p. 102.
[31] Ibid., p. 189.
[32] *Evangelii nuntiandi*, 41.

love it? Are we deeply engaged with this word to the point that it really leaves a mark on our lives and shapes our thinking?"[33] Just as Jesus called the Twelve to be with him (cf. Mk 3:14), and only later sent them forth to preach, so too in our days priests are called to assimilate that "new style of life" which was inaugurated by the Lord Jesus and taken up by the Apostles.[34]

It was complete commitment to this "new style of life" which marked the priestly ministry of the Curé of Ars. Pope John XXIII, in his Encyclical Letter *Sacerdotii nostri primordia*, published in 1959 on the first centenary of the death of Saint John Mary Vianney, presented his asceticism with special reference to the "three evangelical counsels" which the Pope considered necessary also for diocesan priests: "even though priests are not bound to embrace these evangelical counsels by virtue of the clerical state, these counsels nonetheless offer them, as they do all the faithful, the surest road to the desired goal of Christian perfection."[35] The Curé of Ars lived the "evangelical counsels" in a way suited to his priestly state. His *poverty* was not the poverty of a religious or a monk, but that proper to a priest: while managing much money (since well-to-do pilgrims naturally took an interest in his charitable works), he realized that everything had been donated to his church, his poor, his orphans, the girls of his "*Providence*",[36] his families of modest means. Consequently, he

[33] Benedict XVI, *Homily at the Chrism Mass*, 9 April 2009.

[34] Cf. Benedict XVI, *Address to the Plenary Assembly of the Congregation for the Clergy*, 16 March 2009.

[35] Paragraph 12.

[36] The name given to the house where more than sixty abandoned girls were taken in and educated. To maintain this house he would do anything: "*J'ai fait tous les commerces imaginables*", he would say with a smile (Nodet, "Sacerdoce', p. 214).

"was rich in giving to others and very poor for himself".[37] As he would explain: "My secret is simple: give everything away; hold nothing back."[38] When he lacked money, he would say amiably to the poor who knocked at his door: "Today I'm poor just like you, I'm one of you."[39] At the end of his life, he could say with absolute tranquility: "I no longer have anything. The good Lord can call me whenever he wants!"[40] His *chastity*, too, was that demanded of a priest for his ministry. It could be said that it was a chastity suited to one who must daily touch the Eucharist, who contemplates it blissfully and with that same bliss offers it to his flock. It was said of him that "he radiated chastity"; the faithful would see this when he turned and gazed at the tabernacle with loving eyes.[41] Finally, Saint John Mary Vianney's *obedience* found full embodiment in his conscientious fidelity to the daily demands of his ministry. We know how he was tormented by the thought of his inadequacy for parish ministry and by a desire to flee "in order to bewail his poor life, in solitude".[42] Only obedience and a thirst for souls convinced him to remain at his post. As he explained to himself and his flock: "There are no two good ways of serving God. There is only one: serve him as he desires to be served."[43] He considered this the golden rule for a life of obedience: "Do only what can be offered to the good Lord."[44]

In this context of a spirituality nourished by the practice of the evangelical counsels, I would like to invite all

[37] Ibid., p. 216.
[38] Ibid., p. 215.
[39] Ibid., p. 216.
[40] Ibid., p. 214.
[41] Cf. ibid., p. 112.
[42] Cf. ibid., pp. 82–84; 102–103.
[43] Ibid., p. 75.
[44] Ibid., p. 76.

priests, during this Year dedicated to them, to welcome the new springtime which the Spirit is now bringing about in the Church, not least through the ecclesial movements and the new communities. "In his gifts the Spirit is multi-faceted.... He breathes where he wills. He does so unexpectedly, in unexpected places, and in ways previously unheard of ... but he also shows us that he works with a view to the one body and in the unity of the one body."[45] In this regard, the statement of the Decree *Presbyterorum Ordinis* continues to be timely: "While testing the spirits to discover if they be of God, priests must discover with faith, recognize with joy and foster diligently the many and varied charismatic gifts of the laity, whether these be of a humble or more exalted kind."[46] These gifts, which awaken in many people the desire for a deeper spiritual life, can benefit not only the lay faithful but the clergy as well. The communion between ordained and charismatic ministries can provide "a helpful impulse to a renewed commitment by the Church in proclaiming and bearing witness to the Gospel of hope and charity in every corner of the world".[47] I would also like to add, echoing the Apostolic Exhortation *Pastores dabo vobis* of Pope John Paul II, that the ordained ministry has a radical "*communitarian form*" and can be exercised only in the communion of priests with their Bishop.[48] This communion between priests and their Bishop, grounded in the sacrament of Holy Orders and made manifest in Eucharistic concelebration, needs to be translated into various concrete expressions of an effective and affective priestly fraternity.[49] Only

---

[45] Benedict XVI, *Homily for the Vigil of Pentecost*, 3 June 2006.

[46] No. 9.

[47] Benedict XVI, *Address to Bishop-Friends of the Focolare Movement and the Sant'Egidio Community*, 8 February 2007

[48] Cf. no. 17.

[49] Cf. John Paul II, Apostolic Exhortation *Pastores Dabo Vobis*, 74.

thus will priests be able to live fully the gift of celibacy and build thriving Christian communities in which the miracles which accompanied the first preaching of the Gospel can be repeated.

The Pauline Year now coming to its close invites us also to look to the Apostle of the Gentiles, who represents a splendid example of a priest entirely devoted to his ministry. "The love of Christ urges us on—he wrote—because we are convinced that one has died for all; therefore all have died" (2 Cor 5:14). And he adds: "He died for all, so that those who live might live no longer for themselves, but for him who died and was raised for them" (2 Cor 5:15). Could a finer program be proposed to any priest resolved to advance along the path of Christian perfection?

Dear brother priests, the celebration of the 150th anniversary of the death of Saint John Mary Vianney (1859) follows upon the celebration of the 150th anniversary of the apparitions of Lourdes (1858). In 1959 Blessed Pope John XXIII noted that "shortly before the Curé of Ars completed his long and admirable life, the Immaculate Virgin appeared in another part of France to an innocent and humble girl, and entrusted to her a message of prayer and penance which continues, even a century later, to yield immense spiritual fruits. The life of this holy priest whose centenary we are commemorating in a real way anticipated the great supernatural truths taught to the seer of Massabielle. He was greatly devoted to the Immaculate Conception of the Blessed Virgin; in 1836 he had dedicated his parish church to Our Lady Conceived without Sin, and he greeted the dogmatic definition of this truth in 1854 with deep faith and great joy."[50] The Curé would always remind his faithful that "after giving us all he could,

---

[50] Encyclical Letter *Sacerdotii nostri primordia*, par. 116.

Jesus Christ wishes in addition to bequeath us his most precious possession, his Blessed Mother."[51]

To the Most Holy Virgin I entrust this Year for Priests. I ask her to awaken in the heart of every priest a generous and renewed commitment to the ideal of complete self-oblation to Christ and the Church which inspired the thoughts and actions of the saintly Curé of Ars. It was his fervent prayer life and his impassioned love of Christ Crucified that enabled John Mary Vianney to grow daily in his total self-oblation to God and the Church. May his example lead all priests to offer that witness of unity with their Bishop, with one another and with the lay faithful, which today, as ever, is so necessary. Despite all the evil present in our world, the words which Christ spoke to his Apostles in the Upper Room continue to inspire us: "In the world you have tribulation; but take courage, I have overcome the world" (Jn 16:33). Our faith in the Divine Master gives us the strength to look to the future with confidence. Dear priests, Christ is counting on you. In the footsteps of the Curé of Ars, let yourselves be enthralled by him. In this way you too will be, for the world in our time, heralds of hope, reconciliation and peace!

With my blessing.

From the Vatican, 16 June 2009.

BENEDICTUS PP. XVI

---

[51] Nodet, "Sacerdoce", p. 244.

SOURCES

The homilies by Benedict XVI/Joseph Ratzinger in this volume are taken from:

Joseph Ratzinger, *Gesammelte Schriften*, vol. 12 (Freiburg im Breisgau: Herder, 2010), Part C.

Appendix:

https://w2.vatican.va/content/benedict-xvi/en/letters /2009/documents/hf_ben-xvi_let_20090616_anno sacerdotale.html

INDEX